Essential ASP for Web Professionals

ISBN 0-13-030499-9

90000

9 780130 304995

The Prentice Hall Essential Web Professionals Series

- *Essential Design for Web Professionals*
  Charles Lyons

- *Essential Flash 5 for Web Professionals*
  Lynn Kyle

- *Essential Flash 4 for Web Professionals*
  Lynn Kyle

- *Essential ASP for Web Professionals*
  Elijah Lovejoy

- *Essential PHP for Web Professionals*
  Christopher Cosentino

- *Essential CSS & DHTML for Web Professionals*
  Dan Livingston and Micah Brown

- *Essential JavaScript™ for Web Professionals*
  Dan Barrett, Dan Livingston, and Micah Brown

- *Essential Perl 5 for Web Professionals*
  Micah Brown, Chris Bellow, and Dan Livingston

- *Essential Photoshop® 5 for Web Professionals*
  Brad Eigen, Dan Livingston, and Micah Brown

Essential ASP for Web Professionals

Elijah Lovejoy

Prentice Hall PTR
Upper Saddle River, NJ 07458
www.phptr.com

Library of Congress Cataloging-in-Publication Data

Lovejoy, Elijah.
    Essential ASP for web professionals / Elijah Lovejoy.
      p. cm.
    Includes index.
    ISBN 0-13-030499-9
    1. Internet programming. 2. World Wide Web. I. Title.

QA76.625.L68 2000
005.2'76--dc21   00-063702

Editorial/Production Supervision: Donna Cullen-Dolce
Acquisitions Editor: Karen McLean
Marketing Manager: Kate Hargett
Manufacturing Manager: Alexis R. Heydt
Cover Design Director: Jerry Votta
Cover Design: Anthony Gemmellaro
Interior Design Director: Gail Cocker-Bogusz
Series Design: Patti Guerrieri
Composition: April Messina

 © 2001 Prentice Hall PTR
Prentice-Hall, Inc.
Upper Saddle River, NJ 07458

Prentice Hall books are widely used by corporations and government agencies for training, marketing, and resale.

The publisher offers discounts on this book when ordered in bulk quantities. For more information, contact: Corporate Sales Department, Phone: 800-382-3419; Fax: 201-236-7141; E-mail: corpsales@prenhall.com; or write: Prentice Hall PTR, Corp. Sales Dept., One Lake Street, Upper Saddle River, NJ 07458.

Printed in the United States of America

10 9 8 7 6 5 4 3 2 1

ISBN 0-13-030499-9

Prentice-Hall International (UK) Limited, London
Prentice-Hall of Australia Pty. Limited, Sydney
Prentice-Hall Canada Inc., Toronto
Prentice-Hall Hispanoamericana, S.A., Mexico
Prentice-Hall of India Private Limited, New Delhi
Prentice-Hall of Japan, Inc., Tokyo
Prentice Hall (Singapore) P.T.E., Ltd.
Editora Prentice-Hall do Brasil, Ltda., Rio de Janeiro

Contents

Introduction   xi

Acknowledgments   xxi

Chapter 1   Keeping Time   1

Project I: A Simple Date Script   2
New Features   2
Script 1-1
`date_simple.asp`   5
How the Script Works   6

Project II: A More Powerful Date Script   7
New Features   7
Script 1-2
`date_fancy.asp`   9
How the Script Works   10

Chapter 2   Reading and Writing   13

Project I: Add Data from a Text File to a
Web Page   14
New Features   15
Code for Tip of the Day   19
Script 2-1-1
`tips.txt`   20

v

Script 2-1-2
`tip_of_the_day.asp`   *20*
How the Script Works   21

Project II: Writing Form Data to a
Text File   23
New Features   25
Script 2-2
`guest_book.asp`   *30*
How the Script Works   33

Chapter 3   **Database-Driven Pages**   **39**

Project: Generating Web Pages from a
Database   40
New Features   43
Code for View Database Scripts   *68*
Script 3-1
`ch3_include.js`   *68*
How the Script Works   70
Script 3-2
`ch3_view_categories.asp`   *72*
How the Script Works   73
Script 3-3
`ch3_view_records.asp`   *74*
How the Script Works   78

Chapter 4   **Editing Records**   **85**

Project: Using a Web Interface to Edit
Records in a Database   86
New Features   90
Code to Edit Database   *98*
Script 4-1
`ch4_password_form.asp`   *98*
How the Script Works   98
Script 4-2
`ch4_include.js`   *100*
How the Script Works   103
Script 4-3
`ch4_list_categories.asp`   *108*

How the Script Works   109

Script 4-4
ch4_edit_category_form.asp   *110*

How the Script Works   112

Script 4-5
ch4_update_category.asp   *116*

How the Script Works   117

Script 4-6
ch4_delete_category.asp   *121*

How the Script Works   122

Script 4-7
ch4_blank_category_form.asp   *123*

How the Script Works   124

Script 4-8
ch4_insert_category.asp   *127*

How the Script Works   128

Script 4-9
ch4_list_records.asp   *130*

How the Script Works   135

Script 4-10
ch4_edit_record_form.asp   *136*

How the Script Works   140

Script 4-11
ch4_update_record.asp   *145*

How the Script Works   147

Script 4-12
ch4_delete_record.asp   *149*

How the Script Works   149

Script 4-13
ch4_blank_record_form.asp   *150*

How the Script Works   152

Script 4-14
ch4_insert_record.asp   *154*

How the Script Works   155

Script 4-15
ch4_edit_subcategory_form.asp   *157*

How the Script Works   159

Script 4-16
`ch4_insert_subcategory.asp`   *162*
How the Script Works   163

Script 4-17
`ch4_delete_subcategory.asp`   *163*
How the Script Works   164

Chapter 5   Shopping Cart   167

Project: Building a Shopping Cart   168
Security   168
A Quick Tour   169
New Features   175

The ASP Shopping Cart Code   *179*

Script 5-1
`cart_list_items_for_sale.asp`   *179*
How the Script Works   182

Script 5-2
`cart_set_session.asp`   *185*
How the Script Works   186

Script 5-3
`cart_view_contents.asp` *188*
How the Script Works   188

Script 5-4
`cart_change_qty.asp`   *189*
How the Script Works   190

Script 5-5
`cart_remove_all.asp`   *192*
How the Script Works   192

Script 5-6
`collect_shipping_information.asp`   *194*
How the Script Works   196

Script 5-7
`set_shipping_information.asp`   *199*
How the Script Works   201

Script 5-8
`collect_billing_information.asp`   *206*
How the Script Works   208

Script 5-9
`set_cc_billing_information.asp`   *209*
   How the Script Works   211

Script 5-10
`set_pwc_billing_information.asp`   *215*
   How the Script Works   217

   Script 5-11
   `order_complete.asp`   *218*
   How the Script Works   219

Script 5-12
`cart.js`   *220*
   How the Script Works   230

Script 5-13
`view_session_contents.asp`   *245*
   How the Script Works   245

Chapter 6   **Email**   **247**

   Project: Simple Email Script   **247**
      New Features   248
   Code   *252*
   Script 6-1
   `form.asp`   *252*
      How the Script Works   253
   Script 6-2
   `catch_form.asp`   *253*
      How the Script Works   254

Appendix A   **JavaScript Cheat Sheet**   **257**

Appendix B   **Server Configuration**   **265**

   Index   269

Introduction

Welcome to the book.

This is an ASP cookbook. Each chapter contains one or more recipes that work together in a useful way. Briefly:

- Chapter 1 is basically a tutorial, with a couple of very simple scripts that add dates to HTML pages.
- Chapter 2 has two recipes: a tip-of-the-day application (a quick and dirty way to add dynamic content to a Web page) and a guest book.
- Chapter 3 has a complicated recipe for publishing the contents of a database onto a Web site.
- Chapter 4 has a more complicated recipe that creates a Web site that lets you edit the database.
- Chapter 5 has a recipe for a shopping cart. It's the most complicated recipe in this book and the one that's most likely to make you some bucks.
- Chapter 6 gets simple again with a recipe for e-mail.

All of these recipes rely on Active Server Pages (ASP) and JavaScript, which is mostly what this introduction is about.

◆ Before Active Server Pages

Tim Berners-Lee started things off with a great way to publish documents called HTML, which is a wonderful way to publish static documents.

Pretty quickly thereafter, something called CGI was added to Web servers to let programmers generate HTML pages on the fly. With CGI, when the Web server gets a request for page, it starts a program and hands the request to the program. If the program generates any output, that output is returned to the browser.

CGI is a pretty great way to do a lot of things, but it's a very program-ish solution, which is to say it's not very HTML-ish. When you look at a CGI program, most of the time, it doesn't look much like an HTML page, even though that's usually the end result. And if there's a lot of HTML in the program, a lot of the time, it has to be carefully wrapped in quotes to separate the program parts from the HTML parts, which can get tiring.

◆ Too Many CGI Scripts in the Kitchen

Then there's the performance issues: Most CGI programs are written using scripting languages like Perl, which is ideally suited for this kind of thing.

The problem with this is that every time a Web browser asks for a Web page that's generated by a CGI program, a new process is launched on the server. Launching new processes is kind of slow and takes up a lot of resources. Programs with too many simultaneous CGI programs can get very bogged down.

There are, of course, ways around this, but they involve doing fancy technical things that are a lot harder than writing Perl scripts.

So it became clear that there needed to be an easier way to generate dynamic Web pages.

◆ Mixing HTML and Scripts in One Place

The solution that has emerged to the HTML vs. CGI debate is to do both. Increasingly, Web servers are getting smarter, so that it's possible to drop little program snippets inside of Web pages instead of having to maintain programs and HTML separately.

This isn't the end-all, be-all for the Web. Small sites that don't need dynamic content should still be created with HTML.

Very large sites with millions of pages and complicated applications need to be built using complicated publishing systems and application servers.

But for a lot of things, being able to mix HTML and programming is an excellent solution. And that's what ASP is all about.

ASP is probably the best way to mix HTML and simple programming in a Windows environment. ASP pages can also be hosted on a UNIX server, using software from ChiliSoft. But most people use ASP with Windows NT and Windows 2000, because it's built into IIS,[1] it's easy to use, and it's powerful.

ASP is not the only game in town. Other products that let you mix HTML and programming include PHP, Cold Fusion, and JSP. But if you're interested in building dynamic product on the Windows platform, you'll find that ASP is often the first choice for developing dynamic Web sites.

◆ How to Add ASP Code to an HTML Page

If you're comfortable with HTML source code, adding ASP to your arsenal will feel like the logical next step.

Warning
This book assumes that you are comfortable with HMTL source code. If you are not familiar with HTML source code, you will want to get a good HTML book to refer to while you work with this book.

Let's start with a real simple HTML page called hello_world.html:

```
<html>
<head><title>Hello World</title></head>
<body>
```

1. IIS is the Microsoft Web server (Internet Information Server) included with Windows NT and Windows 2000.

```
Hello World

</body></html>
```

If your Web server is IIS (you need IIS or a Web server that supports Active Server Pages for this to work), you can take this file and rename it hello_world.asp:

```
<%@ Language=JavaScript %>
<html>
<head><title>Hello World</title></head>
<body>

<% Response.Write("Hello World") %>

</body></html>
```

Three things have changed:

1. Instead of ending with .html, the file now ends with .asp. This tells the Web server that there may be some code on the page. Instead of just giving the page to a Web browser when someone types in the URL of the page, the Web server checks the page for <% ... %> tags first. If it finds any, it removes the tags and their contents, and replaces them with the output of any program that is inside of them.

2. The first piece of code that the Web server finds is <%@ Language=JavaScript %>. This tells the Web server that the programming language is JavaScript. Because IIS, the Microsoft Web server, often assumes that ASP programs will be written in VBScript, it's always a good idea to tell IIS if you're using JavaScript.

3. The next piece of code that the server finds (remember that it's looking for <% ... %> tags) is the line <% Response.Write("Hello World") %>. The Response.Write() command is a lot like the print() command in many programming and scripting languages. In the context of ASP, this code tells the server to send the string "Hello World" to the browser.

The net result is that the .asp page and the .html shown above have exactly the same result: a Web page with the words "Hello World" on it.

Nevertheless, the two pages are very different. When a browser asks the Web server for an `.html page`, the server passes the page to the browser without much thinking about it. On the other hand, the Web server looks at `.asp` pages to check for small programs to run. This means that any or all of the contents of an `.asp` page can be generated on the fly. This book will explore how this can be useful.

◆ Why JavaScript?

Most books about ASP use the VBScript scripting language. Rather than use VBScript, this book uses JavaScript, for a number of reasons:

- Active Server Pages can be written in VBScript, JavaScript, as well as PerlScript. Because all work pretty much equally well for most things, deciding which language to use is pretty much a matter of taste.
- I'm more used to working in JavaScript than in VBScript, so it's often easier for me to use JavaScript.
- JavaScript is the only practical language to use for client-side programming. I find the idea of switching from one language to another annoying. By using JavaScript on the server side, I can use the same language on both sides. Of course, the browser environment is very different from the ASP environment. Still, using a single language keeps my life simple. Especially because I do hardly any client-side scripting, because it never seems to work right, and figuring out the difference between all the browsers is something I never seem to get around to.
- JavaScript is an open protocol. VBScript is not.
- There are a lot of JavaScript programmers out there and not a lot of resources for using JavaScript on the server side. When I got an opportunity to write a book on ASP, it seemed like a good opportunity to tip the balance the other way.

◆ What's the Difference between JavaScript, JScript, and ECMA Script?

JavaScript first emerged on the scene as a scripting language for the Netscape browser. Later, when you could use JavaScript with Microsoft Internet Explorer, I think they called it JScript (at any rate, Microsoft often calls it JScript now).

Because Netscape and Microsoft couldn't agree on how JavaScript/Jscript should work, it was hard to do anything besides rollover buttons that would work reliably.

For the last couple of years, there's been something called ECMA Script that's supposed to be an open protocol that will bring everything back together or something.

Because all the code in this book was written for Microsoft Active Server Pages, it seems likely that one could argue that the code is JScript. Yet, this book talks mostly about JavaScript, rather than JScript. I've been able to find two reasons why: First, I think JavaScript sounds better than JScript; Second, the code that I use in my scripts to declare the language is `<%@ Language=JavaScript %>`. And this works.

Whatever.

◆ ASP Objects and Other Useful Objects

The reason that ASP, IIS (the Microsoft Web server), and JavaScript are worth using is that they make it easy to create a script quickly, using a suite of tools that let us limit our focus to the specific task confronting us without having to reinvent the wheel.

When our script needs to perform a task, the bulk of the task can often be performed by a built-in ASP object, Microsoft scripting object, or JavaScript object. Some of the important ones are listed below.

A Quick Look at ASP

One of the tasks that used to be a real hassle in the early CGI days was collecting information from a form. For example, if a form collects a variable called `email` that contains an e-mail address, you can easily access it with the Request object:

```
email_address = Request("email");
```

Another fun trick is the ability to redirect a visitor to a different page, using the ASP Response object:

```
Response.Redirect("http://www.lovejoy.com/redirect_page.asp");
```

which is a lot faster way to redirect someone than using a <meta> tag.

And, of course, there are a lot of other neat tricks that make it fun and worthwhile to work with ASP and JavaScript! Thus, this book...

A Quick Tour of the More Important Objects

As the name implies, ASP objects are collections of logically related methods and properties. The table below lists the most commonly used ASP objects and the purposes they serve.

ASP Object	Purpose
Request	Manages information about the request that the browser sends to the Web server. Often, the most important element of this request is incoming form information.
Response	Manages information that is being sent to the browser in response to the browser's request to the Web server. For example, the Response.Write() command can be used to send HTML to the browser.
Server	Manages information that is related to the server. For example, the Server object can be used to find the URL of the current script.
Session	Manages information about a user's total visit. For example, if a user looks at five pages when visiting a site, the Session object can be used to keep track of that user as she looks at the five pages.

In addition to objects that are unique to ASP, it is possible to use Microsoft scripting objects from within the ASP environment. For example:

Microsoft Scripting Object	Purpose
FileSystem	Can be used to read and write information to and from the filesystem, including looking at the contents of existing files and creating new files.
ADODB	A database technology that can be used to read and write information stored in databases such as Microsoft Access, Microsoft SQL Server, or Oracle.
CDONTS	Contains an object called `NewMail` that can be used to send email from a script.

Finally, the JavaScript language includes some built-in objects that help with certain tasks. For example:

JavaScript Object	Purpose
Date	Does the legwork necessary to work with dates—who has time to keep track of days, months, years, etc...?
Math	A variety of useful math tricks such as generating random numbers and rounding off real numbers.

◆ How to Use This Book

This book consists of a series of fully working programs that can usually be set up in a matter of minutes. Unlike CGI scripts, where you often have to worry about permissions and other configuration issues, the ASP scripts in this book can be FTPd to just about any Windows NT or Windows 2000 server (or even a Win95/98 PC with personal Web server installed) and be up and running immediately.[2]

---

2. Some of the scripts in this book require server-side configuration: the database scripts need something called a DSN, which is a database connection thingy. The scripts that write data to the file system will need permission to so. If you have your own Web server, this is easily done; otherwise, your ISP will do it for you.

If you're new to Web scripting/programming, it's probably a good idea to use Chapter 1 as a tutorial.

After that, this book can be used as a cookbook: Simply jump directly to the script that looks interesting or otherwise meets your needs, and you should be up and running quickly, whether you're a novice or an experienced programmer working with ASP for the first time.

The appendixes contain reference information on topics that relate in one way or another to getting ASP scripts up and running quickly and easily.

◆ Conventions

All code examples are identified by the use of the `Courier` fixed width font. If there are line numbers next to an example of code:

```
1.// Some code examples
2. // have line numbers next to them.
```

1,2. The code will usually be followed by detailed explanations of how the code works.

Note that, in some cases, a line of code will wrap to the next line. That does not mean that there is a line break in the code! You can generally tell a wrapped line because there is no line number next to the part of the line that has wrapped. Putting a line break where a line wraps can cause some odd behavior that's surprisingly difficult to track down, so be careful with this one. Don't want to worry about line breaks? Don't! Go to the companion Web site and download the code: http://www.phptr.com/essential/.

How Chapters Are Structured

Each chapter is structured as follows:

1. **Introduction:** Some kind of effort to give you a sense of what the chapter is about.

2. **New Features:** A description of any new ASP or JavaScript features that will be used in the code.

3. **Source Code:** The source code is listed, followed by a detailed description of how it works.

    4. Recap: A brief summary of what was in the chapter.

    5. Advanced Projects: Some ideas on how you could hack the script presented in the chapter.

This book assumes that you've got at least a passing familiarity with HTML. If you haven't worked directly with HTML before, you'll probably want an HTML resource to turn to.

Case Sensitivity

JavaScript is case-sensitive. sO be cAreful about how you type things. If something doesn't work right, you can explore changing the case...

Acknowledgments

In the end, the process of writing this book has taken about a year. During this period, most of the time that has gone into coding and writing has been my own. I can also take credit for all of the bugs and typos. Most of the credit, however, goes to others.

Foremost among them is Rebekah Lovejoy, my wife and business partner. From the beginning, Rebekah has helped me find the time required for this project. For much longer than that, she's been my companion in exploring and delighting in the Internet and other media. Her passion for information architecture has prevented me over and over again from losing track of why technology matters.

Next on the list is Nathan Young, who like myself is easily entertained by a nifty turn of code. Nathan and I have been working together and swapping ideas about technology for several years. He figured out what ASP was well before I did and has always been kind enough to share it with me, comparing notes along the way as we worked on various ASP projects together and separately.

Micah Brown, who started this series and generously asked me to write this book, was there with advice and was willing to commiserate on what a surprisingly difficult thing it is to write so darn much. At Prentice Hall, Karen McLean, Donna Cullen-Dolce, and April Messina were gracious in the face of a sliding schedule and made sure it all came together. Marc Loy provided a necessary and gentle technical edit.

I've always enjoyed working with ASP and JavaScript. These are great tools that are a pleasure to work with. So, to the complete strangers behind this great technology, thanks! Inevitably, there are other members of the community to acknowledge: people whose posts to newsgroups and mailing lists have provided information just when I needed it to get a site up; books and articles that made it possible for me to function in this generous environment where ideas and documentation are widely distributed and highly available.

Michael Boh gave me a job knowing that I was in the middle of writing a book and, along with the rest of the gang at Prepay.com, helped me to keep weekends clear so that I could work on it. At Lovejoy.com, we had great customers who let us practice our licks on their sites. Kristin Kobey, Mike Sale, Gabe Watson, Geoff Price, Karen Enfield, Vicky Firstenberg, David Straede, and Renee Bergan were all part of that adventure, along with Rebekah and Nathan. Stig Berg hasn't gotten to go surfing with me in almost a year.

1 Keeping Time

IN THIS CHAPTER

- Adding ASP code to an HTML file
- Using the JavaScript `Date ()` function
- Sending information to the browser
- Working with numbers, strings, and arrays

Somewhere in the Rocky Mountains last week, the head of marketing and a couple of other suits upstairs rubbed elbows with a deep-thinking guru. A couple of epiphanies later, and you're staring at an email informing you that the company's static Web site is no longer enough. It's time to build a "Dynamic Web Site."

You've been here before: a big, undefined project being dumped in your lap by people who have no idea what it is that they're asking you to do. In fact, the memo that you're looking at actually reads "Dynamic Web Suite." No matter. The solution here is to be proactive and get something dynamic on the site as quickly as possible. Meanwhile, you send out a long email with a detailed list of questions asking for clarification on what kind of dynamic Web site the suits want.

While they're pinned down, you can use the scripts in this chapter to famil-iarize yourself with how Active Server Pages (ASP) work and make your Web site "dynamic" well before the powers that be figure out how to dump more specific demands in your lap. Adding a date to a page is a fairly sim-ple task. As a result, it's a nice way to get started with ASP basics, which makes this section a good tutorial for exploring ASP for the first time.

A date can play a useful role in navigation as a visual clue that informa-tion is fresh: If you publish information on a page on a daily or weekly basis, putting a current date on the page right away tells visitors that at least one piece of information on the page changes once a day.

◆ Project I: A Simple Date Script

This script lets you add a date to a page with only three lines of code. We'll go into a lot of detail about how it works in order to expose basic ASP concepts that will be used time and again in this chapter and those that follow.

Note that the price we pay for simplicity is lack of functional-ity: The date that this script spits out probably isn't formatted exactly the way you'd like, which is where the next script, which produces a *fancy* date (hold on to your hats...) picks up next.

NEW FEATURES

<% ... %> (The ASP Tag)

Any code enclosed in ASP tags will be executed on the server. Furthermore, this code will be removed from the page after it is executed.

For example, the "=" is equivalent to "print" in many lan-guages and is used here to put the words "Hello World" into a page of HTML:

```
1. <HTML><HEAD><TITLE>Simple Date</TITLE></HEAD>
2. <BODY BGCOLOR="#FFFFFF" >
3.
4. <h1><% = "Hello World" %></h1>
5.
6. </BODY></HTML>
```

will generate and send the following HTML page to the browser:

```
1. <HTML><HEAD><TITLE>Simple Date</TITLE></HEAD>
2. <BODY BGCOLOR="#FFFFFF" >
3.
4. <h1>Hello World</h1>
5.
6. </BODY></HTML>
```

Note how line 4 has changed from the source (above) to the code that is actually sent to the browser (below).

ASP vs. HTML: An ASP page is an HTML page with two elements added. First, the file name ends with the ".asp" extension, so that the web server knows that it's an ASP file. Second, the file includes some *server-side* code that contains instructions for tasks that the server should perform before delivering the page to the web browser. In this example, the Web server is inserting the words "Hello World" into the document. In a little bit, we'll look at putting dynamic information (a date) into what would otherwise be a static Web page. For more on the ASP model, see the introduction.

Tip
By using server-side scripting, rather than client side scripting, for Web sites that will be viewed by the general public, you can ensure that visitors to your site won't be confronted with confusing error messages often generated by client-side JavaScript.

<%@ Language=JavaScript %>

Because the default language for ASP code is often VBscript and most of the examples in this book use JavaScript, it is good practice to make JavaScript the default language in all of your scripts. This is done by adding the following line to the beginning of all of your code.

```
<%@ Language=JavaScript %>
```

new Operator

The new operator is used to create a new object.[1] Both ASP and JScript contain a number of built-in objects that make it possible to perform complicated tasks easily. Objects are organized around particular areas of activity (for example, working with dates) and consist of methods that do things for us (methods are a lot like functions) and properties that contain information (numbers or strings).

The next section introduces an object used to work with dates.

Date() Object

The Date object is a JavaScript object that makes it easy to create and manipulate dates. To use the Date object, you must create a Date object using the "new" operator, for example:

```
date_object = new Date ();
```

This generates a Date object that contains the current date. Once a Date object has been created, there is a number of methods that can be used to manipulate the date contained in the object and to obtain information about the date. For example:

```
date_object.toString()
```

will return the date as a human-readable string (as opposed to the number of milliseconds since midnight on January 1, 1970).

Response.Write ( )

Response.Write() is the Write() method of the Response object. The Response object is the ASP object that manages anything that involves delivering information to the browser.

The Write() method is a lot like the "print" command used in many programming languages: It is used to write information to the HTML page that is delivered to the browser. For example:

```
Response.Write("<h1>Hello World</h1>");
```

---

1. The new operator is also used to create a new array.

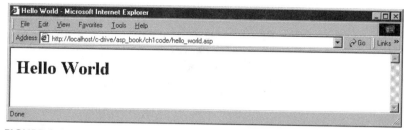

FIGURE 1-1 A simple way of using `Response.Write()`

will create a heading on the Web page that is output from your script (see Figure 1-1).

Note that the Response object is special object that is always available in ASP (you don't have to create it to use it). In contrast, a Date object must be created before it can be used.

Script 1-1
date_simple.asp

```
1. <%@ Language=JavaScript %>
2.
3. <HTML><HEAD><TITLE>Simple Date</TITLE></HEAD>
4. <BODY BGCOLOR="#FFFFFF" >
5.
6. <%
7. date_object = new Date();
8. Response.Write(date_object.toString())
9. %>
10.
11. </BODY></HTML>
```

The Web page that is generated by this scripts looks like Figure 1-2.

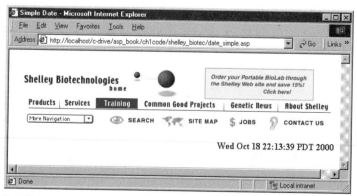

FIGURE 1-2 You thought something this simple would look good? (Try the next script)

HOW THE SCRIPT WORKS

1. The first line sets the default scripting language to JavaScript, in case the ASP interpreter is expecting some other language.

2–5. This is standard HTML.

6. We open the ASP tag in anticipation of the code, which starts on the next line.

7. We create a Date object called `date_object`. By default, this contains the local time on the computer where it's running.

8. There are two things that happen on this line, which consists of two nested functions, executed from the inside out. The first function executed is: `date_object.toString()`. The output of this function is then passed to the `Response.Write ()` function. Here's what happens:

   First, we use the `toString()` method of the date object to turn the date information that's stored in `date_object` and turn it into a string (so called because it consists of a string, or list of human-readable numbers and letters). This generates a string such as "Sat May 22 14:22:55 PDT 1999."

   This string is then handed to the `Response.Write()` function, which lets us add information to the HTML page that we're building. Thus, our string (`"Sat May 22 14:22:55 PDT 1999"`) is added to the HTML page, so that the output of our script is:

```
<HTML><HEAD><TITLE>Simple Date</TITLE></HEAD>
<BODY BGCOLOR="#FFFFFF" >

Sat May 22 14:22:55 PDT 1999

</BODY></HTML>
```

9. Closes the ASP tag, which tells the ASP interpreter that there is no more server-side code to execute and that the rest of the page (lines 10–11) is regular HTML.

◆ Project II: A More Powerful Date Script

Although the simple date script above illustrated how simple it is to use a function that is built into a JavaScript object, this "fancy" script illustrates a more programmatic approach to generate a date on the fly: The approach outlined below can easily be customized so that you can generate a date that is laid out exactly the way you want.

Because this approach is flexible, it involves more code, which gives us an opportunity to examine some new features. The primary focus will be the three data types: numbers, strings, and arrays.

NEW FEATURES

// (Comment)

Code tends to make sense to those who write it, while they're writing it. To others, or even to the person who wrote it a few months later, it starts to look like nonsense. Comments make it easier to share code with others. For example:

```
1. // For some reason, it's traditional to show people
   how to
2. // 'print' things by printing 'hello world'.
3. // In ASP, this is done using the Response.Write ( )
   command
4. // (The Write method of the ASP Response object.
   This looks like:
5. Response.Write ("Hello World");
```

In the above example, lines 1–4 are commented out and are, therefore, ignored by the ASP interpreter. Line 5 is not commented; thus, it gets executed, so that the words "Hello World" appear in someone's browser.

Although I don't know where "Hello World" comes from,[2] it seems like a sensible thing to say after spending too many days and nights in the artificial isolation of a computer screen. I know that I get a little disconnected, maybe a little

---

2. Prentice Hall had this book reviewed by Marc Loy, who wrote me that "Well, computer programming lore has it that this was a popular first message to test new programming languages. It proves two things: 1) you can write/compile/run a program in the language and 2) you can produce output so as to read the results of more interesting programs."

disoriented, until it gets to the point where writing a script that says hello starts to seem downright social. I digress...

Number (JavaScript Data Type)

A number is an integer or real number that can be represented by a literal variable or as a literal:

```
9                       // the number 9
3.45                    // the number 3.45
3 + 2                   // the number 5
number = 12 // the variable "number" has been set to 12
number + 2              // the number 15
```

String (JavaScript Data Type)

A string is a sequence of letters, numbers, spaces, and various other characters, which, like numbers, can be expressed literally or stored in a variable. For example:

```
"Hello World"           // the archetypal string.
"Tel: 805-966-0611"     // another literal string.
Name = "Wilbur"  // a variable called name with a value
                 // of "Wilbur"
```

Array (JavaScript Data Type)

An array is an ordered sequence of values:

```
(1,2,3)              // the numbers one, two, and three
("Wilbur","Fred","Gordon")          // three names.
name_array = ("Wilbur","Fred","Gordon") // a variable
               // called name_array storing three names
```

Because arrays are ordered, it is possible to invoke a particular value in an array by referring to its index value:

```
name_array[0]           // returns "Wilbur"
name_array[2]           // returns "Gordon"
name_array[3] = "Becky"      // name_array is now
               //("Wilbur","Fred","Gordon","Becky")
```

Concatenation (JavaScript "+" Operator)

Concatenation makes it possible to make a single string out of two strings by "concatenating" them:

```
full_name = "jane" + " " + "doe"     // full_name is
                                     //set to "jane doe"
```

Note that in concatenating the strings "jane" and "doe" it was necessary to put a space between them (" ") to prevent the value of full_name being set to "janedoe".

Script 1-2
date_fancy.asp

```
1.  <%@ Language=JavaScript %>
2.
3.  <HTML><HEAD><TITLE>Fancy Date</TITLE></HEAD>
4.  <BODY BGCOLOR="#FFFFFF" >
5.
6.  <%
7.  var now, days, months, day_of_week_int,
    day_of_month_int, month_int, year, today_date;
8.  now = new Date();
9.
10. days = new Array ("Sunday","Monday","Tuesday",
    "Wednesday","Thursday","Friday","Saturday");
11. months = new Array ("January","February","March",
    "April","May","June","July","August","September",
    "October", "November","December");
12. day_of_week_int  = now.getDay();
13. day_of_month_int = now.getDate();
14. month_int = now.getMonth();
15. year = now.getFullYear();
16.
17. today_date = days[day_of_week_int] +", "+
    months[month_int] + " " + day_of_month_int + ", " +
    year;
18.
19. Response.Write (today_date);
20. %>
21.
22. </BODY></HTML>
```

This generates a date that looks like Figure 1-3.

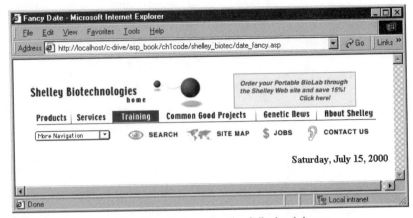

FIGURE 1-3 Now, this will really impress the folks back home

HOW THE SCRIPT WORKS

1. Set default language to JavaScript.

2–5. Start of HTML document.

6. Open ASP tag.

7. This line declares the variables that we will be using with the JavaScript keyword `var`. Although not necessary, this is good practice (one that I'm not particularly good at...).

8. Initialize a new `Date()` object called now. By default, this object contains current date information.

10,11. Creates two arrays—one for days of the week and one for months. We'll need this because the weekdays and months are stored as integer values (0–6 and 0–11) in the now object that we've created.

12. Uses the `getDay()` method of the date object (now) to get an integer value for the day of the week. This assigns a value between 0 and 6 to the variable `day_of_week_int`.

13. Uses the `getDate()` method of the Date object to get an integer value for the day of the month. This assigns a value between 0 and 30 to the variable `day_of_month_int`.

14. Uses the `getMonth()` method of the date object to get an integer value for the month. This assigns a value between 0 and 11 to the variable `month_int`.

15. Uses the `getFullYear()` method of the date object to assign a four-digit value to `year`.

17. In this line, all of the information that we've collected so far is put together into a single string (`today_date`) that contains all of the date information. First, we use `day_of_week_int` to retrieve a single day of the week from the `days` array we created in line 10. For example, if `day_of_week_int` is 3, this returns "Wednesday." Then, the literal string ", " concatenates a comma and a space. We then use the same process to retrieve a month from the `months` array, concatenate a space, then the integer value stored in `day_of_month_int` (which is expressed as a number), throw in another comma and space, and end up with the four-digit `year`.

19. Using the `Write()` method of the Response object, the value in `today_date` is inserted into the HTML output by the script.

20. Closes the ASP tag. That's it for code.

21. Closes the HTML tags.

Recap

This chapter provided a practical introduction to generating dynamic HTML pages using ASP and Javascript.

Topics covered included integrating ASP code with HTML, working with objects that are part of the ASP and JavaScript environment, and printing the output of a script to the page that is sent to a browser.

The second script, `date_fancy.asp`, also provided an introduction to working with strings and arrays in JavaScript.

Advanced Projects

There are numerous ways that `date_fancy.asp` can be modified. Some ideas include:

- The `days` and `months` arrays could be set to different values. For example, the months array could be set to three-letter abbreviations ("Jan," "Feb," "Mar," ..., "Dec"). Alternatively, the language could be changed: ("Dimanche," "Lundi," "Mardi," ..., "Samedi").
- Time information could be added by using the `getHours ( )` and the `getMinutes ( )` methods of the Date object.

- The existing information could be reorganized by changing the order of the elements being concatenated into the `today_date` variable in line 17.

2 Reading and Writing

IN THIS CHAPTER

- Reading from `filesystem`
- Writing to `filesystem`
- Collecting data from forms

The conference room is filled with people who suddenly care passionately about what goes into the Web site, including a couple of people who only last week could think of nothing better to do than to stop by your cubicle to explain in great detail why the Web site thing was just a passing fad. Must be a very slow week for everyone except you.

The conversation quickly boils down to two main issues: Nobody can agree as to what to do with the home page, and everyone agrees that it's vitally important to collect more information from people who visit the site.

You wait a few more minutes to let the windbags do their thing, then you present your solution: a tip-of-the-day script that will randomly cycle any number of greeting messages on the home page of the site and a guest book to collect feedback from people who visit the site. Half the people in the room have no idea what you're talking about, but it's getting close to lunch time, so they agree with your suggestion.

You retreat to your cube, where you sit down to work with the two scripts in this chapter that let you add functionality to your Web site that involves reading from and writing to text files on the Web server.

◆ Project I: Add Data from a Text File to a Web Page

It's common these days for programs to have a feature that displays a tip every time someone starts the program. The tip-of-the-day script lets you add a similar feature to your Web Site—a script that randomly pulls a tip from a database and incorporates it into a Web page.

Figure 2-1 illustrates how the script can be incorporated into a Web site's home page (in this case, a blurb about the softball team, one of several available options, is added to the lower left-hand corner of the home page).

FIGURE 2-1 The softball blurb is dynamic

Adding dynamic information drawn randomly from a pool is a good way to keep a site fresh: With a good sized pool, site visitors will get a different message every time they visit your site.

The tips that the script uses are drawn from the simplest kind of database available—a text data file. The sample data file included with the script includes only a few tips. However, you can use a whole lot more. The script can easily handle a data file that includes several hundred tips.

To use this script effectively, you'll want to integrate it with an existing HTML page. Remember that, to add ASP code to an existing HTML page, all you need to do is to drop the ASP code into the page (anything in the ASP "<%...%>" tags) and change the extension of the file name from .htm or .html to .asp.

NEW FEATURES

Request Object Server Variables

The Request object contains a large number of server variables, information that is specific to the browser request being handled by the script. This script uses the PATH_TRANSLATED variable, which is the fully qualified path to the current script, for example:

```
c:\inetpub\wwwroot\tips\tip_of_the_day.asp
```

The syntax for obtaining this information and assigning it to a variable is as follows:

```
var abs_path =
String(Request.ServerVariables("PATH_TRANSLATED"));
```

The Request object server variables can be used to collect a variety of other information, for example, HTTP header information (HTTP is the protocol used by Web browsers to talk to Web servers) or the name and IP address of the server on which the script is being used.

Knowing the path of a file is critical when accessing a file that is located on the same server as a script. By knowing the full path to tip_of_the_day.asp, it is possible to infer the path of the data file it uses, which is assumed to be located in the same directory.

Regular Expressions (JavaScript)

JavaScript regular expressions make it easy to perform complicated pattern-matching and search-and-replace operations.

This script uses the `replace()` method, a regular expression method that can be applied to any string to replace a pattern found within that string. For example, if we have a string variable called `url`:

```
var url = "htp://www.lovejoy.com";
```

then we can use a regular expression to find and replace a pattern within the `url` variable:

```
Response.Write(url.replace(/htp/,"http"));
```

which would print a correct URL on the HTML page being generated (note how `"htp"` has become `"http"`):

```
http://www.lovejoy.com
```

The `replace ()` method takes two arguments. The first is the regular expression specifying the pattern we are looking for (`"/htp/"`). The second is the string with which we want to replace it (`"http"`). Note that the two arguments are different datatypes: The characters that are encapsulated by forward slashes are a regular expression (a convention shared with other environments, such as Perl), while the characters that are encapsulated in double quotes are a string.

Using a Text File as a Database

A database is a place where you can store data in an organized way, so that it can be effectively used by a program. For large amounts of information, the best way to get things organized is usually to use a database application (a program such as MS SQL Server, Oracle, mySQL, etc. ...). This kind of database application usually provides facilities for normalizing data into related tables, protecting the integrity of data, and efficiently accessing information from very large pools of data.

For small, simple pools of data, however, using a text file as a database is often the best bet. Information stored in a text file should be simple (one or a few fields that can be stored one record per line) and there shouldn't be too much of it, because to retrieve information from it, a script may need to read through the entire file.

The tip database used by `tip_of_the_day.asp` is a good example of a very simple database. It's unlikely that the database will ever grow very large (it can easily accommodate hundreds of tips), and the structure of the data is very simple: Each line in the file is a tip.

while() (JavaScript Statement)

The while() command is used to generate a loop that is repeated so long as a condition is true. The while () command is, thus, ideal when you need your script to pull information from a text file. This is done using the following logic:

```
while ( not end-of-file ){ // this isn't real code!!
        do something with a line from the file…
    }
```

A while() loop set up to loop so long as end-of-file is not true will loop through every line of the file one line at a time and execute the statement inside the loop once for every line in the file. In ASP, this is done using the FileSystemObject, which is described next.

Using FileSystemObject and the TextStream Object to Read Data from a File

The FileSystemObject is an object that is not strictly an ASP object, because it is part of Microsoft's scripting environment, rather than part of the ASP environment. However, this has very little impact on how we use it, because it works much like any other object that is available within ASP.

The code below illustrates how a FileSystemObject can be created, then used to create a TextStream object, which can, in turn, be used to print the contents of a text file to a Web page.

```
1. fso = new
   ActiveXObject("Scripting.FileSystemObject");
2. file_stream = fso.OpenTextFile("c:\docs\file.txt");
3. while (! file_stream.AtEndOfStream){
4.    Response.Write(file_stream.ReadLine());
5. }
6. file_stream.close();
```

Unlike the Request or Response objects, which are always available within ASP, the FileSystemObject needs to be explicitly created (line 1, above). Once the FileSystemObject exists, it can be used to perform any number of file system operations (the kind of thing that you can do with Windows

Explorer: open files, look through the directory structure of a disk drive, etc. ...). In this case, the `OpenTextFile()` method is used to create a `TextStream` object called `file_stream` (line 2).

Once a `TextStream` object is created, a `while()` loop can be used to loop through the file, line by line (lines 3–5). Here, the contents of the text file are added to an HTML page, using the `Write()` method of the Response object.

JavaScript `if` … `else` Statements

`if` statements and their cousins, `if/else` statements, are probably the most common way to get a script to do different things, depending on how events are unfolding.

An `if` statement will be executed if a condition is true. For example:

```
1. if (1 > 0){
2.        // code here should always be executed
3.        // since 1 is always greater than zero.
4. }
```

Alternatively, a script might perform one task if a condition is true and another task if it isn't. Given a variable called number:

```
1. if (number > 0){
2.        Response.Write("number is greater than zero");
3. }
4. else {
5.        Response.Write("number is less than or equal to
           zero");
6. }
```

If you're new to programming, the first critical thing to understand is how an `if` statement works. It defines a block of code that will be executed only if a condition is true:

```
1. if (condition){
2.        statement // this could be many lines of code
3. }
```

The second critical thing to remember is that you've got to get the parentheses and the curly brackets straight: You need to put parentheses "`()`" around the condition, and curly brackets around the statement "`{}`."

Generating a Random Integer with the JavaScript Math Object

Javascript includes a built-in Math object that makes it easy to take advantage of a number of mathematical functions that are built into the JavaScript language.

For example, the `Math.random()` function returns a random number between 0.0 and 1.0:

```
random_number = Math.random();
```

This might output one of the following values: 0.18359177861083936, 0.1663040438840987, 0.7250774196619358, 0.45072710578013564, 0.19805329447345815, 0.6124185344364772, 0.23355290088725944, etc. ...

Because integers are often more useful than floating point values, the floating point output of `Math.random()` can be rounded to the nearest integer:

```
random_number =  Math.round(Math.random());
```

The random number generated this way will always be either one or zero. To obtain numbers drawn from a larger pool, all you need to do is multiply the output of `Math.random()` by an integer greater than one.

For example, the code below will generate a number between zero and five:

```
random_number =  Math.round(5 * Math.random());
```

CODE FOR TIP OF THE DAY

Important! This script requires a data file in order to work:

- `tip_of_the_day.asp` contains all of the code.
- `tips.txt`, the data file, contains any number of tips from which the script randomly selects one to print. Each line in the data file should include one tip.

Both files must be placed in the same folder.

Script 2-1-1
tips.txt

1. What do 8 of the 10 most profitable pharmaceutical companies in the world have in common? Successful partnerships with Shelley Biotechnologies, Inc.
2. Need to talk to a sales engineer that will actually understand the technical requirements of your project? <a href="contact.asp">Contact Us</a>
3. With a 3-1 record, the Shelley Softball team shows how teamwork can develop great results even outside the lab.

Script 2-1-2
tip_of_the_day.asp

```
1. <%@ Language=JavaScript %>
2. <HTML><HEAD><TITLE>Tip of the day</TITLE></HEAD><BODY
   BGCOLOR="#FFFFFF" >
3. <center><h1>Tip Of The Day:</h1>
4.
5. <%
6. tips_file = "tips.txt"
7.
8. // this gives us the absolute path of this script
   which we'll use
9. // to get the path to the current directory so we
   can open a
10. // file in it (the tips_file, above).
11. var abs_path =
    String(Request.ServerVariables("PATH_TRANSLATED"));
12.
13. // get rid of script name in absolute path
14. // and replace with name of file we want to open
15. var file_to_open =
    abs_path.replace(/\\\w*\.asp/,"\\") + tips_file;
16.
17. fso = new
    ActiveXObject("Scripting.FileSystemObject");
18.
19. //Make sure we can find tips file before we get
    carried away
20. if (fso.FileExists(file_to_open)){
21.
22.    // open file and read contents:
23.    file_stream = fso.OpenTextFile(file_to_open);
24.
25.    tips_array = new Array ();
```

```
26.    // loop through file and collect tips
27.    while (! file_stream.AtEndOfStream ){
28.                 line_num = file_stream.Line;
29.                 tip = file_stream.ReadLine();
30.                 tips_array[line_num-1] = tip;
31.    }
32.    file_stream.close();
33.
34.    // generate random number based on number of
tips
       we found and print one.
35.    random_number = Math.round((tips_array.length-1)
       * Math.random());
36.    Response.Write("<p>" +
       tips_array[random_number]);
37.
38. } // end of if file exists
39.
40. // if we can't find file
41. else {
42.    Response.Write("<p>Sorry, the tips file seems to
       be missing")
43. }
44. %>
45. </center></BODY></HTML>
```

HOW THE SCRIPT WORKS

Note

The tips file has to be in same directory as the script.

1. Tell the ASP server that we'll be coding our page in JavaScript.

2–4. Normal HTML, kept simple for clarity.

5. Open ASP tag marks the beginning of the script.

6. Create a variable `tips_file` to store the name of the file we're going to open. This makes it easy to change the name of the data file later if we want to.

11. Rather than hard-code the location of the data file (`tips.txt`), which would mean having to modify the script any time it is moved, the script assumes that the

data file will be located in the same directory as the script. Because an absolute path is required to open a file, first the script uses the PATH_TRANSLATED server variable to find out the path of the script. This path is stored in the abs_path variable.

15. Next, a regular expression is used to substitute the name of the data file that we need to open for the name of the script in the abs_path variable. This gives us the absolute path of the data file. The regular expression, /\\\w*\.asp/, matches a back slash (\\), followed by any number of of word characters (\w*) and then the string ".asp." This will match the name of the script, then substitute it with the name of the file we want to open. This string is stored in a variable called file_to_open.

17. A FileSystemObject object called fso is created. This object lets the script access the file system of the Web server.

20. Before getting carried away, we use the FileExists() method of the FileSystemObject to verify that the file we want to open exists.

23. The OpenTextFile() method of the FileSystemObject is invoked on the fso object to create a text stream object called file_stream. This is a little confusing if you're new to objects, so I'll rephrase: To do anything with the file system, first we need to create a FileSystemObject, which is fso. Next, we need to use the FileSystemObject to create a TextStream object (which lets us read information from a specific file, which is file_stream). OpenTextFile() is the method which lets us create a TextStream object (remember that a method is a function that is assigned to an object). Note that we have to tell the OpenTextFile () function which file we want to open using the file_to_open variable.

25. Here a new array, tips_array, is initialized. We will use this array to store all of the tips that we find in the data file.

27–31. This while loop goes through the text file one line at a time until reaching the end of the file, when the AtEndOfStream property of the file_stream object will be true. For each line in the data file, the value of the line is placed into tips_array. First, the Line property of the file_stream object is assigned to a new variable line_num, which is an integer equal to the current line in the file. Next, the `readline()` method is used to place the value of the current line into a variable called `tip`. Finally, the value of `tip` is placed into the appropriate position in the array, based on the value of line_num-1. One is taken off of line_num so that the array will start at zero (as is conventional) rather than at one. Note that it is possible to express this more concisely as follows (at the expense of clarity):

```
1. while (! file_stream.AtEndOfStream ){
2.       tips_array[file_stream.Line-1] =
         file_stream.ReadLine();
3. }
```

32. Having placed the contents of the data file into an array, we no longer need the TextStream object, so it is closed, using the `close()` method.

35. To determine which tip to display, a random number is generated, based on the number of elements in tips_array (determined by using the `length` property).

36. Using the random number found in line 35, a single tip is sent to the browser, using the `Write()` method of the ASP Response object.

38–43. Finally, the `if` statement that was opened in line 20 is closed, followed by an `else` statement that will display a useful error message, if for some reason the tips file is missing.

44. The ASP tag is closed.

◆ Project II: Writing Form Data to a Text File

The guest book script is a nice way to collect comments from people who visit a Web site. Visitors can look at comments that others have submitted, as well as post their own.

The guest book script can perform three tasks required to maintain a guest book (which, in turn, generates three separate pages, shown in Figures 2-2, 2-3, and 2-4).

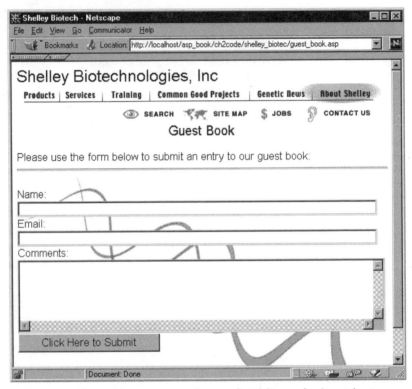

FIGURE 2-2 The script generates a form to let visitors submit entries to the guest book...

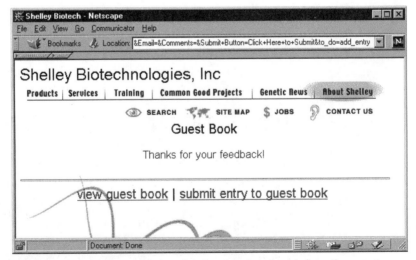

FIGURE 2-3 ... collects an entry from a visitor and adds it to the guest book...

FIGURE 2-4 ... then displays the contents of the guest book as an HTML page

NEW FEATURES

Note

Many of the new features introduced for the previous script (Request object server variables, regular expressions, the FileSystemObject object, the TextStream object, and if/else statements) are also used in this script.

Working with HTML Forms

Forms are the most widely used mechanism by which people visiting your Web site can submit information to you. The guest book script illustrates two of the most common uses of forms.

1. Submitting information that the visitor types into a form to a script (the guest book form lets visitors add information to the guest book).

2. Submitting instructions embedded within a link or a form that tells a script what to do.

COLLECTING INFORMATION SUBMITTED BY A VISITOR

I'm going to go out on a limb here and assume that you've used or at least looked at forms and have a sense of how they can be used to collect information that is then sent to a Web server. This type of form includes several elements: Form tags that tell the browser where to submit the form (lines 1 and 4, below; the action attribute of the form tag specifies the URL of the script that will process the form), one or more form elements that let the visitor put information into the form (line 2), and a submit button (or image) that lets the visitor submit the information they've typed into a form (line 3). For example, a very simple form that lets a visitor submit an email address:

```
1. <form action="script_url.asp">
2. Email: <input type=text name=email value="">
3. <input type=submit name=submit_button value="Click
   Here to Submit">
4. </form>
```

Note that information in a form consists of key/value pairs: The form above contains two pairs. The first, called "email," has a default value of " ", and should contain an email address when the form is submitted. The second is called "submit_button" and has a value of "Click Here to Submit". Thus, a script that wants to collect the email address submitted by the form above would look for a form variable called "email".

INSTRUCTIONS TELLING A SCRIPT WHAT TO DO

Unlike information typed into a form by someone visiting a Web site, instructions are usually hidden inside forms or URL. For example, both the form and link below will do the same thing:

```
1. <form action="script_url.asp">
2. <input type=hidden name=to_do value="perform_task">
3. <input type=submit name=submit_button value="Perform
   Task">
4. </form>
```

or, as a link:

```
<a href="script_url.asp?to_do=Perform+Task"> Perform Task </a>
```

In both cases, the script is given the form element named "to_do" with a value of "Perform Task" (spaces in URLs are converted to plus signs). Assuming that the script is expecting to be told what to do, it will then be able to perform the appropriate task.

USING THE REQUEST OBJECT TO COLLECT INCOMING FORM INFORMATION

The ASP Request object makes collecting form information a breeze. For example, if a script needs to collect the value of the form element to_do and put this into a variable called "form_instruction", you could do this:

```
var form_instruction = String(Request("to_do"));
```

Note that three things are happening in the line above:

1. The to_do property of the Request object is being passed as an argument to the a JavaScript function called String ().

2. The String() function is converting this value into a string.

3. The resulting string is being assigned to the variable form_instruction.

Because all form information is stored in the Request object, finding the value of a form element is simply a matter of obtaining that property of the Request object.

Tip

If you're planning on using that value in a string context, as is usually the case, you'll also want to use the String() function to avoid getting an error or cryptic results. Although using the String() function is not always necessary, you'll see that I almost always use it when collecting form information, which has saved a great many hours of debugging time.

undefined, A Special JavaScript Value

If a script collects a form variable that has not been set, its value will be set to undefined. For example, consider:

```
var form_instruction = String(Request("to_do"));
```

if "to_do" was not set in the form or link that points to the script, this will return undefined. As a result, if a script is using a form variable that may not have been set, it is sometimes necessary to check for the value undefined. The guest book script does this, because when people first go to the script, it receives no form variables and needs to react appropriately by creating a form that lets visitors add an entry to the guest book.

APPENDING INFORMATION TO A FILE

There are two ways to write information to a file: A script can overwrite any information that might exist in a file or it can append information to a script that already contains information.

The guest book script appends information to the data file where entries are stored, because we want to preserve existing entries in the guest book. Appending is a nice way to go, because you don't have to worry about deleting anything by accident. Writing to a file is more tricky, because it's very easy to lose information accidentally.

The code used to append information to a file is similar to the code used to read information from a file, discussed with regard to the tip_of_the_day.asp script earlier in this chapter. After a FileSystemObject object has been created, a TextStream object is created and set to ForAppending mode. A string can then be added to the file using the Write () method of the TextStream object:

```
1. fso = new
   ActiveXObject("Scripting.FileSystemObject");
2. fs_stream =
   fso.OpenTextFile("c:\file.txt",ForAppending);
3. fs_stream.Write("hello world");
```

The above code would append the string "hello world" to the text file c:\file.txt.

Tip

Often, when appending to a file, you'll also want to throw in a line break (described next) to keep things readable. For example:

```
fs_stream.Write("\n hello world");
```

Working with Linebreaks, Special Characters, and Escaping with "\" in JavaScript

It is often necessary to deal with linebreaks, tabs, and other special characters when creating a script. For example, to create the string containing the following:

He said "No way!"

there are two solutions. Either the string must be enclosed in single quotes, or the double quotes must be escaped using the backslash character:

```
var dialog = 'He said "No Way!"';
```

or

```
var dialog = "He said \"No Way!\"";
```

Add a linebreak, and it gets a little more tricky. To create a string that contains the following:

He said "No way!"
She said "Way!"

it is now necessary to use a linebreak "\n" symbol:

```
var dialog = 'He said "No Way!" \nShe said "Way!"';
```

Table 2-1: Common escape sequences

\n	Newline
\t	Tab
\'	Single quote
\"	Double quote
\\	Backslash

Script 2-2
guest_book.asp

```
1.  <%@ Language=JavaScript %>
2.  <HTML><HEAD><TITLE>Guest Book</TITLE></HEAD><BODY
    BGCOLOR="#FFFFFF" >
3.  <center><font size=+1>Guest Book</font></center>
4.
5.  <%
6.  var to_do = String(Request("to_do"));
7.  var this_script_url =
    String(Request.ServerVariables("SCRIPT_NAME"));
8.
9.  /////////////////////////////////////////////////////
10. // If the "to_do" variable does not contain any
    instructions, create
11. // a form that lets visitors add an entry to the
    guest book.
12.
13. if (to_do == "undefined"){
14.
15.    // since most of the next few lines are html,
       the ASP tag is closed
16.    // and normal html is added to the page. Only
       the name of the script is
17.    // dynamically generated, so that the script
       will still work if its name
18.    // is changed down the road.
19.    %>
20.    <p>Please use the form below to submit an entry
       to our guest book:<hr>
21.    <form action = "<% = this_script_url %>">
22.    Name: <br><input type=text name="Name" value=""
       size=50><br>
23.    Email: <br><input type=text name="Email" value=""
       size=50><br>
24.    Comments: <br><textarea name="Comments" cols=50
       rows=5></textarea><br>
25.    <input type=submit name="Submit Button"
       value="Click Here to Submit">
26.    <input type=hidden name="to_do" value="add_entry">
27.    </form>
28.
29.    <%
30. } // end if (to_do == "undefined")
31. else {
32.
33. /////////////////////////////////////////////////////
34. // If the "to_do" variable is defined, we need to
    create a file system
```

```
35. // object that will let us read or write to the
    guest book file
36.
37. // this is the file that will store the guest book
    data. This file
38. // must exist for the script to work. It should be
    placed in the same
39. // directory as the script.
40. var guest_book_file = "guest_book.txt";
41.
42. // this gives us the absolute path of this script
    which we'll use
43. // to get the path to the current directory so we
    can open a
44. // file in it.
45. var abs_path =
    String(Request.ServerVariables("PATH_TRANSLATED"));
46.
47. // get rid of script name in absolute path
48. // and replace with name of file we want to open
49. var file_to_open =
    abs_path.replace(/\\\w*\.asp/,"\\") +
    guest_book_file;
50.
51. fso = new
    ActiveXObject("Scripting.FileSystemObject");
52.
53. if (fso.FileExists(file_to_open)){
54.
55.
56.    ////////////////////////////////////////////////
57.    // If the "to_do" is set to "print_contents", we
       print the entire
58.    // contents of the guest book file to the web
       page we're building
59.
60.    if (to_do == "print_contents"){
61.
62.        // create a text stream object
63.        fs_stream2 =
           fso.OpenTextFile(file_to_open);
64.        //copy the contents of opened file into the
           variable "temp_file"
65.        var temp_file = fs_stream2.ReadAll();
66.        // close  the text stream object
67.        fs_stream2.close();
68.
69.        // add contents of guest book to web page
70.        Response.Write("<pre>" + temp_file +
           "</pre>");
71.
```

```
72.    } // end if (to_do == "print_contents")
73.
74.    ////////////////////////////////////////////////
75.    // If the "to_do" is set to "add_entry", we
       append the new guest
76.    // book entry to the guest book file and thank
       the visitor for
77.    // taking the time to do so.
78.
79.    if (to_do == "add_entry"){
80.
81.        // create TextStream object set to append
           mode
82.        var ForReading = 1, ForWriting = 2,
           ForAppending = 8;
83.        fs_stream =
           fso.OpenTextFile(file_to_open,ForAppending);
84.
85.        // collect date and form information
86.        date_object = new Date();
87.        date_string = date_object.toString()
88.        var message = "Name: " +
           String(Request("Name"));
89.        message += "\nEmail: " +
           String(Request("Email"));
90.        message += "\nComments: " +
           String(Request("Comments"));
91.
92.        // append date and form information to
           guest book data file
93.        fs_stream.Write("\n" + date_string + ": \n"
           + message + "\n");
94.        // close TextStream object
95.        fs_stream.close();
96.
97.        // Print a thank-you message
98.        Response.Write("<p>Thanks for your feed-
           back!<p>");
99.    } // end if (to_do == "add entry"){
100.
101. } // end if file exists
102.
103. // if the file doesn't exist, print an error message
104. else {
105.    Response.Write("<p>can't find file <b>" +
        guest_book_file + "</b><p>");
106.    }
107. } // end else (where to_do != undefined)
108. %>
109.
110. <hr><center><font size=+1>
```

```
111.  <a href="<% =  this_script_url
      %>?to_do=print_contents">view guest book</a>
112.  | <a href="<% =  this_script_url %>">submit entry
      to guest book</a>
113.  </font></center>
114.  </BODY>
115.  </HTML>
```

HOW THE SCRIPT WORKS

Note
The guest book file (guest_book.txt) must be in same directory as the script. This should initially be an empty text file.

1. Tell the ASP server that we'll be coding our page in JavaScript.

2–4. Normal HTML, kept simple for clarity.

5. Open ASP tag marks the beginning of the script.

6. Because the script performs several distinct tasks (display guest book form, accept submissions, and display contents of guest book, all illustrated above), the first thing to do is to find out which of the tasks need to be performed. This is done by looking at the value of the form variable to_do: if no value is set, the guest book submission form is displayed. The value can be set to print_contents to tell the script to display the contents of the guest book or to add_entry in order to submit a new entry to the guest book.

7. The script generates both forms and links that point back to itself. Rather than hard-code this value so that it needs to be changed if the script is moved, the script collects the value of the SCRIPT_NAME server variable (through the ASP Request object) and assigns it to a variable called this_script_url.

13. If no value is assigned to the form variable to_do, it will be undefined (a special JavaScript value, discussed in the New Features section, above). If this is the case, the code in lines 13–29 will be executed.

Tip
Note that these lines include both ASP code and standard HTML: ASP can be used to determine whether to include the HTML portions of an ASP page in the page that is sent to the browser.

19. Here, the ASP tag is closed, because the bulk of lines 20–28 consist of HTML. Because most of this HTML is fairly standard, I won't go into a lot of detail about it.

21. This is the only place in lines 20–28 where we use ASP. It is used to assign a value to the action attribute of the form tag, using the variable `this_script_url` that was set in line 7.

25. Although the submit button in a form is a key/value pair that is sent to the script, the script does not make use of it because it's nice to be able to edit the text that appears in the button without having to worry about it having an impact on how the script works.

26. The hidden form tag `to_do` on this line is used to tell the script what to do when it receives this form. The value `add_entry` indicates that the script should insert the contents of the form into the guest book.

29. Open the ASP tag because most of what follows will be code.

30. End of the `if` statement that started on line 13.

31. If a value is assigned to `to_do`, the balance of the script is executed (lines 31–107).

40. Create a variable `guest_book_file` to store the name of the file we're going to open. This makes it easy to change the name of the data file later if we want to.

45. Rather than hard-code the location of the data file (`tips.txt`), which would mean having to modify the script any time it was moved, the script assumes that the data file will be located in the same directory as the script. Because an absolute path is required to open a file, first the script uses the `PATH_TRANSLATED` server variable to find out the path of the script. This path is stored in the `abs_path` variable.

49. Next, a regular expression is used to substitute the name of the data file that we need to open for the name of the script in the `abs_path` variable. This gives us the absolute path of the data file. The regular expression, `/\\\w*\.asp/`, matches a backslash (`\\`), followed by any number of word characters (`\w*`) then the string `".asp"`. This will match the name of the script, and then substitute it with the name of the file we want to open. This string is stored in a variable called `file_to_open`.

51. A FileSystemObject object called `fso` is created. This object lets the script access the file system of the Web server.

53. Before getting carried away, we use the `FileExists()` method of the FileSystemObject to verify that the file we want to open exists.

60. If `to_do` is set to `print_contents`, the script will execute lines 62–70.

63. The `OpenTextFile()` method of the FileSystemObject is invoked on the `fso` object to create a Textstream object called `file_stream2`. This is a little confusing if you're new to objects, so I'll rephrase: To do anything with the file system, first we need to create a FileSystemObject, which is `fso`. Next, we need to use the FileSystemObject to create a TextStream object (which lets us read information from a specific file, which is `file_stream2`. `OpenTextFile()` is the method which lets us create a TextStream object (remember that a method is a function that is assigned to an object). Note that we have to tell the `OpenTextFile ()` method which file we want to open using the `file_to_open` variable.

65. The `ReadAll()` method of the TextStream object is used to put the contents of the file into a string called `temp_file`.

67. `fs_stream2` is closed, now that we've collected its contents.

70. The contents of the file are written to the HTML page that is being generated. To preserve the formatting of the text file, `<pre> </pre>` tags are concatenated to either end of the `temp_file` string.

72. End of the statement started on line 60.

79. If `to_do` is set to `add_entry`, the script will execute lines 80–99.

82–82. Create a new TextStream object called `fs_stream`, set to `ForAppending` mode.

86–87. To log when entries to the guest book are made, a date object and then a date string are created using the JavaScript `Date()` object.

88–90. The guest book information collected by the form (`Name`, `Email`, and `Comments`) is concatenated into a string called `message` with a newline between each piece of information.

93. The `Write()` method of the TextStream object is used to write the `date` and `message` strings created above to the guest book file. Three newlines are added to keep things tidy.

95. The TextStream object is closed.

98. A thank-you message is sent to the browser to let the visitor know that the entry was successfully received.

104,105. If we were unable to find the guest book file (line 53), the script prints a useful error message. Once you've got the script up and running, you might want to edit this message for end-user consumption.

107. End of the `else` statement started on line 31.

108. Close the ASP tag to create an HTML footer.

111. This line contains two URLs to the guest book script. The first, which sets the `to_do` form variable to `print_contents`, lets visitors view the contents of the guest book. The second, which does not set a value to the `to_do` variable, lets visitors go the guest book form. In both cases, the URL of the script is set dynamically, using the `this_script_url` variable.

RECAP

The scripts in this chapter provide a good overview of how to use the FileSystemObject object and the TextStream object to read from and write to text files.

The guest book script also introduced working with forms, both as a way for the visitor to submit information to the Web server, as well as a way to give the script instructions on which task to carry out.

IDEAS FOR HACKING THIS SCRIPT

- If you have a big site, use the tip-of-the-day script to provide links to different parts of your site that a visitor might not otherwise find.
- Modify the guest book script so that, after receiving a submission, it automatically displays the contents of the guestbook.
- Using the email code described in Chapter 4, add code that automatically sends a thank-you message to visitors who submit information to your guest book.
- Modify the guest book script so that visitors cannot view contents of the guest book.
- Modify the script so that the most recent submissions are placed at the top of the page. The best way to do this is to modify how data is written to the data file so that the data file becomes a tab- or pipe-delimited file with one record per line. The records could then be written to an array and reversed, using the JavaScript `reverse ()` method. You can then loop through the array (described in Appendix A) and write the contents of the array to the HTML page being generated.

3 Database-Driven Pages

IN THIS CHAPTER

- Introduction to relational databases
- Getting started with SQL
- Microsoft Access
- ASP database tools: Creating a DSN, working with the database Connection and Recordset objects
- JavaScript functions, objects, and `for()` loops
- Using includes to merge more than one file into a single script.

Relational databases are among the most exciting tools that are at our disposal, whether it's lightweight tools like MS Access or Filemaker that are designed for the desktop or heavy duty server applications like Oracle or MS SQL Server.

By organizing information in a database, two things happen. First, it becomes possible to build tools that will automatically perform certain tasks for us, such as organizing information into categories and performing searches. Second, it becomes possible to store large amounts of data, from phone books with a few dozen entries to databases with tens of thousands of records or more.

This chapter covers what you need to know to build an ASP script that retrieves information from a database and publishes it to an HTML page. If you're new to databases, you'll find a lot of new concepts here, including an introduction to relational databases. If you've already got experience with databases, you should be able to skim parts of this chapter and focus on those sections that discuss material that is specific to ASP.

The scripts in this chapter use information that is stored in a Microsoft Access database. Although it is probably helpful to open the database in Access if you have a copy of this program, it is not required to use these scripts. Together with the scripts in the next couple of chapters, you can view and edit the contents of the database without ever using Access. All you need is a DSN (explained in this chapter) to connect your scripts to the database, which you can download from this book's Web site.

◆ Project: Generating Web Pages from a Database

The scripts in this chapter use a simple database that stores three kinds of information: people, Web sites, and events.

Each type of information is stored in a different category, which can be selected from a menu that is presented in Figure 3-1.

FIGURE 3-1 Visitors can browse events, people, and Web sites

Because the data stored in each category is different, it needs to be presented in a different manner.

For events, by default, the script displays the name of the event, the principal date with which the event is associated, a description of the event, as well as a start and end date. Events are organized into subcategories, then listed by date (see Figure 3-2).

FIGURE 3-2 Event information

The database stores a fairly standard set of contact information about people (see Figure 3-3).

The script generates a link so that users can go to Web sites stored in the database (see Figure 3-4).

FIGURE 3-3 People and their contact information

FIGURE 3-4 Web site information stored in the database

NEW FEATURES

Relational Databases

In Chapter 2, the tip-of-the day script used a text file to maintain a list of tips (one tip was kept on each line of the file). This is just about as simple as data gets. It is often the case, however, that it is necessary to store data that is sufficiently complicated that it is difficult to store in a flat text file. This is where relational databases come in.[1] I won't try to explain in great detail what a relational database is, but I will review certain aspects that are critical to understanding how the scripts in this chapter interact with a database.

You'll want to understand two concepts: First, how information is stored in tables and, second, how information in one table can be related to information in another table.

STORING INFORMATION IN TABLES

The first step in creating a database is to organize information so that it can be stored in a database. For example, the tables below show how two kinds of information used by the scripts in this chapter are organized into tables.

Table 3-1 stores information about categories (the database stores three categories of information). Table 3-2 is a list of the actual people, events, and Web sites that are stored in the database.

Note the following about the tables and the information stored in them:

- Each row in the table is stored information about one piece of information and is called a **record**.
- Each record is broken up into a number of **fields**. The names of the fields are listed in the top row of each table. Deciding how many fields to use when building a

---

1. Relational databases perform a great deal of tasks that are outside the scope of this book. For example, they usually store information more compactly than does the normal file system, making it possible to store large amounts of information efficiently. By organizing data, databases also make it possible to search large amounts of information more efficiently than if they were stored in text files. Advanced database servers also include a host of administrative and transactional tools that make managing large databases a wonderful challenge. All fun stuff, but far beyond the scope of an ASP book.

Table 3-1 The categories table stores information about the kinds of information stored in the database used in this chapter

category_uid	category_name	category_description
1	People	A list of people, their phone numbers, and information about them
2	Events	A list of scheduled events and important dates
3	Web sites	Web sites that relate to our industry or are of general interest

Table 3-2 The data table stores information about the people, events, and Web sites stored in the database

data_uid	data_name	data_category	data_subcategory	data_description
1	lovejoy.com	3	General Interest	overrated Web site
2	yahoo!	3	General Interest	old-school search engine
3	jane doe	1	Employees	VP of something or other
9	new event	2	Company Events	new product release

database is one of the key issues of database design (not covered in this book).

- Each field contains a different type of information. For example, in the data table, the data_uid and data_category fields contain integers. The data_name and data_subcategory fields contain short strings, while the data_description field contains a longer string. Most databases also support date/time, floating point, boolean, and binary fields. Because the kind of information stored in a field is fixed, it is possible to write a script that will know how to manipulate correctly stored information in a database.

RELATING INFORMATION STORED IN DIFFERENT TABLES

As the name suggests, relational databases can keep track of the relationship between different pieces of information. In the case of the tables shown above, the tables are related because the information stored in the data table (Table 3-2) is related to one of the categories listed in the categories table (Table 3-1).

The relationship is established by comparing the value of the `category_uid` field in the categories table with the value of the `data_category` field in the data table. Where the values are the same, there is a relationship.

For example, the first two records in the data table are Web sites. As a result, the value of the `data_category` field for both records is 3, which is the value of the `category_uid` in the categories table that corresponds to Web sites.

This relationship illustrates two ideas that are critical to the function of relational databases: **primary keys** and **foreign keys**.

A primary key is a field that can be used to uniquely identify a record in a table. The `category_uid` field is a good example of this: In order for the use of categories to be effective, each category must be unique (it wouldn't make much sense to have two categories for Web sites, given that the purpose of the categories table is to organize data from the data table into categories that are broadly the same—people, Web sites, and events).

More specifically, the primary key (a unique identifier, remember?) for each category must be unique. In addition to playing a role in the broader organization of data, a primary key is very useful when it is necessary to work with a specific record in a table. Because each value in the `category_uid` field is unique, it can be used to identify explicitly a specific record in a table. For example, if I want to change the description of the Web sites category, I can tell the database that I want to modify the value of the `category_description` field of the record where the value of `category_uid` is 3 (Table 3-3).

Table 3-3 The `category_uid` field is the primary key for the categories table. In this case, the `category_uid` field uniquely identifies the Web sites category

category_uid	category_name	category_description
3	Web sites	Web sites that relate to our industry or are of general interest

A foreign key is a field that can be used to relate fields in a table to the primary key of a record in another table. Because the value in a foreign key field relates one or more records to a specific record in another table, the relationship that is established is very well defined, which makes it quite useful. For example, there are two records in the data table whose foreign key (the data_category field) indicate that they are related to the Web sites category, shown in Table 3-4.

Table 3-4 The foreign key field in the data table, data_category, establishes a relationship with the category_uid field in the categories table

data_uid	data_name	data_category	data_subcategory	data_description
1	lovejoy.com	3	General Interest	overrated Web site
2	yahoo!	3	General Interest	old-school search engine

Unlike a primary key field, which is unique, it is not uncommon for many records in a table to have the same foreign key. When this happens, those records share a relationship to a single record in another table. In this example, two records in the data table are both related to the same record in the categories table.

Structured Query Language (SQL)

SQL is a language used for database programming supported by many of the most common database applications. Like many programming languages, SQL can be used to do both simple and complicated things. In this chapter, we'll use SQL in an ASP script to retrieve information from a database. Note that there are entire books written on the use of SQL, so I'm just scratching the surface here.

You'll notice that there is no information about context: how the SQL statements are used, or how, when results are returned, those results are collected. This context is covered a little bit later in this chapter when we discuss using the database Connection object and the database Recordset object, which, like the other objects we've looked at so far in this book, are easy to use from within the ASP environment.

Using SQL to Retrieve Data from a Database

The most basic SQL operation consists of a statement called a "query," which retrieves information from a database. This is done using a **select** statement. For example, to select all of the information in the data table above, you could use the following query:

```
select * from data
```

This can be translated as "Give me all of the fields in the table called data." The result would be that the database would return a set of records, called a **recordset**, which would look like the following table:

data_uid	data_name	data_category	data_subcategory	data_description
1	lovejoy.com	3	General Interest	overrated Web site
2	yahoo!	3	General Interest	old-school search engine
3	jane doe	1	Employees	VP of something or other
9	new event	2	Company Events	new product release

Frequently, it's useful to narrow the scope of a query. For example, to limit the scope of the query to Web sites (category 3), a **where clause** can be applied to the select statement, limiting the scope of the statement to those records where the value of a field meets a specific criterion:

```
select * from data where data_category = 3
```

This limits the resulting recordset to two records:

data_uid	data_name	data_category	data_subcategory	data_description
1	lovejoy.com	3	General Interest	overrated Web site
2	yahoo!	3	General Interest	old-school search engine

Other times, it might be not be necessary to get all of the fields in a table. In this case, the query can request specific fields instead of using the "*" wildcard. For example:

```
select data_name, data_description from data where
data_category = 3
```

This would generate the following recordset:

data_name	data_description
lovejoy.com	overrated Web site
yahoo!	old-school search engine

Finally, it's often useful to sort a recordset so that the results will be in order. This is done by appending an `order by` clause to a query:

```
select data_name from data order by data_name
```

This would return an alphabetically sorted list of names:

data_name
Jane doe
lovejoy.com
new event
yahoo!

Microsoft Access

The database used in this chapter was created using Microsoft Access 97, an inexpensive database-authoring application suitable for building small single- and multiuser databases. I used MS Access for three reasons:

1. Because MS Access is widely used on Windows and Windows NT platforms (it is often bundled with Microsoft Office), there is a good chance that many readers of this book will already own a copy.

2. The ODBC drivers (discussed below) for MS Access are bundled with Windows and Windows NT, which means

that, even if you do not own MS Access, you can use an MS Access database to set up the scripts in this chapter.

3. A MS Access database is a single file that is easy to put on this book's Web site, so that you can download it and use it with the scripts in this chapter.

MS Access, like most of the MS Office products, is a pretty big product with an awful lot of features that are entirely beyond the scope of this book. MS Access can be used not only to build databases to store data, but also to build GUI interfaces to work with that data. It includes both GUI and programmatic tools for building database applications and is often used to build large, complicated programs. Fortunately, it can also be used to build small, simple databases, which is what I did to create the small database that is used in this chapter.

If you have a copy of MS Access, you will be able to use Access to edit directly the database that is used by the scripts in this chapter. This is useful if you need to add a lot of records to the database: Although the Web interface (next chapter) is often easier to use to add or edit a small number of records, working directly with the database might save you time if you need to add an entire phone list. You'll also want to use Access to create new fields or tables.

If You Don't Have MS Access

You can still use the scripts in this chapter if you don't own a copy of MS Access: You won't be able to edit the database or edit the data in the database directly, but since the scripts in the next chapter let you edit the data stored in the database, you can do quite a lot without ever opening the database.

If you own a different database that you can connect to using ODBC (most database products include an ODBC driver), you should be able to get the scripts in this chapter to work with it by creating the tables described in this chapter.

If You Have MS Access

Note
Having MS Access is not required to use the scripts in this chapter!

If you have MS Access 97, this is the window that you'll see when you open the database. The tabs across the top list the various database objects that are available in Access (tables, queries, forms, reports, macros, and modules). From the Forms tab, you can open the Categories Form and the Data Form as in Figure 3-5.[2]

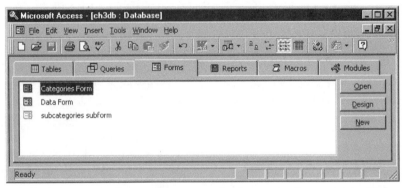

FIGURE 3-5 Use the Forms tab to open the Categories Form and the Data Form

The Categories form can be used to edit existing categories and to create new categories. The subcategories subform (the little window in the form that looks like a spreadsheet) can be used to edit existing subcategories and to create new subcategories (see Figure 3-6).

The data form looks and works a lot like a spreadsheet: Each record is on its own line, some records have dropdown menus, and others can be edited directly. This interface is useful for doing bulk data entry, for example, if you need to type in an entire phone list for your intranet (see Figure 3-7).

If you get really excited about the scripts in this chapter, you may decide that you want to customize the database, for example, by adding fields that are not currently in the database. To do this, you'll need to edit the tables where the data is stored. This is done from the Tables tab of the database window, where you'll find three tables: categories, data, and subcategories (see Figure 3-8).

---

2. You can also open the database using MS Access 2000. The interface looks a little different, but things work the same.

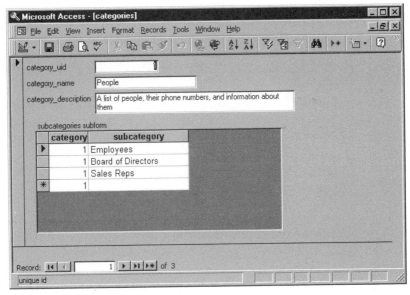

FIGURE 3-6 The Categories Form

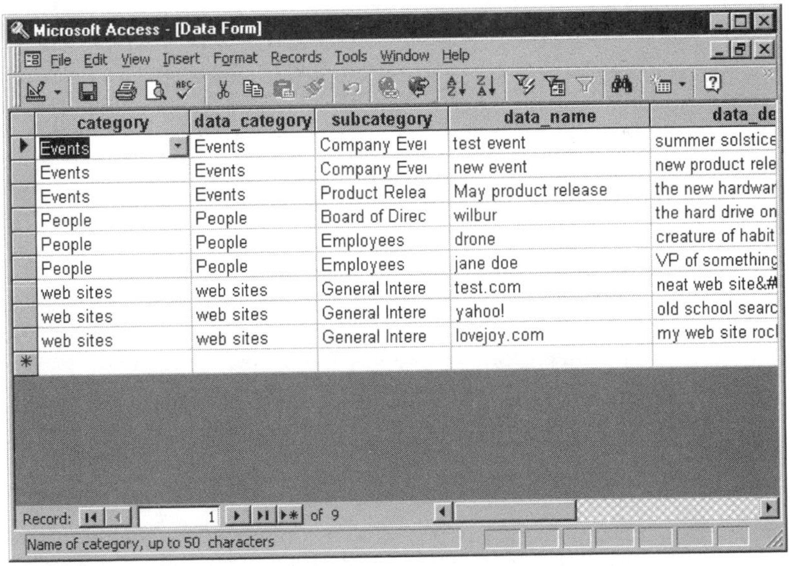

FIGURE 3-7 The Data Form is useful for bulk data entry and editing

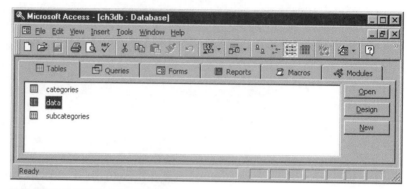

FIGURE 3-8 The Tables tab

As discussed earlier in this chapter in the overview of relational databases, data is stored in tables where information is broken up into fields. MS Access provides an visual interface that lets you edit the properties of a table (see Figure 3-9).

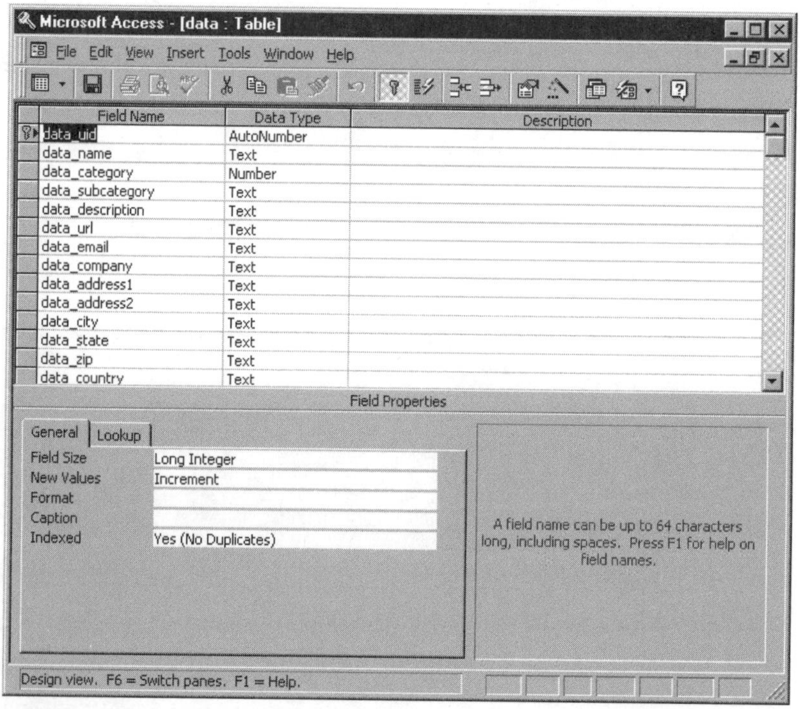

FIGURE 3-9 The MS Access tables editor

Each field has a unique name and is assigned a data type that corresponds to the information that will be stored in the fields. In this case, most of the fields are text fields, with the exception of the primary key field (data_uid) and the foreign key field (data_category), which contain numbers. The data_uid field data type is set to AutoNumber, a MS Access data type that automatically generates a unique integer value.

New fields can be added to a table simply by typing in a field name at the end of the field list and selecting a data type. In some cases, you may also want to configure some of the field properties, using the interface at the bottom of the screen.

ADO, ADODB, ODBC, DSN, Etc....

When an ASP script connects to a database, a lot of different technologies are involved, including at least all of the acronyms above. Rather than go into a lot of detail about how all of these technologies work, I'm just going to stick to covering those things that you'll need to know in order to use them. The point of all of these technologies is that you and I can write a script that connects to a database without having to worry about how they work or exactly what they do.

However, it is nice to have a big picture. There are three steps involved in creating database-driven ASP pages:

1. Create a database (this could be an Access database or any other database that has an ODBC driver).

2. On your Web server, create a DSN (a Data Source Name, which is an ODBC data source). This makes it possible for your script to find your database and connect to it.

3. Write an ASP script that uses ADO (ActiveX Data Objects) to create one or more recordsets and perhaps give SQL instructions to your database.

The database for this chapter is downloadable from this book's Web site, so that takes care of the first step. This leaves creating a DSN, then writing a script. I cover each in turn next.

Creating a DSN (Data Source Name)

A DSN is a device that makes it easy for your script to connect to a database, thanks to a technology called ODBC (Open DataBase Connectivity, an open protocol for connecting to SQL data sources).

When you create a DSN, you are assigning a unique name to a database and telling the ODBC software how to connect to the database. In the case of an MS Access database, this is simply a matter of telling it the file name and path of the database file.

Once you've created a DSN for a database, any number of programs and scripts that know how to use ODBC data sources will be able to connect easily to your database.

If you are running these scripts on your own Web server, you will need to create a DSN yourself (it's easy). If you are running them on someone else's server (an ISP, a friend, a server maintained by your company's system administrator...) you will need to have them create the DSN.

GETTING SOMEONE TO CREATE A DSN FOR YOU

If someone else will be setting up your DSN (or if it is being created by a script that your ISP has set up), all you need to do is upload the database for this chapter to your Web account and tell the person setting up the DSN where you put the file and what it's called.

For example, if you ftp to your server, create a folder called db and put ch3db.mdb into that folder, you would tell your ISP or system administrator that you need a DSN called ch3db created for the MS Access database db/ch3db.mdb.

Note that some ISPs have a system for how DSN names are assigned. If you get a different name for your DSN, you will need to change the name of the DSN in the script (it's a variable near the top of the script).

CREATING A DSN YOURSELF

Creating a DSN is done via the ODBC control panel:

1. If you have not downloaded the database from this book's Web site, you should do so now. Put the database (by default it's called ch3db.mdb, but you can change the name to something that makes more sense to you) somewhere where you're not likely to move it, because you'll need to modify the DSN if you move it later.

2. In the Start menu, select Settings/Control Panel. This opens the Control Panel window, which contains a number of Control Panel icons.

3. Double-click on the ODBC icon (called `32bit ODBC` or `ODBC Data Sources`). This opens the ODBC control panel.

4. Go to the System DSN tab. It should look something like Figure 3-10, although it is not likely that you will have so many DSNs already set up.

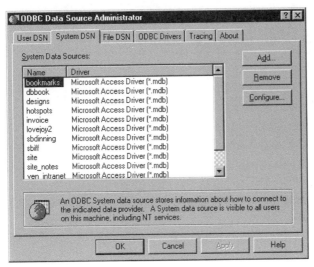

FIGURE 3-10 The system DSN table

5. Click on the Add... button. This pops up a window that lists the different ODBC drivers that are available on your computer. You may not have as many options as shown in Figure 3-11, but this is not important: All you need is the driver for MS Access, which should be available.[3]

6. Select `Microsoft Access Driver` (`*.mdb`), then click on the Finish button. This opens the ODBC Microsoft Access 97 Setup window (Figure 3-12).

---

3. If you do not have a driver for Microsoft Access available (it's been installed on every Win95, Win98, and WinNT system I've looked at), you should be able to download it from Microsoft. You might start by downloading any operating system updates that have been released since your system was set up. If that doesn't do it, try downloading an updated version of ADO (Active Database Objects, a package of Microsoft database technologies).

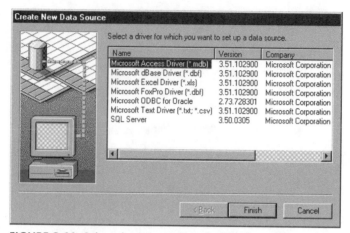

FIGURE 3-11 Select the Microsoft Access Driver

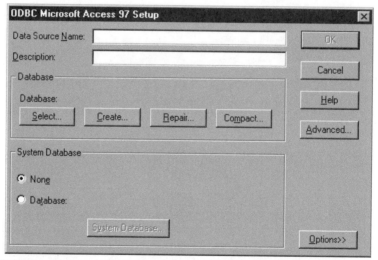

FIGURE 3-12 You'll need to give your data source a name and a path

You'll need to do two things in this window: Assign a name to your data source and give the ODBC software the path to your database.

7. In the top field (Data Source Name), type in a name for your DSN. I used ch3db, but you can use any name that makes sense to you. You'll need to modify the scripts in this chapter if you use a different name.

8. Optional: You can use the `Description` field to note the purpose of the DSN.

9. Click on the Select button. This brings up a dialog box that lets you select the path to your database.

10. When you're finished, you should have something that looks like Figure 3-13.

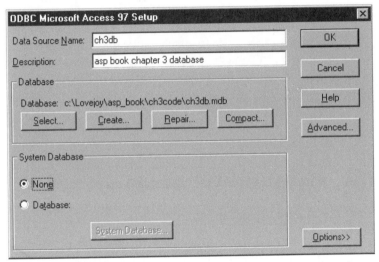

FIGURE 3-13 Once the DSN is set up, it should have a name and point to a database file

To reiterate: You need only two things to set up a DSN: a name (in this case, `ch3db`) and the path to the MS Access database file (in this case, `c:\Lovejoy\asp_book\ch3code\ch3db.mdb`).

11. Click on the OK button to close the Setup window.

12. Click on the OK button to close the ODBC Data Source Administrator window.

The Database Connection Object

To work with a database from an ASP script, the first thing you have to do is set up a connection to a database. Once you have a connection, you can execute SQL statements and/or create a recordset.

As with most things ASP, this is done by creating an object. For example, to create a connection to a DSN called `ch3db`:

```
1. DSN = "DSN=ch3db";
2. Conn = Server.CreateObject("ADODB.Connection");
3. Conn.Open(DSN);
4. // now that the connection is open
5. // you can do something with it here
6. Conn.Close ();
```

In line 1, a variable called DSN is created. It will be used in line 3 to tell the database Connection object the name of the DSN that is being used. Note the syntax: The value of DSN is not ch3db, but the string DSN=ch3db. The reason for this is that, in some cases, it is also necessary to give the database Connection object username and password information. Thus, information handed to the Open() method is labeled.

Next, in line 2, the CreateObject() method of the Server object is used to create an object called Conn. The parameter ADODB.Connection is used to specify what kind of object is being created.

In line 3, the Open()method is applied to the Conn object, using the DSN variable that was created in line 1.

Finally, in line 6, the Close()method closes the connection that was opened in line 3.

Of course, it's not much use to create a connection with a database if you're not going to do something with it. There are two things you can do, once you have a connection:

- Execute SQL statements that do not return records.
- Create a Recordset object to collect the results of an SQL select statement.

I'll cover the first here and deal with recordsets in the next section.

The scripts in this book use three kinds of SQL statements that do not return records: insert statements, update statements, and delete statements. Once a connection is established, the Execute() method of the Connection object can be used to execute an SQL statement:

```
Conn.Execute(SQL_statement);
```

For example, the following code executes three sample statements:

```
1. DSN = "DSN=ch3db";
2. Conn = Server.CreateObject("ADODB.Connection");
```

```
 3. Conn.Open(DSN);
 4.
 5. Conn.Execute("delete from data where data_uid = 9");
 6.
 7. Conn.Execute("update categories set
    category_description = 'Spiffy sites!' where
    data_uid = 3");
 8.
 9. var insert_statement = "insert into data (data_name,
    data_category, data_subcategory, data_description)
    values ('prentice hall', 3, 'General Interest', '
    web site for this book')";
10. Conn.Execute(insert_statement);
11.
12. Conn.Close ();
```

Note how, in lines 5 and 7, the SQL statement is passed direct-ly to the `Execute()` method as a string, whereas in line 10, a variable (which is set in line 9) is used.

The Recordset Object

Where the SQL statements covered in the previous section per-form operations on a database without generating any out-put, the purpose of `select` statements is to generate a list of records, often referred to as a "recordset." In ASP, recordsets are handled with Recordset objects.

For examples of different `select` statements, see the discus-sion of SQL, earlier in this chapter.

Once a recordset has been created, it is necessary to do some-thing with it. Most frequently, the goal is to scroll through the recordset one record at a time to put information from the recordset into a Web page. For example, given the categories table in Table 3-5.

Table 3-5 The categories table

category_uid	category_name	category_description
1	People	A list of people, their phone numbers, and information about them
2	Events	A list of scheduled events and important dates
3	Web sites	Web sites that relate to our industry or are of general interest

The following code can be used to add its contents to a Web page:

```
1.  <%@ Language=JavaScript %>
2.  <%
3.  DSN = "DSN=ch3db";
4.  Conn = Server.CreateObject("ADODB.Connection");
5.  Conn.Open(DSN);
6.
7.      sql = "SELECT * FROM categories ";
8.      rs = Server.CreateObject("ADODB.RecordSet");
9.      rs.Open (sql, Conn);
10.
11.     out = "<table border=1>";
12.     out += "<tr><td><pre>category_uid</pre></td>
        <td><pre>category_name</pre></td>
        <td><pre>category_description</pre></td></tr>";
13.     while (! (rs.EOF)){
14.             out += "<tr><td>";
15.             out +=
                String(rs.fields.item("category_uid")) +
                "</td><td>";
16.             out +=
                String(rs.fields.item("category_name")) +
                "</td><td>";
17.             out +=
                String(rs.fields.item("category_
                description")) + "</td><tr>";
18.             rs.move(1);
19.     } // end while recordset
20.     out += "</table>";
21.
22.     rs.Close ();
23.
24. Conn.Close ();
25. %>
26. <html><head><title>recordset
    example</title></head><body>
27. <%= out %>
28. </body></html>
```

The output of the script is shown in the Figure 3-14. First, a word about this code.

Lines 3–5 and line 24 take care of creating and later closing the connection to the database. Remember that you always create a connection to the database before you create a recordset.

Lines 7–9 deal with the mechanics of creating a recordset. First, in line 7, I create a string called `sql`, which is a simple `select` statement. Next, in line 8, I create a recordset called `rs` using the `CreateObject()` method of the Server object. Note that the syntax is similar to that used to create a database connection, except that, in this case, the argument passed to the method is `"ADODB.RecordSet"`. Finally, in line 9, I use the `Open()` method of the Recordset object I just created to open the recordset. Two parameters are passed to the `Open()` method: `sql` and `Conn`. `sql` is the `select` query that was created in line 7, and `Conn` is the database Connection object that was opened in line 5.

At this point, the recordset has been created, and most of the balance of the code has to do with getting the information out of the Recordset object and onto the Web page generated by the script. This is done by means of a string variable called `out`, to which information is added bit by bit throughout the rest of the script.

In lines 11 and 12, HTML is added to `out`. This is not particularly good ASP programming: The point of ASP is that you're able to switch back and forth between code and HTML easily, so a better way of doing it would be something like:

```
1. %>
2. <table border=1>
3. <tr><td><pre>category_uid</pre></td>
   <td><pre>category_name</pre></td>
   <td><pre>category_description</pre></td></tr>
4. <%
```

Problem is, when I write the script part of an ASP page, transitioning back to HTML is confusing somehow, so I tend not to do it all that much unless I have a big chunk of HTML, which is too awkward to put into a string like `out`. I'm rambling...

In line 13, I initiate a `while` loop that continues through line 19. The `while` statement will loop until it reaches the end of the recordset, which is determined by the value of `rs.EOF` (the end-of-file property of the `rs` object).

Inside the `while` loop, the information that is obtained from the recordset is concatenated into the `out` string. This is a matter of building the table that is used to organize the recordset's output and grabbing the value of specific fields using the expression:

```
rs.fields.item("field_name")
```

Here, the `item()` method of the `fields` object, itself part of the Recordset object `rs`, is used to collect the value of the field `field_name`. In lines 15–17, this method is used to collect the successive values of the fields `category_uid`, `category_name`, and `category_description` as the `while` loop iterates through the recordset.

Line 18 is very important: It tells the `rs` object to move to the next record in the recordset. Forget line 18, and the `while` loop will never reach the end of the recordset, continuing until the script times out (ASP does a nice job of protecting us from ourselves: If a script runs too long, typically around 30 seconds, it will time out instead of chewing up system resources indefinitely or crashing your server).

In line 22, the recordset is closed, using the same syntax used to close the Connection object, which is, in turn, closed in line 24. Finally, in line 27, the `out` string is dropped into a plain vanilla HTML page. The result looks like Figure 3-14.

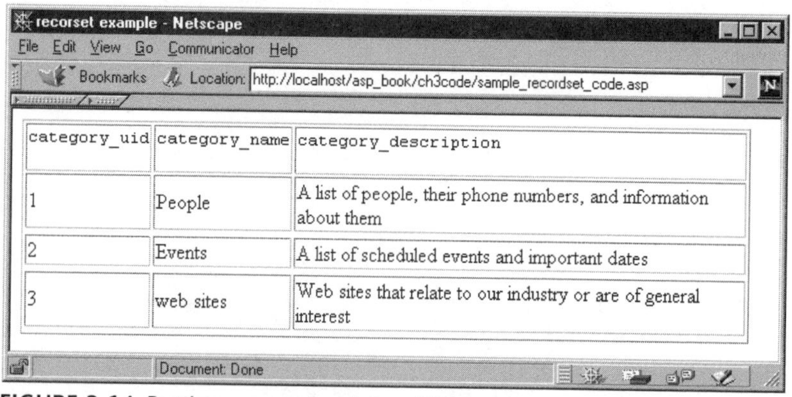

category_uid	category_name	category_description
1	People	A list of people, their phone numbers, and information about them
2	Events	A list of scheduled events and important dates
3	web sites	Web sites that relate to our industry or are of general interest

FIGURE 3-14 Putting a recordset into a Web page

Collecting Field Names from a Recordset Object

Although the code above is perfectly adequate for many situations, it suffers from a significant drawback: In order to put a field into a page, you have to know the name of that field. This make sense if you know what all of the fields in your table are, which is usually the case. The problem is that, if you change your mind and later add another field to your database, you then have to go back into your code and update it to reflect the new field.

The script below solves this problem by dynamically collecting the field names from the recordset itself. Although this is not always appropriate, because it can be used only when the output of the script is being placed in a fairly structured output, such as the table used by this script, it is sometimes useful:

```
1.  <%@ Language=JavaScript %>
2.  <%
3.  DSN = "DSN=ch3db";
4.  Conn = Server.CreateObject("ADODB.Connection");
5.  Conn.Open(DSN);
6.
7.      sql = "SELECT * FROM categories ";
8.      rs = Server.CreateObject("ADODB.RecordSet");
9.      rs.Open (sql, Conn);
10.
11.     out = "<table border=1><tr>";
12.     field_array = new Array()
13.     for ( field_number = 0; field_number
        < rs.fields.count ; field_number++ ){
14.         out += "<td><pre>" +
            rs.fields(field_number).Name +
            "</pre></td>";
15.         field_array[field_number] =
            rs.fields(field_number).Name;
16.     }
17.     out += "</tr>";
18.
19.     while (! (rs.EOF)){
20.         out += "<tr>";
21.         for (i=0; i<field_array.length ; i++)
22.                 {
23.                     out +="<td>" +
                        String(rs.fields.item(field_
                        array[i])) + "</td>"
24.             }
25.         out += "</tr>";
26.         rs.move(1);
27.     } // end while recordset
28.     out += "</table>";
29.
30.     rs.Close ();
31.
32.  Conn.Close ();
33.  %>
34.  <html><head><title>recordset
        example</title></head><body>
```

```
35. <%= out %>
36. </body></html>
```

Most of this script is identical to the preceding script, so I'll limit my discussion to the code I've added.

The `for` loop on lines 13–16 loop through the field names that are stored within the recordset object, dynamically "discovering" what fields have been collected. Field information is stored in `rs.fields`. Because each field in `rs.fields` has an index value, the name of each field can be obtained using the expression `rs.fields(n).name`, where n is an integer. Beginning at zero, the `for` loop continues until the `field_number` variable is no longer less than `rs.fields.count`, which returns the number of fields in the recordset.

Within the loop, line 14 outputs field names into the first row of the table that is being created, while line 15 creates an array called `field_array` that stores the names of all the fields in the recordset.

Having created the first row of the table, the next task is to use the contents of the recordset to populate the balance of the table. This takes place in lines 19 to 27. For each record, the `for` loop on lines 21 to 24 loops through `field array`. Since the contents of `field array` provide the name of all the fields in the recordset, it's easy to use `rs.fields.item(field_name)` to do so.

Creating a JavaScript `for()` Loop

`for()` loops are useful when you need to iterate through a known number of items. For example, to count from one to ten:

```
for (i=1; i<=10; i++){
    Response.Write(i + "<br>");
}
```

which creates results shown in Figure 3-15.

How it works: `for()` loops iterate using a counter. Inside the parentheses, first a counter is set (in this case "i" is set to 1), then a condition is established (the `for()` loop will continue so long as i is less than or equal to 10), then the counter is modified (in this case, incremented by one, using the "++" operator). So long as the condition is true, the code within the curly brackets will be executed, in this case, sending the value of i and a break tag to the browser.

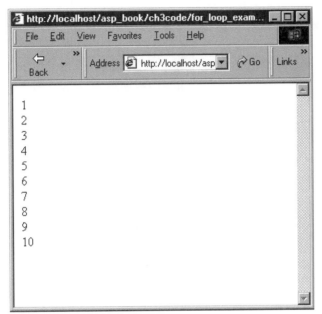

FIGURE 3-15 Counting with `for()`

A similar system can be used to iterate through an array using the `length` property of arrays, which contains the integer value for the number of elements in the array. For example,

```
1. names_array = new Array
     ("bob","marla","jonathan","dede");
2. for (i=0; i<names_array.length ; i++) {
3.        Response.Write(names_array[i] + "<br>");
4. }
```

will create the results shown in Figure 3-16.

Creating a JavaScript Function

A function is a way of encapsulating code that is frequently used. For example, let's say you were working on a really implausible project where you constantly had to send the string "Hello World" to the browser. You might get tired of constantly typing:

```
Response.Write("Hello World");
```

As a truly slothful and improbable programmer, you'd decide to create a function that would do this for you:

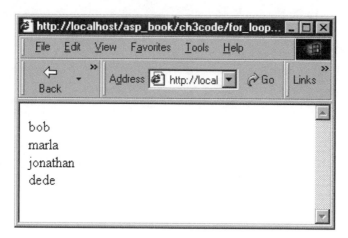

FIGURE 3-16 Looping through an array

```
Function hello (){
      Response.Write("Hello World");
}
```

so that now, all you'd have to type would be:

```
hello();
```

See how much easier that is? (I'll use a function to do something that makes more sense later in this chapter). Note that this function works exactly like any other JavaScript function.

Using Include Files for Shared Code

If you find yourself using the same code over and over in different scripts, you may want to consider using include files to share the same set of code among many files. Because the two scripts used in this chapter do a lot of the same database stuff, this comes in handy.

When you use an include, it's just like pasting the contents of a file into another file. This happens before the file goes to the ASP interpreter, so if your include file has code in it, it gets interpreted just as it would if it were in the file.

For example, let's say you have a file with an include:

```
<%@ Language=JavaScript %>
<html><head></head><body>
<!-- #include file="include.js" -->
```

```
<p>example asp page
</body></html>
```

and the include file consisted of a small amount of ASP code:

```
<%
Response.Write("Yet another")
%>
```

This would be the same as having a single file:

```
<%@ Language=JavaScript %>
<html><head></head><body>
<%
Response.Write("Yet another")
%>
<p>example asp page
</body></html>
```

Obviously, not a very useful example. But, as you'll see in this chapter (and the next couple of chapters, too), includes can make a big difference in terms of keeping things simple when several scripts share functionality.

Creating a JavaScript Object to Store Information

I'd probably make a fool of myself it I tried to go into details about object-oriented programming, so I'll keep it brief. The basic problem with programming is that programs tend to get long and complicated, and this even happens to scripts that are supposed to be short and simple.

Objects were supposed to change all that by organizing information in logical groups of properties (variables) and methods (functions).

Well, it turns out that, even with objects, scripts get long and complicated, but a well-crafted object can be a big help. I won't cover methods here, but I'll show you how to store information in an object.

For example, let's say that you need to keep track of information about Bill in a script. You could write:

```
bill = new Object();
bill.name = "bill smith";
bill.age = "8";
bill.favorite_colour = "purple!";
```

```
bill.birthday = "10/18/99";
```

Then it would be easy to use this information later. For example:

```
Response.Write("Happy Birthday, " + bill.name + ". I
can't believe you're already" + bill.age );
```

which would send the string "Happy Birthday bill smith. I can't believe you're already 8" to the browser.

If all you're doing is keeping track of information about Bill, this might not make so much sense. But if you needed to keep track of the same information for Miranda and Wilbur and Veronica as well, all of a sudden, using an object might help make keeping track of everything a lot easier. Knowing, for example, that we had objects named after each with the appropriate age stored in each object, we could then access their ages using a consistent syntax: `bill.name`, `miranda.name`, `wilbur.name`, and `veronica.name`.

CODE FOR VIEW DATABASE SCRIPTS

To get these scripts to work, make sure that you've covered the following bases:

- You'll need four files: the database (`ch3db.mdb`) and three asp files (`ch3_include.js`, `ch3_view_categories.asp`, and `ch3_view_records.asp`).
- You need to create a DSN (see instructions above) so that the scripts can connect to the database via ODBC.

Script 3-1
ch3_include.js

```
1.  <%
2.  var out = "";
3.  var current_category =
    String(Request("current_category")); // category uid
4.  var view_categories_script =
    "ch3_view_categories.asp";
5.  var view_records_script = "ch3_view_records.asp";
6.
7.  ///////////////////////////////////////////////////////
8.  // create connection to database
9.
10. DSN = "DSN=ch3db";
11. Conn = Server.CreateObject("ADODB.Connection");
```

```
12.  Conn.Open(DSN);
13.
14.  /////////////////////////////////////////////////
15.  // create cat_object, the category object. Because
     category information is used
16.  // on almost every page, this code is executed every
     time.
17.
18.  sql = "SELECT * FROM categories order by
     category_name";
19.  rs = Server.CreateObject("ADODB.RecordSet");
20.  rs.Open (sql, Conn, 2,3);
21.      if (rs.EOF){        // check to see if rs is empty
22.              out += "no records found in categories
                 table. something is probably wrong.";
23.      }
24.      else{                    // rs not empty
25.              cat_object = new Object ();
26.              temp_counter = 0;
27.
28.              while (! (rs.EOF)){
29.                      cat_object[temp_counter] = new
                         Object ();
30.                      cat_object[temp_counter].uid =
                         parseInt(rs.fields.item
                         ("category_uid"))
31.                      cat_object[temp_counter].name =
                         String(rs.fields.item
                         ("category_name"))
32.                      cat_object[temp_counter].desc =
                         String(rs.fields.item
                         ("category_description"))
33.
34.                      rs.move(1);
35.                      temp_counter ++;
36.              } // end while recordset
37.              cat_object.qty = (temp_counter);
38.      } // end else (rs not empty)
39.  rs.Close ();
40.
41.  /////////////////////////////////////////////////
42.  //  slash_date (), a function used to clean up
     dates
43.
44.  new function slash_date (temp_date){
45.  if (temp_date != ""){
46.      temp_date2 = new Date(temp_date);
47.      temp_date3 =  temp_date2.getMonth()+1 + "/" +
         temp_date2.getDate() + "/" +
         temp_date2.getFullYear();
48.      return (temp_date3);
```

```
49. }
50. else{
51.     return "--/--/--";
52. }
53. }
54. %>
```

HOW THE SCRIPT WORKS

The include file is used to perform tasks that are shared by the display scripts described later in this chapter. By using an include file, we are able to avoid having duplicate code. This saves some effort when creating the display scripts discussed in this chapter and a great deal of effort when you consider that the include file will eventually be used not only by the display scripts covered in this chapter, but also by the scripts used to edit the database discussed in the next chapters.

1. Open the ASP code tag. This is necessary, because the include tag is outside of the ASP code below.

2–5. Several variables that are shared by both scripts are declared here.

- out is a string used to store any output generated during the execution of the script that is not immediately sent to the browser.
- Current_category is used to store the id of the current category, if a category is defined.
- View_categories_script and view_records_script are used to store the URL of the two scripts discussed below. By using these variables, rather than hard-coding the file names, it'll be a lot easier to change the names of the files later, something that seems to happen a lot.

10–12. These three lines create a database connection object called Conn. Note that, if your DSN is not called ch3db, you should change the value set in line 10.

18–39. Because both scripts in this chapter need information about categories, category information is collected in the include file rather than in the individual scripts. This is done by creating an object called cat_object and putting all of the category data that we'll need into this data: the uids, names, and descriptions of all the categories in the database. Later, the information can be retrieved by iterating through cat_object.

19,20. Here, I create a recordset called `rs` that contains all of the fields of all of the records in the table `categories`, sorted alphabetically using the `category_name` field.

21–23. Although it's not particularly likely that there won't be any categories in the database, things always seem to break, and catching an error here makes it easier to figure what is going on when I do something stupid in six months, long after I've forgotten how this script works. You may want to change the error message in line 22 so that it says something that will make sense to you.

24–38. If we do have records in `rs`, we collect the information from `rs` and put it into `cat_object`.

25. Create the variable `cat_object`.

26. Create the variable `temp_counter` and set its value to zero. `cat_object` is a lot like an array that contains a number of objects, except that it also has a property called `qty`. The first category we find will be `cat_object[0]`, then `cat_object[1]`, and so on.

28–37. A `while()` loop that loops through the recordset `rs` so long as `rs.EOF` (end of the recordset) is not true.

29. On each iteration, a new object is created that will contain information about one of the categories in the database. For example, the first category will be `cat_object[0]`.

30–32. Store the uid, name, and description of the current category.

For example, `cat_object[0].uid` might be the integer `"1"`, `cat_object[0].name` might be the string "Events", and `cat_object[0].description` the string "A list of scheduled events and important dates".

34. The `move()` method takes us to the next record in the recordset. Without this, we end up with one of those oh-so-delightful endless loops.

35. Increments the `temp_counter` variable.

36. End of the `while` loop.

37. Creates a property of `cat_object` called `qty`, which is set to the number of categories we found. This makes it easy to loop through `cat_object` later.

38. End of the `else` started in line 24.

39. Closes the recordset created on line 19.

44–48. These lines define a function called `slash_date()`, which converts the date output by an Access database to a format that is easy to read.

44. Declares a new function and specifies that it expects a single argument, which is set to `temp_date`.

45. If string `temp_date` is not empty, lines 46–48 are executed.

46. Using the string `temp_date` that was passed as an argument, a new date object called `temp_date2` is created.

47. Here, the `temp_date2` is used to create a new string called `temp_date3` that contains a date that's easy to read (xx/xx/xx). To do this, the `temp_date2` object is used to get numeric values for the month, day of the month, and year. This is done using three methods that are built into JavaScript date objects: `getMonth()`, `getDate()`, and `getFullYear()` (see Chapter 1 for more date stuff). Note that the month value needs to be incremented by one because a value between 0 and 11 is returned instead of the 1–12 that most of us are used to.

48. Finally, the `return()` function is used to return the string `temp_date3` that was just created.

50–52. If `temp_date` turns out to be empty, the string --/--/-- is returned.

53. End of the `slash_date()` function.

50. Close ASP tag.

Script 3-2
ch3_view_categories.asp

```
1.  <%@ Language=JavaScript %>
2.  <!-- #include file="ch3_include.js" -->
3.
4.  <html><head><title>View
    Categories</title></head><body>
5.
6.  <center><font size="+2"> View Contents of Database
    </font>
7.  <br>Select a category to see records in that
    category<hr>
8.
9.  <%
```

```
10.
11. for (i = 0; i < cat_object.qty; i++){
12.     %>
13.     <a href="<% = view_records_script
        %>?current_category=<% = cat_object[i].uid %>"
        ><b><% = cat_object[i].name %></b></a>
14.     <br><% = cat_object[i].desc %><br>
15.     <%
16. }
17.
18.Conn.Close ();
19. %>
20. </center>
21. </body></html>
```

HOW THE SCRIPT WORKS

Because category information is put into `cat_object` in the include file, creating a list of categories is simply a matter of looping through `cat_object` to retrieve information that has already been collected. As a result, `ch3_view_categories.asp` is a fairly short script.

As per convention, I'll only discuss the ASP portion of the script and assume that you're familiar enough with HTML that I don't need to go into it.

1. Specify that this script is written in JavaScript.

2. Use an `include` tag to include `ch3_include.js` (previous script, discussed above).

11–16. A `for()` loop is used here to loop through `cat_object`, which is created in `ch3_include.js`, and create a list of categories with descriptions and links to `ch3_view_records.asp` (next script, below).

11. The loop is initiated on line 11, using a counter called `i`, which is incremented from zero, so long as it is less than `cat_object.qty`. Thus, if we have three categories in our database, `cat_object.qty` will be 3, and `i` will go from zero to 2.

13,14. The `uid`, `name`, and `desc` properties of `cat_object` are dropped into an HTML template. Note how ASP tag is closed on line 12 and reopened on line 15, with variables dropped in using the `<% = variable %>` syntax. The `view_records_script` string, also set in the include file,

is used to specify the name of the script that the link being
created will link to.

16. End of the `for()` loop.

18. The `Conn` object, which was created in the include file, is
closed here.

19. End of ASP code.

Script 3-3
ch3_view_records.asp

```
1.  <%@ Language=JavaScript %>
2.  <!-- #include file="ch3_include.js" -->
3.
4.  <html><head><title>List
    Categories</title></head><body>
5.
6.
7.  <%///////////////////////////////////////////////////////
8.  // Create Header %>
9.
10. <div align="center"><font size="+2">
11. <%
12. // loop through cat_objects to get category name
    based on value
13. // of current_category
14. for (i = 0; i < cat_object.qty; i++){
15.     if (cat_object[i].uid == current_category)
        { Response.Write(cat_object[i].name);}
16. }
17. %>
18. </font><br><a href="<% = view_categories_script
    %>">Back to list of Categories</a>
19. </div><hr>
20.
21. <%
22. ///////////////////////////////////////////////////////
23. // Create dynamic subcategory navbar
24.
25. sql = "SELECT distinct data_subcategory FROM data
    where data_category = " + current_category + " order
    by data_subcategory";
26. rs = Server.CreateObject("ADODB.RecordSet");
27. rs.Open (sql, Conn, 2,3);
28.     if (rs.EOF){      // check to see if rs is empty
29.            out += "no subcategories in this
               category.";
30.     }
```

```
31.    else{                    // rs not empty
32.            Response.Write("<center>");
33.            while (! (rs.EOF)){
34. %>
35.                    <a href="#<% =
                       String(rs.fields.item
                       ("data_subcategory"))%>"><% =
                       String(rs.fields.item
                       ("data_subcategory"))
                       %></a>     
                        
36. <%
37.                    rs.move(1);
38.            } // end while recordset
39.            Response.Write("</center><HR>");
40.    } // end else (rs not empty)
41. rs.Close ();
42.
43. ////////////////////////////////////////////////////
44. // Create list of records:
45.
46. sql = "SELECT * FROM data where data_category = " +
    current_category + " order by data_subcategory,
    data_name";
47.
48. // events should be ordered by date so slightly
    different query:
49. if (current_category == 2){
50.    sql = "SELECT * FROM data where data_category
           = " + current_category + " order by
           data_subcategory, data_main_date, data_name";
51. }
52.
53. rs = Server.CreateObject("ADODB.RecordSet");
54. rs.Open (sql, Conn, 2,3);
55. if (rs.EOF){        // check to see if rs is empty
56.    Response.Write("<p>There are no records in
           this category");
57. }
58. else{                        // rs not empty
59.
60. temp_subcat= ""; //this string used to group records
    by subcategory
61. fields = new Object(); // this object used to store
    fields in records
62.
63. while (! (rs.EOF)){
64.
65.    // clean up data and put it into the fields
           object:
```

```
66.    for ( field_number = 0; field_number <
       rs.fields.count ; field_number++ )
67.        {
68.            temp_field =
               String(rs.fields(field_number).Name);
69.            temp_content =
               String(rs.fields.item(temp_field));
70.            if (temp_content == "null")
               {temp_content = ""; }
71.            if (temp_field.search(/date/) > 0 )
               // check for date fields
72.                    {temp_content =
                       slash_date(temp_content);}
73.            fields[temp_field] = temp_content
74.    } // end looping through fields in current
       record
75.
76.    // when we get to a new subcategory, display
       its name
77.    // and create an anchor
78.    if (temp_subcat != fields.data_subcategory){
79.            temp_subcat = fields.data_subcategory;
80. %>
81.            <div align="center"><b><a name="<% =
               temp_subcat %>"><% = temp_subcat
               %></a></b></div>
82. <%
83.    }
84.
85.            ////////////////////////////////////////
86.            // What happens next is entirely
               category dependent
87.            ////////////////////////////////////////
88.
89.            ////////////////////////////////////////
90.            // PEOPLE (1)
91.            if (current_category == 1){
92. %>
93. <p><b><% = fields.data_name%></b> -  <% =
    fields.data_description %>
94. <table width=80%>
95. <tr><td width=50%>
96.    Company: <% = fields.data_company %>
97.    <br>Address1: <% = fields.data_address1 %>
98.    <br>Address2: <% = fields.data_address2 %>
99.    <br>City: <% = fields.data_city %>
100.   <br>State: <% = fields.data_state %>
101.   <br>Zip: <% = fields.data_zip %>
102.   <br>Country: <% = fields.data_country
       %>
103. </td><td>
```

```
104.      Email: <% = fields.data_email %>
105.      <br>Work Phone: <% =
          fields.data_phone_work %>
106.      <br>Fax: <% = fields.data_phone_fax %>
107.      <br>Cell Phone: <% =
          fields.data_phone_cell %>
108.      <br>Home Phone: <% =
          fields.data_phone_home %>
109. </table>
110.<%
111.              } //end if cat is 1
112.
113.
114.              //////////////////////////////////////
115.              // EVENTS (2)
116.              else if (current_category == 2){
117.
118.
119. %>
120. <p><b><% = slash_date (fields.data_main_date)
     %>: <% = fields.data_name%></b>
121. <br>Description: <% = fields.data_description
     %>
122. <br>Start Date: <% = fields.data_start_date %>,
     End Date: <% = fields.data_end_date %>
123.
124. <%
125.              } // end if category is 2
126.
127.              //////////////////////////////////////
128.              // WEB SITES (3)
129.              else if (current_category == 3){
130. %>
131. <p>
132. <a href="<% = fields.data_url %>">
133. <b><% = fields.data_name%></b></a>
134.
135. <br><% = fields.data_description %>
136. <%
137.              } //end if cat is 3
138.
139.              //////////////////////////////////////
140.              // CATCH-ALL TEMPLATE
141.              else {
142. %>
143. <p>
144. <a href="<% = fields.data_url %>">
145. <b><% = fields.data_name%></b></a>
146. <br><% = fields.data_description %>
147. <br>Note: no template has been created for
     this category
```

```
148. <%
149.            }
150.
151.                rs.move(1);
152. } // end while recordset
153. } // end else (rs not empty)
154.
155. rs.Close ();
156. Conn.Close ();
157.
158. %>
159. </body></html>
```

HOW THE SCRIPT WORKS

This script is fairly long, so it's worth taking the time to review what it does before jumping in. I always have an easier time dealing with big chunks of code if I know that, ultimately, what's happening isn't all that complicated:

1. Create a header: This contains the title of the page.

2. Create a subcategory navbar: Because this script lists all the records in a category, it can get fairly long. The subcategory navbar lets a user jump to a specific subcategory.

3. Create a list of all the records in the category. This makes up the bulk of the script, in large part, because there is a separate template for each category.

Here goes...

CREATING A HEADER

1. Set ASP language to be JavaScript.

2. Pull in the include file (discussed earlier in this chapter).

10–21. Create header. The header consists of two things: the title, which is the name of the current category, and a link back to the list of categories (the previous script, above).

The only required parameter for this script is the uid of the category whose records are being displayed, which is is stored in the `current_category` variable, which is collected in the include file (`ch3_include.js`). To find the name of the current category, it is necessary to loop through `cat_object` (created in the include file) and find the category whose uid matches `current_category`. This starts on line14.

14. Start a `for()` loop that loops through `cat_object`.

15. For each category record in `cat_object`, check to see whether the current record's uid is equal to `current_category`. If it is, that record's name is sent to the browser.

16. End of the `for()` loop.

18. This line uses the `view_categories_script` variable to create a link back to the categories list script (previous script).

CREATE SUBCATEGORY NAVBAR

25–41. The next step is to create the subcategory navigation bar, which consists of links to all of the subcategories in the current category.

25. The SQL string created on this line uses the `distinct` keyword to create a recordset that consists of an alphabetical list of the subcategories that exist in the database for the current category.

26–27. Create the recordset `rs`, then open it using the SQL string from line 25.

28–30. If no subcategories are found, create an error message. This shouldn't happen, unless something is broken or there are no records in a category.

Most of the time, there will be at least one subcategory, and lines 32–39 will be executed.

32. Send a `<center>` tag to the browser.

33. Start of a `while()` loop to loop through the recordset.

35. Using the name of the subcategory (`String (rs.fields.item("data_subcategory"))`), create a link to an anchor that has the same name as the subcategory.

37. `move()` to the next record in the recordset.

38. End of the `while` loop.

39. Close the `<center>` tag opened in line 32.

40. End of the `else` on line 31.

41. Close the recordset opened on line 27.

<small>DISPLAY RECORDS</small>

46–156. The balance of the code deals with the work involved in collecting all the records in the current category, cleaning up the data, and formatting it before sending it to the browser.

46–51. One of two different SQL queries is used to collect the relevant records from the database. Both collect the same set of records—all the records in the table `data` where the `data_category` field is equal to `current_category`. The difference is that if `current_category` is set to 2, the records are sorted chronologically, using the `data_main_date` field. In both cases, records are grouped by subcategory.

53,54. A recordset called `rs` is created, using the query defined above.

55–57. If no records are found, an error message is displayed.

58–154. If records are found (which is what will almost always happen, once the script is up and running correctly), the code on lines 57–153 will be executed.

60. A variable called `temp_subcat` is set to empty string (`""`). This variable will be used to keep track of the current subcategory. Any time that the value of `temp_subcat` changes, the script will generate a subcategory header.

61. This line creates a new object called `fields`. The purpose of this object is to make it easier to work with the information that we are collecting from the database. For example, when sending the name of a record to the browser, instead of having to type `String(rs.fields.item(data_name))`, the same information will be accessible by typing `fields.data_name`. Because each category has its own template that needs to be modified from time to time, this is a nice convenience.

63. Start the `while()` loop that will loop through the recordset. This executes the code between line 64 and line 153, which makes up the bulk of this script.

66–75. The first step in displaying the data is to clean it up and put it into the `fields` object that was created on line 61. This is done using a `for()` loop.

66. This `for()` loop goes through all of the fields of the current record, which is relatively easy to do, thanks to the `rs` object, which tells us how many fields we're dealing with in its `rs.fields.count` property. Starting at 0, we can then loop through the fields, using `field_number` as a counter.

68. The `temp_field` variable is used to store the name of the current field.

69. The `temp_content` variable is used to collect the value of the current field, using the `temp_field` value we just collected.

70. If the value of `temp_content` is the special value `null`, `temp_content` is set to "" (empty string), which makes more sense, especially to nonprogrammers.

71,72. If the name of the current field includes the string `"date"` (using a regular expression), the `slash_date()` function is used to express the date in a format that is easy to read. The `slash_date()` function is described in the description of the include file earlier.

73. Finally, the `temp_field` and `temp_content` fields are used to put the value of the field into the `fields` object. For example, if the field `data_description` contains the string `"A really neat site"`, then `fields[data_description]` (which is the same thing as `fields.data_description`) will be set to the value `"A really neat site"`.

78–83. These lines create a subcategory header every time the subcategory changes. Because records are ordered by subcategory, this has the effect of grouping records.

78. The `temp_subcat` variable is used to keep track of transitions from one subcategory to another. Any time that a new subcategory is found, it will not be equal to `temp_subcat`; lines 79–82 are executed.

79. `temp_subcat` is set to the new subcategory.

81. A subcategory header is printed, inside of an anchor tag (so that users can jump directly to subcategories from the top of the page).

91–149. The templates on these pages create a different page, depending on the category. Note that if you create a new category in the database, you will probably want to create a new template. A set of `if/else if/ else` statements are used to determine which templates, based on the value of the `current_category` variable.

The templates consist of standard HTML, along with information drawn from the `fields` object. For example, to add the `data_name` field to the HTML code, the following code is used:

```
<% = fields.data_name %>
```

151. The all-important `move()` method of the recordset object, without which endless loops seem to sneak in. Not that I'd ever make such an elementary mistake. :)

Well, if you've gotten this far, I'm gonna bet that you can pretty much figure out the rest. First, the `while()` loop runs out of steam, then the `else` thing we started way back on line 58. Finally, it's time to close things: the recordset, the Connection object, the ASP tag, the <body> tag, and, ultimately, the <html> tag.

RECAP

Separating content from interface is at the core of publishing large amounts of information on the Web. This chapter covers the basics of using ASP and an ODBC database to publish a simple data structure. The scripts can easily be extended to handle more complicated data structures.

Critical issues covered include:

- Using ASP to get data via ODBC
- Displaying the resultant data in templates
- Passing instructions between scripts using form variables
- Using an SQL database

IDEAS FOR HACKING THIS SCRIPT

- Create new categories (see next chapters)
- Modify templates in display script.

- Create a search page that performs a keyword search on one or more fields. This is done using a where clause, for example:

```
sql = "select * from data where data_category = " +
current_category + " and where data_name like '%" +
search_term + " %'";
```

Note that you'll need to create a form that collects a search_term variable.
- Use if() statements to check to see whether a field has information in it before displaying it.

4 Editing Records

IN THIS CHAPTER

- Using a Web interface to edit records in a database
- SQL `insert`, `update`, and `delete` statements
- The ASP Session object
- Password-protected Web pages with ASP
- The Request.QueryString object
- Regular expressions
- Dynamically generated forms

The previous chapter covered a set of scripts that published information stored in a relational database to the Web. This chapter discusses a set of scripts that create a password-protected interface that can be used to edit the contents of that database.

By abstracting the contents of a Web site, storing these contents in a database, and creating an interface that is usable by nontechnical users, it becomes possible to create sites that can effectively publish large amounts of dynamic information.

Applied effectively, the approach outlined in this chapter goes a long way toward solving the biggest problem of Web design—maintaining the site after it's finished.

By abstracting the structure of a site (HTML templates, scripts, databases, servers, etc. ...) from the information that is published within that structure (ideally, information stored in a database, but often, information that is trapped in a static HTML page), this chapter illustrates the extent to which all but the smallest Web sites have become collaborative projects.

Those of us concerned with technology need to coordinate with designers, strategists, marketers, copywriters, support people, and, of course, whoever is in charge of the purse strings. Increasingly, it's becoming important to set up a technical infrastructure that we can walk away from, leaving the other parties to manage the site. So you can dive into your next project and solve yet another puzzle.

This chapter illustrates one approach.

◆ Project: Using a Web Interface to Edit Records in a Database

Chapter 3 covered a lot of the basics of connecting a Web site to a database: creating a connection to a database, collecting a set of data, cleaning up that data, then dropping it into a template that generates the HTML page that a visitor actually sees.

If you have a database where data entry is performed using a front end, such as the MS Access front end described in Chapter 3, that may be all you need. But there are several reasons that you might prefer to use a Web interface to manage the data. If a lot of different people will be editing information in the database, it'll be a heck of a lot easier to set up a script on a Web server than to set everyone up with a database front end (MS Access, for example), show them how to use it, and help them every time they run into to trouble getting connected to the database located on your Web server. You could save some money on licensing costs, as well. Perhaps most critically, you'll be able to edit the database from any computer with a Web browser that can establish a TCP/IP connection to the Web server where you host the database.

Hmm... Sounds like I'm writing a commercial for why the Internet matters. Maybe this should've gone on the back cover of the book instead of here in the middle. If this is old hat, my apologies for subjecting you to another tired rant. If not, file this away with all the other arguments you'll use next time you're trying to get your boss to give you a raise.

:)

So let's take a quick tour of the Web interface generated by the scripts in this chapter.

First thing to consider is security: If you're going to let people edit a database, you want to make sure some spiteful recreant can't delete the information you've worked so hard to create. The scripts in this chapter use a very simple password mechanism, as in Figure 4-1.

FIGURE 4-1 To edit the database, a Web user has to know the password

If a user knows the correct password, the first thing she'll see is a list of categories similar to the list displayed by the scripts in the previous chapter. This time, however, she'll have the option of either clicking on a category name to view the records in that category, or of editing the information for the category itself (see Figure 4-2).

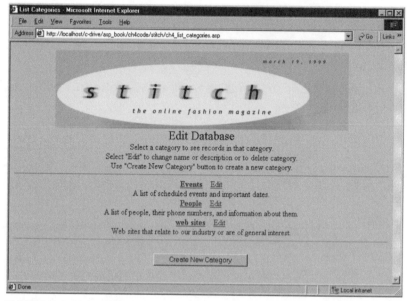

FIGURE 4-2 Users with access to this script can now edit category information

Using the category edit form in Figure 4-3, users can change the name or description of a category.

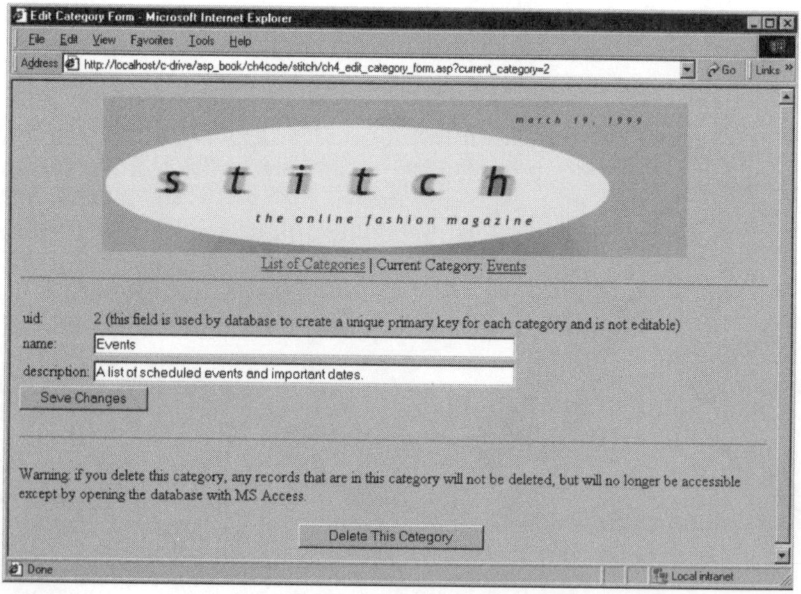

FIGURE 4-3 This form lets users edit the category names and descriptions

Just as with the category list (Figure 4-2), the list of records within a category lets you select a specific record for editing, as in Figure 4-4.

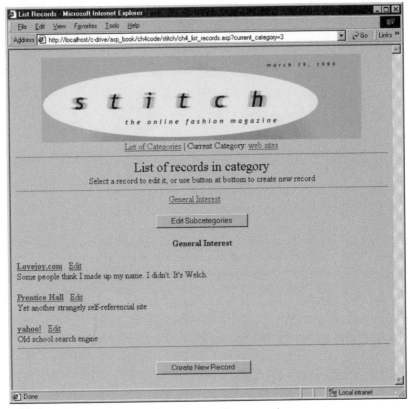

FIGURE 4-4 The "Edit" link lets a user edit a record

The edit record form creates an HTML as in Figure 4-5 from the field for every editable field in the database (note that the `uid` field, which is maintained by the database, is not editable).

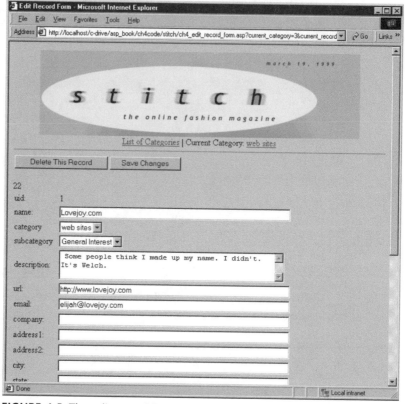

FIGURE 4-5 The edit record form

So let's take a look at the new features that make these scripts tick.

NEW FEATURES

`Response.Redirect()`: Redirecting Users to Another Page with the Response Object

In Chapter 1, I described how the `Write()` method of the Response object could be used to send a string of HTML code or content to the browser.

The Response object can also be used to send HTTP header information to a browser. HTTP headers are used to exchange a variety of information. For example, browsers use headers to tell Web servers what kind of files they're prepared to handle. Likewise, Web servers use headers to communicate about various things, including, for example, whether a file contains text, HTML, a binary image, etc. ....

An HTTP header can also be used to **redirect** a browser from one page to another page. In ASP, this is done through the Response object:

```
Response.Redirect("Page.asp")
```

This would redirect a browser from the current script to a page called `Page.asp` (the same code could just as easily be used to send visitors to an HTML page called `Page.html`).

Note
As the word "header" implies, HTTP headers need to be sent to the browser before the page can be sent. You'll note in this chapter that `Response.Redirect()` is always used before the `<body>` tag is opened.

ASP Session Object

HTML was designed as an open protocol that would allow computer users to share documents, regardless of the program used to create the document or the computer used to view the document. To make it easy to use, HTML was set up so that servers did not necessarily need to keep track of who was visiting a site or whether a visitor requesting a document had previously requested another document from the same server.

What made the protocol ideal for making it easy to publish documents has since made it difficult for certain situations where it's nice to know that a person who requested one page then requests another page. For example, shopping cart scripts need to know whether visitors have any items in their shopping carts. Another case where it's necessary to maintain information about a user (sometimes referred to as maintaining "state") is when it's necessary to authenticate a user, then to give that user access to more than one Web page or script.

Confronted with the need to keep track of information about site visitors, Netscape introduced a browser feature called "cookies," which was subsequently built into Internet Explorer and is now supported by most browsers. Cookies make it possible for a Web server to store small amounts of information on a browser, which can then be used to keep track of site visitors.

ASP includes a built-in facility for keeping track of unique visitors (using cookies): the Session object. Because the ASP Session object keeps track of unique visitors, once a user has been authenticated using a password check, it is very easy to use the Session object to verify that a user requesting access to a script does, in fact, have permission to use that script.

Session Password Mechanism

Using the Session object to exclude nonauthenticated users from using certain scripts requires two elements:

1. Code that sets a value in the Session object when a user matches a certain criterion (in this case, when a user knows a password).

2. Code that checks to make sure that the desired value is stored in the Session object before granting a user access to a sensitive script or HTML page.

COLLECTING A PASSWORD AND SETTING A Session VARIABLE

The first step is to create a simple script that collects a password, checks to make sure it is correct, then assigns the value of the password to a Session object variable so that subsequent scripts will be able to verify that a user is, in fact, authenticated. The following script does the trick.

```
1. <%@ Language=JavaScript %>
2. <%
3. if (String(Request("password")) == "password")
4.     {
5.        Session("edit_db_pass") =
          String(Request("password"));
6.        Response.Redirect("yet_another_page.asp");
7. }
8. %>
9. <html><head></head><body>
10. <form action="<% =
    String(Request.ServerVariables("SCRIPT_NAME")) %>">
11. <p>Password Please:
12. <input type=password name=password >
13. <input type=submit name="toss" value="Submit">
14. </form>
15. </body></html>
```

Lines 9–14 consist of a very simple form that contains a text box and a Submit button, allowing the user to type in a password. Note that, on line 12, the `type` attribute of the input tag is set to `password` (as opposed to `text`), so that the password is not displayed when a user types it in.

When the password is submitted, it is reviewed by the `if()` statement on line 3. If the correct value is typed in, which, in this case, is the string `"password"`, lines 5 and 6 are executed.

Line 5 creates a `Session` variable called `edit_db_pass` and assigns to it the value that was collected by the `password` box on the form.

Line 6 uses a `Response.Redirect()` statement (discussed above) to forward the browser to `yet_another_page.asp`.

Thus, if the correct password is entered, a user is forwarded to `yet_another_page.asp`, whereas, if the wrong password is typed in (or if no password is typed in, as when this script is invoked for the first time), the user is given the form and an opportunity to type in a valid password.

CHECKING FOR VALID **Session** VARIABLE

Once a `Session` variable has been set, the next step is to check for it any time a script is generating a page to which you want to control access. In the case of the code above, this is done by checking to make sure that the value of the `Session` variable `edit_db_pass` is set to the correct value:

```
1. <%@ Language=JavaScript %>
2. <%
3. if (Session("edit_db_pass") != "password"){
4.
5. Response.Redirect("password_form.asp");
6. }
7. %>
8. //… balance of the script
```

On line 3, an `if()` statement is used to compare the value stored in `Session("edit_db_pass")` to the string `"password"`. If the values are not the same, the browser is redirected to the page `password_form.asp`, which would contain a script similar to the script shown above, which would collect a valid password from the user.

A QUICK NOTE ON SECURITY

Note that the password system described here offers very limited security, based on using a single password, which is passed unencrypted across the network and might be shared by many users.

Although adequate for many applications, this type of security is mainly useful where the point of the password is more to prevent someone unfamiliar with how the scripts work from accidentally deleting or modifying records than to prevent malicious users from accessing or modifying information stored in your database.

Using SQL to Update Records

Chapter 3 included a brief introduction to SQL and described how to use SQL to retrieve records from a database. This section briefly discusses how an existing record can be edited using an `update` statement.

This is applied to a specific record by constraining the `update` statement to affect only a record whose primary key is a specific value.

For example, an `update` statement can be used to change the description field of a specific record in the categories table.

Category_uid	category_name	category_description
3	Web sites	Web sites that relate to our industry or are of general interest

To do this, the statement is written so that it applies to only those records where the value of `category_uid` is 3. Because the `category_uid` field is the primary key of the table and can, therefore, contain only unique values, this effectively constrains the statement to acting on the single record shown above. To wit:

```
update categories set category_description = 'Spiffy
sites!' where data_uid = 3
```

This statement modifies the value of a single field, `category_description`. As a result, the record is modified so that it now looks like this:

Category_uid	category_name	category_description
3	Web sites	Spiffy sites!

Using the Request.QueryString Object to Collect Form Data

In Chapters 2 and 3, the Request object was used to collect form data that was submitted by the user or included in a form or link in order to give a script instructions on what task to perform. In every case, the script had to identify specifically the name of the field for which a value was expected. For example, earlier in this chapter, a script retrieved a form variable called `password` by using the expression:

```
Request("password")
```

Well, actually, the script used an expression that included the `String()` function, because that helps to keep things simple:

```
String(Request("password"))
```

Either way, the point here is that it's pretty easy to get the Request object to collect a specific form variable. But what if you're too lazy to enumerate specifically every form variable that you're working with?

Fear not, for ASP gives us the Request.QueryString object, which contains all of the form information that was passed to the server using the HTTP `Get` method.[1] All that's required to collect all the information sent to a script via the `Get` method is to iterate through the Request.QueryString object:

```
1. <%@ Language=JavaScript %>
2. <html><head></head><body>
3. <%
4. for ( field_number = 1; field_number <=
   Request.QueryString.count ; field_number++ ){
5.
6.     temp_field =
       String(Request.QueryString.Key(field_number));
7.     temp_content =
       String(Request.QueryString.item(temp_field))
8. %>
9.     <br><% = temp_field %>: <% = temp_content %>
```

---

1. The HTTP Get method is when form information is passed to the server in the URL, which is the default method. The alternative, the `Post` method, passes information to the server via the HTTP headers that were discussed earlier in this chapter. Scripts can collect form information passed to the server by the `Post` method using the Request.Form object.

```
10. <%
11. }
12. %></body></html>
```

Here's how it works:

- `Request.QueryString.count` returns the number of form variables in the incoming form.
- If we give `Request.QueryString.Key()` a number less than the number of incoming form variables, the Request object gives us the name of a field.
- If we put that field name in `Request.QueryString.item()`, we get the value of that field.

Thus, line 4 opens a `for()` statement that loops from 1 to `Request.QueryString.count`.

Warning

Note that here the ASP `Request` goes off into left field, starting at 1 rather than at the more traditional 0. Duh.

On each iteration, the `field_number` is incremented by one, retrieving a different field name and value (lines 6 and 7) on each successive occasion. Finally, on line 9, the key/value pair is added to the Web page.

Iterating through form variables like this is useful in two cases. The first is while writing a script, when it's often useful to see what form variables are being passed for debugging purposes. The second is when dealing with a large number of fields that can be manipulated in a systematic fashion. One such scenario will be explored later in this chapter.

Using a Regular Expression to Examine the Contents of a String (`String.search(//," ")`)

Chapter 2 touched briefly on regular expressions, showing how a regular expression could be used to perform pattern matching and substitutions within a string.

Regular expressions can also be used to check to see whether you can find a pattern within a string in order to make a decision.

For example, let's say that you have a variable called name, and that you want to check to see whether it contains the string "Bob" so that your script can react appropriately:

```
1. if (name.search(/Bob/) >= 0 ){
2.      Response.Write("Bob! \n<p>So how the heck are
        you?")
3. }
4. else{
5.      Response.Write("Oh.<p>Hi.<p>How are you?")
6. }
```

When you apply the search() method to a string (regular expressions are methods of the generic JavaScript string object), this returns a "-1" if nothing is found, and the index value of where the pattern starts if it is found. Thus, if the "Bob" exists within the string name, the regular expression will return a value of 0 or more and trigger a familiar greeting. Non-Bobs will be relegated to the merely courteous "Hi".

To check for more than one value, you can separate patterns with the pipe ("|") symbol:

```
if (name.search(/Bob|Dolores/) >= 0 ){
    //… do something
}
```

The JavaScript substring() Function

The substring( ) function lets you remove a small piece of a string. For example, it can be used to remove the last character from a string:

```
sentence = "Nothing will happen here."
sentence = sentence.substring(0,(sentence.length-1));
```

which will remove the period from the string sentence, leaving you with the string "Nothing will happen here".

The two arguments passed to the substring() function are the index values of the first character and the last character that you want to cut out of the string that you start with.

CODE TO EDIT DATABASE

The code to edit the records in the database is a little more involved than the code in Chapter 3 used to display information in the database. Figure 4-6 illustrates the point.

UTILITY STUFF: PASSWORDS AND INCLUDES

Stuff that's like, you know, useful:

- A script that collects a password and checks to see whether it's any good.
- An include file that is shared by most of the scripts in this chapter that does different things.

Script 4-1
ch4_password_form.asp

```
1. <%@ Language=JavaScript %>
2.
3. <%
4. if (String(Request("password")) == "password"){
5.
6.     Session("edit_db_pass") = "OK";
7.     Response.Redirect("ch4_list_categories.asp");
8. }
9. %>
10.
11. <html><head></head><body>
12. <form action="<% =
    String(Request.ServerVariables("SCRIPT_NAME")) %>">
13. <p>Password Please:
14. <input type=password name=password >
15. <input type=submit name="toss" value="Submit">
16. </form>
17. </body></html>
```

HOW THE SCRIPT WORKS

The ch4_include.js file, which is used by most of the scripts in this chapter, checks to see whether a Session variable called edit_db_pass is set to a value of OK. If it's not, users are sent to this script, which asks them for a password. If they can enter a valid password, the edit_db_pass variable will be set, and they'll be redirected to ch4_list_categories.asp.

1. Set language to JavaScript.

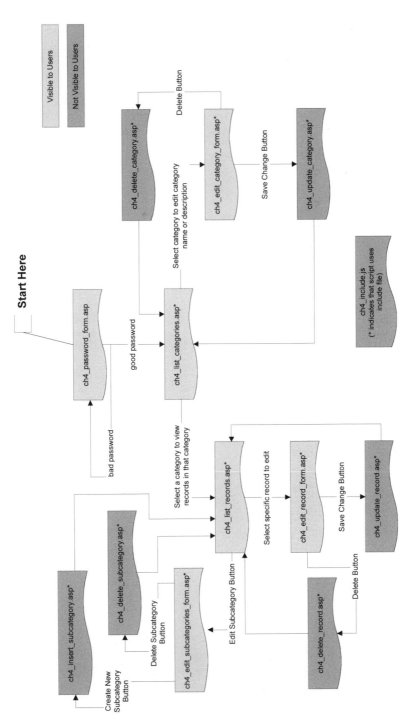

FIGURE 4-6 How the scripts fit together

4. Check the password, whether a form variable called `password` is set to an arbitrary string value, in this case, the string `"password"` (you might want to pick a different password).

If the password is correct, lines 5–8 are executed.

If no password is set or the password is incorrect, the rest of the script is run, which consists of a form that collects a password and submits it to this script.

6. Because a correct password was collected, this line sets the user's `Session` variable `edit_db_pass` to the value OK. This will give the user access to the other scripts in this chapter.

7. The user is redirected to the script `ch4_list_categories.asp`. Note that the `Response.Redirect()` command must be used before any HTML is sent to the browser, because it is implemented via an HTTP header.

Script 4-2
`ch4_include.js`

```
1. <%
2. if (Session("edit_db_pass") != "OK"){
3.
4.     Response.Redirect("ch4_password_form.asp");
5. }
6.
7. var out = "";
8.
9. var this_script_url =
   String(Request.ServerVariables("SCRIPT_NAME"));
10.
11. var current_category =
    String(Request("current_category")); // category uid
12. var current_subcategory =
    String(Request("current_subcategory")); //
    subcategory string
13. var current_record =
    String(Request("current_record")); // data uid
14.
15. // display scripts
16. var list_categories_script =
    "ch4_list_categories.asp";
17. var list_records_script = "ch4_list_records.asp";
18.
```

```
19. var edit_record_form_script =
    "ch4_edit_record_form.asp";
20. var blank_record_form_script =
    "ch4_blank_record_form.asp";
21.
22. var edit_category_form_script =
    "ch4_edit_category_form.asp";
23. var blank_category_form_script =
    "ch4_blank_category_form.asp";
24.
25. var edit_subcategories_form_script =
    "ch4_edit_subcategories_form.asp";
26.
27. // db scripts
28. var update_record_script = "ch4_update_record.asp";
29. var insert_record_script = "ch4_insert_record.asp";
30. var delete_record_script = "ch4_delete_record.asp";
31.
32. var update_category_script =
    "ch4_update_category.asp";
33. var insert_category_script =
    "ch4_insert_category.asp";
34. var delete_category_script =
    "ch4_delete_category.asp";
35.
36. var insert_subcategory_script =
    "ch4_insert_subcategory.asp";
37. var delete_subcategory_script =
    "ch4_delete_subcategory.asp";
38.
39. /////////////////////////////////////////////////////
40. // create connection to database
41. DSN = "DSN=ch3db";
42. Conn = Server.CreateObject("ADODB.Connection");
43. Conn.Open(DSN);
44.
45.
46. /////////////////////////////////////////////////////
47. // create cat_object, the category object. Because
    category information is used
48. // on almost every page, this code is executed every
    time.
49. sql = "SELECT * FROM categories order by
    category_name";
50. rs = Server.CreateObject("ADODB.RecordSet");
51. rs.Open (sql, Conn);
52.     if (rs.EOF){       // check to see if rs is empty
53.             out += "no records found in categories
                table. something is probably wrong.";
54.     }
55.     else{                         // rs not empty
```

```
56.          cat_object = new Object ();
57.          temp_counter = 0;
58.
59.      while (! (rs.EOF)){
60.              cat_object[temp_counter] = new
                Object ();
61.              cat_object[temp_counter].uid =
                parseInt(rs.fields.item
                ("category_uid"))
62.              cat_object[temp_counter].name =
                String(rs.fields.item
                ("category_name"))
63.              cat_object[temp_counter].desc =
                String(rs.fields.item
                ("category_description"))
64.
65.              rs.move(1);
66.              cat_object.qty =
                (temp_counter + 1);
67.              temp_counter ++;
68.          } // end while recordset
69.      } // end else (rs not empty)
70. rs.Close ();
71.
72. /////////////////////////////////////////////////////
73. // Create nav_header
74. nav_header = '<div align="center">';
75. nav_header += '<a href="' + list_categories_script
    +'">List of Categories</a> '
76.
77. if (current_category > 0){
78.     nav_header += ' | Current Category: <a
        href="' + list_records_script +
        '?current_category='
        + current_category + '">'
79.     for (i = 0; i < cat_object.qty; i++){
80.             if (cat_object[i].uid ==
                current_category){
81.                     nav_header +=
                        cat_object[i].name + '</a>'
82.             }
83.     }
84. }
85.
86. nav_header += '</div><hr>'
87.
88. /////////////////////////////////////////////////////
89. // slash_date()
90. new function slash_date (temp_date){
91. if (temp_date != "" && temp_date != "null" ){
92.     temp_date2 = new Date(temp_date);
```

```
93.      temp_date3 =  temp_date2.getMonth()+1 + "/" +
         temp_date2.getDate() + "/" +
         temp_date2.getFullYear();
94.      return (temp_date3);
95. }
96. else{
97.      return "--/--/--";
98. }
99. }
100.
101. %>
```

HOW THE SCRIPT WORKS

This include file is used by most of the scripts in this chapter to perform the following tasks:

- Check to make sure that the user is authorized to use the current script.
- Define shared variables.
- Create the `cat_object` object, which stores information about the categories that the database knows about.
- Creates a header that is used to navigate around the scripts in this chapter.
- Define a function called `slash_date()` that seems to have something to do with formatting dates.

2-5. The first four lines deal with checking that the current user is authorized to use whatever script is invoking the `ch4_include.js` file.

2. An `if()` statement is used to check whether the `Session` variable `edit_db_pass` is not equal to `OK`. If this is true (its not being equal, that is), lines 3–4 are used to make sure that the user is authorized before anything else happens.

3,4. This block of code consists of a single line, which, if executed, redirects the user to the script `ch4_password_form.asp`, described above, which will ask the user for a password.

7-37. These lines declare a bunch of variables that are useful. Some have fixed values, others are set on the fly by the script.

7. Creates a variable called `out` with a value of empty string (`""`). This allows scripts to concatenate stuff to `out` later without worrying about whether `out` exists.

9. `this_script_url` uses the ASP Request object to create a URL that points to the current script. Note that this will point to the script that uses this include file, not to the include file. Which is what we want.

11–13. These lines collect the form variables `current_category`, `current_subcategory`, and `current_record` and stuff them into local variables of the same name. Because these variables are not always set, they'll sometimes end up being "undefined".

16–37. These lines map script names to variables to make it easy to rename scripts later. This tends to be handy in projects like this one, where there are a lot of scripts floating around.

41–43. These lines create a database connection called `Conn` that allows the scripts in this chapter to communicate to the database.

41. The DSN variable contains a string that defines the name of the DSN that is used to connect to the database. See the previous chapter for an explanation of what a DSN is.

42. Next, an object called `Conn` is created using the `Server.CreateObject()` method. As the argument implies, the `Conn` object has something to do with being a connection and the acronym ADODB, which is a Microsoft database technology.

43. Using the DSN variable created in line 41, the `open()` method is applied to the `Conn` object to connect to the database that we want to play with, at which point we have a database connection that can be used to create recordsets or to execute SQL `insert`, `update`, or `delete` statements.

49–70. These lines create an object called `cat_object` that contains useful information about the categories of information that are stored in the database. For example, the default categories in the database are people, events, and Web sites.

`cat_object` is created by collecting all the fields that are stored in the `categories` table of the database (described in the previous chapter) into a recordset, then looping though the recordset and adding the information in the recordset to `cat_object`. Specifically:

49. This line creates an SQL statement that will grab all the records stored in the `categories` table and order them alphabetically according to the field `category_name`.

50. Creates a recordset object called `rs`.

51. Using the `Conn` object and the SQL statement created above, the recordset is populated using the `open()` method.

52–55. Before looping through the recordset, this line checks to make sure that `rs.EOF` is not true. This would be true only if the recordset were empty (meaning there are no categories in the database). If this is the case, an error message is added to the `out` variable in line 53.

In most cases, there will be categories in the database, and lines 55–69 will be executed as a result of the `else` statement on line 55.

56,57. At this point, `cat_object` is created, which is, of course, the main attraction at this point. Another variable called `temp_counter` will be created, which will be used to organize the category records that are stored in `cat_object`.

59. The `while()` loop that starts here will run until the recordset is empty and the script has collected all the category information from it. It encompasses lines 60–67.

60. The first thing the loop does is create a nested object inside of `cat_object` called `cat_object[temp_counter]`. For example, if there are three records in the recordset, three nested objects will be created: `cat_object[0]`, `cat_object[1]`, and `cat_object[2]`.

61–63. Information is stored in the `category_uid`, `category_name`, and `category_description` fields of the recordset are passed to the appropriate property of the nested object being created.

65. Having collected the information we needed, the `move()` method is applied to the Recordset object to go to the next object. Note that, without this line, the `while` loop would run until the Web server times it out.

66. The `qty` property of `cat_object` is set to one more than `temp_counter`, which is the number of categories found so far. Theoretically, it might be more efficient to do this outside of the `while` loop, so that it happens only once.

67. Finally, `temp_counter` is incremented so that the next nested object created on line 60 will have a new name.

70. Having finished with the recordset, the `Close()` method is used to get rid of it. At this point, `cat_object` is good to go and can be used any time it's necessary to get information about the categories stored in the database.

74–86. These lines create a variable called `nav_header` that contains a string of HTML that creates a very simple header that looks like Figure 4-7.

The header has two links. The first goes back to the list of all of the categories in the database—the home page of the scripts in this chapter, if you will. The second link is the name of a specific category and takes the user to a list of the records that are in that category.

Much of the code on these lines is HTML that I won't discuss here.

75. This line uses the variable `list_categories_script`, defined earlier in this file to build a link.

77. This line checks to make sure that the `current_category` is set to a value greater than zero before executing lines 78–84. This is necessary because the `current_category` variable is not always set, for example, when a user logs in for the first time, and the code on lines 78–84 will generate an error when this happens.

78. The variables `list_records_script` and `current_category` are used to create some HTML.

79–83. These lines loop through `cat_object` to find a category whose uid matches the value of `current_category` so that we can find out what that category's name is (creating a link to a category called "Events" is fine. Creating a link to category "2" might alienate some users).

79. The `for()` loop on this line will iterate through `cat_object` based on the number of categories stored in `cat_object`.

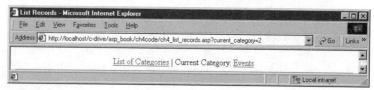

FIGURE 4-7 The header stored inside of the string nav_header

80. The `if()` statement on this line checks to see whether the uid of the current category matches the value in `current_category`. If it does, line 81 adds the name of that category to the HTML string `nav_header`.

86. A bit more HTML, and `nav_header` is good to go.

90–99. The last bit of code in this file defines a function called `slash_date()`. The purpose of the function is to translate the rather indecipherable date information stored in the database into a more human-readable string. For example, Wed Jan 5 00:00:00 PST 2000 will be transformed to 1/5/2000. How it works:

90. This line tells the computer that a new function is being created called `slash_date` and that it takes a single argument, which will be stored in a local variable `temp_date`.

91. The first thing to do is to make sure that we're dealing with an actual date. This line checks to make sure that we're not dealing with an empty string or the value `"null"`. Note that `"null"` is in quotes, because the script is checking for a `"null"` from the database, not the special JavaScript value `null`.

If `temp_date` doesn't look like it's likely to be a date, the `else` clause (lines 96–98) will return the string `"--/--/--"`. Otherwise, the script assumes we've got a date, and lines 92–94 get executed.

92. This line creates a new object called `temp_date2`, which is created by creating a JavaScript `Date()` object by parsing the `temp_date` variable.

93. Next, a string called `temp_date3` is used to collect the month, day, and year information stored in `temp_date2`. See Chapter 1 for more on working with the JavaScript `Date()` object.

The slashes that are added to the string here were the inspiration for the name of this function.

94. Our work complete, the function returns the variable `temp_date3`.

99. End of the function.

101. End of the include file.

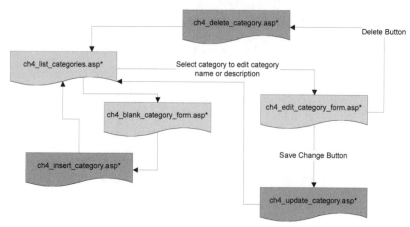

FIGURE 4-8 Scripts involved in editing categories

CODE TO EDIT CATEGORIES

The scripts illustrated in Figure 4-8 are used to review and edit category information as detailed below.

- `ch4_list_categories.asp`: Displays a list of categories in the database and lets user go to `ch4_list_records.asp`, `ch4_edit_category_form.asp`, or `ch4_blank_category_form.asp`.
- `ch4_edit_category_form.asp`: Lets user change category information or delete a category.
- `ch4_update_category.asp`: Updates the database with edits created, using `ch4_edit_category_form.asp`.
- `ch4_delete_category.asp`: Deletes a category.
- `ch4_blank_category_form`: Creates a blank form that users can use to create a new category.
- `ch4_insert_category.asp`: Inserts a new category using information typed into `ch4_blank_category_form.asp`.

Script 4-3
ch4_list_categories.asp

```
1. <%@ Language=JavaScript %>
2. <!-- #include file="ch4_include.js" -->
3.
4. <html><head><title>List Categories</title></head>
5. <body>
6.
7. <center><font size="+2"> Edit Database </font>
```

8.
Select a category to see records in that category.
9.
Select "Edit" to change name or description or to delete category.
10.
Use "Create New Category" button to create a new category.<hr>
11.
12. <%
13. for (i = 0; i < cat_object.qty; i++){
14.   %>
15.   <a href="<% = list_records_script %>?current_category=<% = cat_object[i].uid %>"><b><% = cat_object[i].name %></b></a>
16.   <a href="<% = edit_category_form_script %>?current_category=<% = cat_object[i].uid%>">Edit</a>
17.
<% = cat_object[i].desc %>
18.   <%
19. }
20. %>
21.
22. <hr>
23. <form action="<% = blank_category_form_script %>">
24. <input type="submit" name="toss" value="Create New Category">
25. </form>
26. </center>
27.
28. <%
29. Conn.Close ();
30. %>
31.
32. </body></html>

HOW THE SCRIPT WORKS

If this script looks familiar, it's because it's almost identical to ch3_view_categories.asp that was described in the last chapter. There are only three significant differences: first, some copy that tells users how to use this page. Tedious as it is to take the time to write documentation, it beats having to stop what you're doing to explain to someone how to use the page for the twelfth time. Second, next to every category name, there's a link called "Edit" that takes users to ch4_edit_category_form.asp. Finally, there's a form at the bottom of the page that creates a "Create New Category" button.

Because this is mostly a repeat of the Chapter 3 script, I'll address only those portions of the script that are new:

16. This is where the "Edit" link is created. This is done using the `edit_category_form_script` variable that was created in the include file and setting the `current_category` variable so that the script will know which category is being edited.

23–25. The small form here is used to display a button that says "Create New Category" on it. Note that there is no particular reason to use a button here rather than a link. For example, a link might have looked like:

```
<a href="<% = blank_category_form_script %>">Create
New Category</a>
```

Either way works fine: It's largely a matter of interface design, which, as you've probably figured out by now, I'm not paying a whole lot of attention to in the scripts. I'm not saying that interface design isn't important. It is. In a lot of ways, it's more important than writing code, because people will be more willing to use a terrible script with a great interface than good code that looks like junk. It's just that this is a book about writing code, and to make it look really good would mean cluttering up the scripts in this book with a bunch of HTML code that would make things a lot less readable.

Once again, I'm using the name `"toss"` for a button whose value I don't care about. This way, six months down the road, it'll be easy for me to know at a glance that the button is there just for looks.

Script 4-4
ch4_edit_category_form.asp

```
1.  <%@ Language=JavaScript %>
2.  <!-- #include file="ch4_include.js" -->
3.
4.  <html><head><title>Edit Category
    Form</title></head><body>
5.
6.  <% = nav_header %>
7.
8.  <%
9.  // create recordset "rs"
10. sql = "SELECT * FROM categories where category_uid =
    " + current_category ;
11. rs = Server.CreateObject("ADODB.RecordSet");
```

```
12. rs.Open (sql, Conn);
13.
14. // check to see if rs is empty
15. if (rs.EOF){
16.     out += "no records found. This shouldn't
        happen unless multiple people are using the
        database simultaneously and somebody just deleted
        the category you were about to edit.";
17. }
18.
19. // rs not empty, we have a record to edit, so
    create form:
20. else{      %>
21.
22. <form action="<% = update_category_script%>">
23. <table>
24.
25. <%
26. for ( field_number = 0; field_number <
    rs.fields.count ; field_number++ ){
27.
28.     temp_field =
        String(rs.fields(field_number).Name);
29.     temp_content =
        String(rs.fields.item(temp_field));
30.
31.     //data cleanup: nulls
32.     if (temp_content == "null") {temp_content =
        ""; }
33.
34.     // we can get rid of "category_" on labels,
        but not in the form fields
35.     temp_field_label = temp_field.replace
        (/category_/,"");
36.
37.     // uid field should not be editable:
38.     if (temp_field.search(/uid/) >= 0){
39.         out += '\n\n<tr><td>' +
            temp_field_label + ': </td><td>' +
            temp_content + ' (this field is used by
            database to create a unique primary key
            for each category and is not
            editable)</td></tr>';
40.     }
41.
42.     // standard text box for name and description
        fields
43.     else {
44.         out += '\n\n<tr><td>' +
            temp_field_label + ': </td><td><input
            type=text name="' + temp_field + '"
```

```
                             value="' + temp_content + ' "
                             size=60></td></tr>';
45.    }
46. }// end of looping through incoming form fields
47.
48. } // end else (rs not empty)
49. rs.Close ();
50. %>
51. <% = out %>
52. </table>
53.
54. <input type="hidden" name ="current_category"
    value="<% = current_category %>">
55. <input type="submit" name ="toss" value="Save
    Changes">
56. </form>
57.
58. <hr>
59. <p>Warning: if you delete this category, any records
    that are in this category will not be deleted, but
    will no longer be accessible except by opening the
    database with MS Access.
60. <center>
61. <form action="<% = delete_category_script%>">
62. <input type="hidden" name ="current_category"
    value="<% = current_category %>">
63. <input type="submit" name ="toss" value="Delete This
    Category">
64. </form></center>
65.
66. <%
67. Conn.Close ();
68. %>
69. </body></html>
```

HOW THE SCRIPT WORKS

This script lets users edit the name and description fields of category records, as well as lets users delete a category entirely. Note that when a category is deleted, the records within that category will no longer be accessible using the scripts in this chapter, so you want to be a little careful about that (if you think the people using this script might do this by accident, you can always pull lines 59–65 out of the script.)

The URL that invokes this script must tell the script what the unique id of the category being edited is (this is done using a form variable called current_category, which is used by most of the scripts in this chapter).

This script includes a nifty trick that I'm partial to: rather than hard-coding a form that is populated by a recordset, the form that is generated by this script is generated dynamically, based on the fields that are found in the recordset. As a result, it is entirely possible that you could add a field to the table `categories` (this is the database table where the category information is stored) and be able to edit information in that field without having to modify this script.

Note that this means that the field labels on the form are derived from the field names, so you'll need to give any new fields a reasonably human-readable name for this system to work.

The fine print:

1,2. Set script language to be JavaScript and import include file that is discussed earlier in this chapter.

6. Add the `nav_header` variable to the page being generated. This contains a link back to `ch4_list_categories.asp`, as well as a link to the list of records for the current category (`ch4_list_records.asp`).

10. Creates an SQL string (the variable `sql`) that selects all records from the table categories where the field `category_uid` is equal to the form variable `current_category`. Because `category_uid` is the primary key for `categories`, this will return only a single record. Thus, it will be unnecessary to loop through the recordset that we retrieve, as we would if we were getting more than one record.

11,12. First, the Recordset object `rs` is created. On the next line, the `Open()` method is used to pass the SQL string `sql` to the `Conn` object and place the resultant recordset into the `rs` object.

15–17. Checking to see whether the recordset is empty (if `rs` is empty, `rs.EOF` would be true) won't be all that useful most of the time. But it could come in handy if multiple users are sharing the database or if you decide to extend these scripts and unexpected things start happening.

20. If, as expected, the `rs` object is not empty, this `else{}` statement executes lines 20–49.

22. Because the script is collecting information from the user, a form is required. The form generated by this script will be sent to the script defined as the `update_category_script` in `include.js`.

26–47. Starting on line 26, a `for()` loop is used to loop through every field in the first (and only) record that is stored in the `rs` object. Field names and contents are retrieved using the `rs.fields` object.

In the case of this script, three fields will be retrieved from the `categories` table: `category_uid`, `category_name`, and `category_description`. The field names are retrieved from `rs.fields` using the counter `field_number`, which will increment from 0 to 2, so that, in line 28, `temp_field` is set, in turn, to `String(rs.fields(0).Name)`, `String(rs.fields(1).Name)`, and `String(rs.fields(2).Name)`.

On line 29, `temp_field` is then used to set the contents of the field into the variable `temp_content`, which is thus set first to `String(rs.fields.item("category_uid"))` (when `field_number` is 0), then `String(rs.fields.item("category_name"))` (when `field_number` is 1), and finally to `String(rs.fields.item("category_description"))` (when `field_number` is 2).

32. If a field is empty, the value of that field will be set to `null`. For some reason, the word "null" seems to confuse some users, and replacing it with an empty string seems to keep them happy, and it's easy enough to do.

35. All the fields in the database are prefixed: Fields in the `categories` table all start with `category_`, fields in the `data` table start with `data_`, etc. ... Again, this is something that could confuse users, who would then want to talk about it, so it's better just to get rid of the prefix. This is done using a simple regular expression, the `replace()` method, which in JavaScript can be applied to any string. In this case, the regular expression `/category_/` is replaced with an empty string.

The purpose of the prefix is to keep field names as unambiguous as possible. You'll notice that there are not a lot of weird variables like `rsFldLstWrd` in my code. Sure, I spend a little more time typing than some of you freaks who like to abbreviate everything. On the other hand, when I go back to my code six months later and try to figure out what I was doing, maybe I save a little time. And maybe it makes this book a little easier to read, too. At any rate, that's how I'll do it until I change my mind or arguments about naming conventions stop reminding me of conversations about which operating system is best.

Finally, having retrieved the fields we need and cleaned them up a bit, it's time to send information to the browser. How this happens depends on what field we're talking about:

38–40. Because the `uid` is a field whose value is set by MS Access (called an "Autonumber" field by Access; other SQL databases offer a similar feature), it should not be editable. A `search()` regular expression is used to check for `/uid/`, and if the current field is the primary key field, it will be displayed but not be editable. In some cases, it may make sense to comment out line 39 so that this information is not displayed in order to streamline the interface.

43–45. All other fields are displayed in the same way: The `temp_field_label` variable is used to label a text box, whose `name` attribute is set to the name of the current field (`temp_field`) and whose `value` attribute is set to the value of the current field (`temp_content`).

Lines 46 and 48 close some curly brackets that were opened earlier.

49. Closes the Recordset object.

51. The `out` variable that was used to store most of the good stuff that's being sent to the browser is dumped here.

54. The `current_category` variable is passed to the next script using a hidden form variable. `current_category` is the same thing as `category_uid` and will be required by the next script, which commits the edits made on this form to the database, so that it can make changes to the correct record.

55. As is the case with all of the scripts in this chapter, the copy on the Submit button, in this case, "Save Changes", can be changed without affecting how the scripts work. Because people always want to change what buttons say, you want to avoid assigning any more functionality to buttons, aside from the fact that when someone clicks on a Submit button, the current form is submitted to a script.

61–64. The small form here is used to delete a category. The key stuff here is that the `action` attribute of the `<form>` tag is set to `delete_category_script` (defined in the include file) and that the primary key of the category to be deleted (`current_category`) is passed as a hidden variable. The same information could be passed as a link:

```
<a href="<% = delete_category_script
%>?current_catego-ry=<% = current_category
%>">Delete This Category</a>
```

67. Database connection is closed.

Script 4-5
ch4_update_category.asp

```
1.  <%@ Language=JavaScript %>
2.  <!-- #include file="ch4_include.js" -->
3.
4.  <%
5.  temp_update = "";
6.  for ( field_number = 1; field_number <=
    Request.QueryString.count ; field_number++ ){
7.
8.      temp_field =
        String(Request.QueryString.Key(field_number));
9.      temp_content =
        String(Request.QueryString.item(temp_field))
10.
11.     if (temp_field.search
        (/uid|current_category|toss/) < 0 ){
12.             // check for null values
13.             if (temp_content == "null" ||
                temp_content == "")
14.                 {temp_update += " "+ temp_field
                    + " = null,";}
15.
16.             else {
17.
18.                 temp_content =
                    temp_content.replace(/'/g,"&#039;");
19.                 temp_update += " "+ temp_field
                    + " = '" + temp_content +"',";
20.             }
21.     } // end if()
22. }// end for()
23.
24. // remove last character, which is a trailing
    comma that we don't want
25. temp_update =
    temp_update.substring(0,temp_update.length-1);
26.
```

```
27. update_sql = "update categories set " + temp_update
    + " where category_uid = " + current_category;
28.
29. Conn.Execute(update_sql);
30.
31. Conn.Close ();
32.
33. Response.Redirect(list_categories_script)
34.
35. //Response.Write("<hr>\n\n\n" + update_sql +
    "\n\n\n<hr>");
36. //Response.Write(list_records_script)
37. %>
```

HOW THE SCRIPT WORKS

ch4_update_category.asp performs a relatively simple task—
it collects the edits that were carried out using the form generated
in the previous script (ch4_edit_category_form.asp) and
writes them to the database.

This means doing two things: First, collecting the form information being forwarded from the previous script. Second, creating an SQL statement that will save this information to the
database.

Just as the previous script dynamically generated a form
based on the fields that it found in the database, this script is
smart enough to dynamically collect the form information it
receives and generate an SQL statement without knowing what
those fields are. Again, this means that form fields need to be
named in a specific way (in this case, they need to be named the
same as the fields into which their data is to be inserted. This is
easy enough, because the form fields in the previous scripts were
generated on the fly, based on the field names that the script
found in the database). Again, this means that you can add new
fields to the category table in the database and not have to
worry about updating this script. And if that's not fun, I guess I
just don't know what is.

One more thing before I dive into it. The SQL statement to edit
a single record whose primary key is known is an update statement and has the form:

```
update table set field_1='value_1', field_2='field_2',
... where primary_key_field=value
```

Thus, the riddle that this script needs to solve is figuring out a
relatively easy way to collect incoming form fields and values,

and plugging that information into an SQL statement that itself consists of a series of fields and values.

That means collecting incoming database field names and values into a comma-separated string (field_1='value_1', field_2='field_2', ...) while the where clause will assign the changes to that record where the category_uid field is equal to the value current_category.

This is how it works:

5. The meat of the script starts by creating an empty string variable called temp_update.

6–22. These lines encompass a for() loop that executes once for every field in the Request.QueryString object (discussed in the New Features section of this chapter). The Request.QueryString object contains all of the form information passed to the current script using the Get method (form stuff in the URL).

Just as the rs.fields object was used to collect field names and values in the previous script, the Request.QueryString object tells us how many form variables were collected (the count property), what their names are (by passing an index value to the Key() method), and what their values are (by passing a field name to the item() method).

Thus, in line 6, the for() loop increments from 1 to Request.QueryString.count, looping through each of the incoming form variables in turn, so that the information that's going to get written to the database can be put into the temp_update string. [2]

8. temp_field is set to a form variable (or key), using Request.QueryString.Key().

9. temp_content is set to the content of that form variable, using Request.QueryString.item().

11. Having collected form information, the first step is to eliminate form information that doesn't get written to the database. Line 11 uses a regular expression to search for expressions that match form variables that should **not** go in the database: /uid/, /current_category/, and /toss/. Using a regular expression makes it easy to add

---

2. Note that the index value for the QueryString object starts at 1 instead of 0.

new variables that we want to exclude. For example, this line started out as:

```
if (temp_field != "toss"){
```

Then I realized that I also needed to check for the field current_category. Thus:

```
if (temp_field != "toss" && temp_field !=
"current_category"){
```

Later, when I was passing a form variable category_uid (which was superfluous, because I already had current_category, but it took me a while to realize that), the idea of adding yet another "logical and" (&&) got me thinking; thus, the regular expression.

At any rate, if the regular expression finds a match, it returns the index value of where it found the match, which will be zero or higher. Without a match, it returns a value of -1, so that the if() resolves to true (minus one is less than zero), and the code on lines 12–20 is executed.

13,14. Nulls and empty strings get special treatment: null is a special value in SQL. String fields in the database (in SQL terminology: char, varchar, text/memo, etc. ...[3]) that are storing a zero-length string ("") are, in fact, storing a string. On the other hand, fields that are set to null are empty. For the sake of simplicity, it's nice to have consistent data in the database.

Furthermore, null is better behaved than is an empty string, because integers, date fields, strings, etc. can be set to null, and, whereas a string field can be set to an empty string, an integer field cannot.

14. At any rate, if temp_content is empty, whatever field we're dealing with gets set to null. For example, if the category_description field is set to an empty string, the result is equivalent to:

```
temp_update += " category_description = null,"
```

---

3. char, varchar, text, and memo are SQL data types that can store strings.

Note the preceding space and the trailing comma, so that any number of fields can be concatenated into the `temp_update` string.

16. Empty or null fields are all handled the same way:

18. First, a regular expression is used to replace single quotes—which are special characters used to delimit strings in SQL statements—with the string `"&#039;"`, the HTML expression for single quotes. Note the use of the `"g"` operator to replace every occurrence of a single quote, rather than only the first one.

19. Next, the field name and value are concatenated into the `temp_update` string. For example, if the field `category_name` is set to `"Events"`, line 19 would be equivalent to the statement:

```
temp_update += " category_name='Events',";
```

21. End of the `if()` on line 11.

22. End of `for()` loop. At this point, the script has reviewed all of the incoming form variables, used some to concatenate field names and contents into the `temp_update` variable, and discarded those fields that do not need to be updated in the database.

25. Because a trailing comma (`","`) is included every time information is added to the `temp_update` string, there will always be an extra comma that needs to be removed to avoid generating an error. This is done using the JavaScript `substring()` function (actually a method that can be applied to any string, which makes a string kind of like an object... but that's another story).

The `substring()` method takes two arguments: the index values of where the substring starts and the where it ends. We want everything from the very beginning (`"0"`) to the next-to-last character (`"temp_update.length-1"`: The `length` property of a string returns the number of characters in a string. By subtracting one, the offending comma is eliminated.).

27. At last, the SQL string `update_sql` is generated. The `temp_update` string provides a list of field names and values, while the `current_category` variable provides the value of the primary key field, so that the appropriate record in the database is updated.

29. The SQL statement assembled in line 27 is executed using the `Execute( )` method of the `Conn` database connection object (created in the include file).

31. The `Conn` object is closed.

35,36. These two lines may be useful in the future for debugging purposes. For example, if you decide to make some changes to the form that submits information to this script, and all of a sudden you start getting an error, most likely it will have something to do with attempting to execute the SQL statement on line 29. Should this happen, you can comment out lines 29 and 33 and uncomment lines 35 and 36, which will show you the two pieces of information that you're most likely to need when things stop working: What the SQL statement you're trying to execute looks like and where the form is being redirected to afterward. For example, if you're getting some kind of error from the `update_sql` string, there's a good chance you'll be able to eyeball the problem when you see the statement. If you're new to SQL and all looks like gibberish, you may want to take the opportunity to learn some more about SQL, or it might be time to call in a favor with a friend who's more familiar with it than you are (my favorite programming trick any time I'm stumped). Newsgroups are also often good with this kind of thing.

Script 4-6
ch4_delete_category.asp

```
1.  <%@ Language=JavaScript %>
2.  <!-- #include file="ch4_include.js" -->
3.  <%
4.
5.  delete_sql = "delete from categories where
    category_uid = " + current_category;
6.
7.  Conn.Execute(delete_sql);
8.
9.  Conn.Close ();
10.
11. Response.Redirect(list_categories_script)
12.
```

```
13. //Response.Write("<hr>\n\n\n" + delete_sql +
    "\n\n\n<hr>");
14. //Response.Write(list_categories_script)
15.
16. %>
```

HOW THE SCRIPT WORKS

For this script to work, the form variable `current_category` needs to exist. For example, a valid URL would be:

```
ch4_delete_category.asp?current_category=2
```

Deleting something is, of course, easier than creating it or editing it, and this script is correspondingly simple.

The critical issue with an SQL `delete` statement is to make sure that its scope is sufficiently restricted that you are unlikely to delete something that you would prefer to keep around. For example, you want to be real careful not to execute a statement like `"delete from table_name"`, which would delete every single record in the table `table_name`.

On the other hand, by restricting the scope of the `delete` statement to those records whose primary key field matches a specific value, you'll never delete more than one record (remember that primary key fields, by definition, contain unique values). So when you're creating a `delete` statement, pay attention to the `where` clause.

How it works:

1,2. Standard housekeeping: Language is JavaScript, and we need the include file because it creates the database Connection object (`Conn`) for us.

5. This is where the SQL statement `delete_sql` is created (discussed above).

7. SQL statement is executed.

9. `Conn` object is closed.

11. Browser is redirected to `list_categories_script`, a variable that is set in the include file, discussed earlier in this chapter.

13,14. These two lines can be uncommented if this script starts giving you error messages. You'll want to comment out lines 7 and 11 at the same time.

Script 4-7
ch4_blank_category_form.asp

```
1.  <%@ Language=JavaScript %>
2.  <!-- #include file="ch4_include.js" -->
3.
4.  <html><head><title>Blank Category
    Form</title></head><body>
5.
6.
7.  <% = nav_header %>
8.  To create a new category, type in a name and
    description below, and then click on the "Create New
    Category" button.<hr>
9.
10. <%
11. sql = "SELECT * FROM categories where
    category_uid=0" ;
12. rs = Server.CreateObject("ADODB.RecordSet");
13. rs.Open (sql, Conn, 2,3);
14. %>
15.
16. <form action="<% = insert_category_script
    %>"><table>
17.
18. <%
19. // loop through form fields and create a form based
    on fields we found
20. // in recordset.
21. for ( field_number = 0; field_number <
    rs.fields.count ; field_number++ ){
22.
23.     temp_field =
        String(rs.fields(field_number).Name);
24.
25.     // we can get rid of "category_" on labels,
        but not in the form fields
26.     temp_field_label =
        temp_field.replace(/category_/,"");
27.
28.     // if not uid field, create text box:
29.     if (temp_field.search(/uid/) < 0){
30. %>
31.             <tr><td><% = temp_field_label %>:
                </td><td><input type=text name="<% =
                temp_field %>"value="" size=60></td></tr>
32. <%
33.     }
34.
35. }// end of looping through incoming form fields
```

```
36. rs.Close ();
37.
38. Conn.Close ();
39. %>
40.
41. </table>
42. <input type="submit" name="toss" value="Create New
    Category">
43. </form>
44.
45. </body></html>
```

HOW THE SCRIPT WORKS

This script dynamically generates a form that can be used to create a new category.

The best way to talk about this script is to start off by noting that it is unnecessary. It would be considerably simpler just to create an HTML page to do the same task. For example, you could use the HTML generated by this script (I removed a few spaces and line breaks):

```
1. <html><head><title>Blank Category
   Form</title></head><body>
2.
3. <div align="center"><a
   href="ch4_list_categories.asp">List of Categories</a>
4. </div><hr>
5. To create a new category, type in a name and
   description below, and then click on the "Create New
   Category" button.<hr>
6.
7. <form action="ch4_insert_category.asp"><table>
8. <tr><td>name: </td><td><input type=text
   name="category_name" value="" size=60></td></tr>
9. <tr><td>description: </td><td><input type=text
   name="category_description" value=""
   size=60></td></tr>
10. </table>
11. <input type="submit" name="toss" value="Create New
    Category">
12. </form>
13.
14. </body></html>
```

So why use a script? Here are a few reasons:

1. I'm lazy.

2. Writing JavaScript code that maintains itself is more fun than changing HTML.

3. This book isn't about HTML programming.

Actually, I could probably have stuck to points 1 and 2: Once again, this script builds a form based on the fields that it discovers in the database. Which means that if I add a field to the `categories` table in the database, not only will that field show up in the form generated by this script, it'll also be automatically handled by `ch4_edit_category_form.asp` and `ch4_update_category.asp`.

Remember

Much of the purpose of putting scripts on top of a database is to avoid having to generate dozens, hundreds, or even thousands of HTML pages by hand. To limit the number of trees chewed up to make this book, this script deals with a relatively simple database—it generates a form with only two fields in it. However, it could be used to create a record with many more fields. Which is, in fact, what will happen later in this chapter in `ch4_blank_record_form.asp`.

Enough rambling. Let's look at the script:

1,2. Declare language and grab include file.

7. Drop in `nav_header` string (from include file, described earlier in this chapter). This creates a link back to `ch4_list_categories.asp`.

11. The SQL string does not need to be all that specific, because all the script really cares about is retrieving the names of the fields in the `categories` table. For example, the where clause is not required, and the following statement could also be used:

```
sql = "SELECT * FROM categories";
```

However, setting a where clause restricts the size of the recordset that is returned by the query, which reduces the load placed on the database and, presumably, the amount of memory required to store the recordset. (I haven't tested this, so you never know. But it seems likely that an empty recordset would use less memory than a recordset with several records in it.)

12,13. Create recordset `rs`.

16. As with all the scripts in this chapter, the URL in the `<form>` tag is a variable that is set in the include file to make it as easy as possible to change file names.

21. This is the start of a `for()` loop that will run from line 22 to line 35. The loop will be executed once for every field in the `categories` table. Because there are currently three fields in the table (`category_uid`, `category_name`, `category_description`), the hope is that it will run three times and that `field_number` will increment from 0 to 2.

This is the same mechanism used to loop through the fields in `ch4_edit_category_form.asp`.

23. `temp_field` is set to the current field name, based on the index value `field_number`.

24. A regular expression is used to strip the prefix `category_` from `temp_field` and to create the variable `temp_field_label`.

29. The script will create a text form element for every field that does not match the regular expression `/uid/`. (If the `search()` method finds the expression `/uid/`, it'll return a value of zero or higher, and lines 30–33 will not be executed.)

The same thing could also have been accomplished using a different test, such as:

```
if (temp_field != "category_uid")
```

31. The heart of this script: the variables `temp_field_label` and `temp_field` are used to create a label and a text box where the user will be able to type in information.

36,38. `rs` and `Conn` are closed.

42. A Submit button needs to be included so that users can submit the form. The `name` attribute is set to toss and won't be used by the script that processes this form.

Script 4-8
ch4_insert_category.asp

```
1.  <%@ Language=JavaScript %>
2.  <!-- #include file="ch4_include.js" -->
3.
4.  <%
5.  fields = "";
6.  values = "";
7.
8.  // loop through incoming form fields to build sql
    statements
9.  for ( field_number = 1; field_number <=
    Request.QueryString.count ; field_number++ ){
10.
11.     temp_field =
        String(Request.QueryString.Key(field_number));
12.     temp_content =
        String(Request.QueryString.item(temp_field))
13.
14.     if (temp_field.search(/toss/) < 0 ){
15.
16.             fields += ' ' + temp_field + ',';
17.
18.             // check for null values
19.             if (temp_content == "null" ||
                temp_content == ""){
20.                 values += " null,";
21.             }
22.             // this works for non-null char fields
23.             else {
24.                 temp_content =
                    temp_content.replace(/'/g,"&#039;");
25.                 values += " '" + temp_content +"',";
26.             }
27.     } // end if we want to add to update string
28. } // end looping through incoming form fields
29.
30. // remove last character, which is a trailing comma
    that we don't want
31. values = values.substring(0,values.length-1);
32. fields = fields.substring(0,fields.length-1);
33.
34. insert_sql = "insert into categories (" + fields +
    ") values (" + values + ")";
35.
36. Conn.Execute(insert_sql);
37.
38. Conn.Close ();
39.
```

```
40. Response.Redirect(list_categories_script)
41.
42. //Response.Write("<hr>\n\n\n" + insert_sql +
    "\n\n\n<hr>")
43. //Response.Write(list_records_script)
44.
45. %>
```

HOW THE SCRIPT WORKS

Like a script discussed earlier (ch4_update_category.asp), this script collects data from a form (in this case, the form created by ch4_blank_category_form.asp, above), organizes it into an SQL statement, submits the SQL statement to a database, and redirects the user to the category list, where, if all went according to plan, the user will find the new category that was just created.

Once again, form information is collected using the Request.QueryString object by iterating through the object, cleaning up the data thus collected, and dropping it into the SQL.

The syntax for an insert statement is:

```
insert into table_name (field_1, field_2, …, field_n)
values (value_1, value_2, …, value_n)
```

Thus, the task of the script is primarily to create two lists: a list of fields and a list of values. Both must be separated by commas. Here's how it works:

1,2. Set language and grab include file.

5,6. Declare the eponymous variables that will be used to collect fields and values.

9. Start of the for loop that will iterate through the Request.QueryString object and collect incoming form information.

11,12. Assign name and value of current form variable to temp_field and temp_content.

14. The regular expression here is used to exclude any fields that should not be integrated into the SQL statement that is being created (in this case, any field that matches /toss/).

16. The current value of temp_field is simply concatenated into the fields variable.

19,20. As discussed earlier with `ch4_update_category.asp`, both string `"null"` and the empty string ("") are set to the SQL special value `null` in `values`.

23–26. Otherwise, after replacing single quotes with their HTML analog, `temp_content` is concatenated into `values`, with a space in front and a comma behind it.

27,28. Close blocks that were opened earlier.

31,32. At this point, the information that is going into the database has been put into the variables `values` and `fields`. Because both have an extra trailing comma, the `substring()` method is applied to both, removing the last character.

CODE TO EDIT RECORDS

The interactions between the scripts that are used to edit records are illustrated in Figure 4-9.

Just as the scripts discussed in the previous section allow users to review, create, edit, and create categories, the scripts in this section let Web users look at a list of records in a category, create new records, as well as edit or delete existing records. Briefly:

- `ch4_list_records.asp`: Lists the records for a given category. Provides a link to edit a specific record (`ch4_edit_record_form.asp`) and a button to create a new record (`ch4_blank_record_form.asp`).

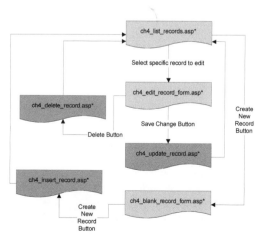

FIGURE 4-9 Scripts used to edit records

- ch4_edit_record_form.asp: A form used to edit a specific record. Edits are forwarded to ch4_update_record.asp.
- ch4_update_record.asp: Saves changes made to a record using ch4_edit_record_form.asp.
- ch4_delete_record.asp: Deletes a single record when a user hits the Delete Record button on chr_edit_record_form.asp.
- ch4_blank_record_form.asp: Creates a blank form that lets user create a new record.
- ch4_insert_record.asp: Saves a record created using ch4_blank_record_form.asp.

Although this section has a good deal of code in it, much of it is similar or identical to code already described earlier in this chapter (code to edit information in the database) or the previous chapter (code to display information stored in the database). As a result, in discussing the code, I won't go into great detail to describe code that is more carefully described elsewhere.

Script 4-9
ch4_list_records.asp

```
1.  <%@ Language=JavaScript %>
2.  <!-- #include file="ch4_include.js" -->
3.
4.  <html><head><title>List Records</title></head><body>
5.
6.  <% = nav_header %>
7.  <center><font size="+2"> List of records in <% =
    cat_object.current %> category </font><br>Select a
    record to edit it, or use button at bottom to create
    new record
8.  </center>
9.  <hr>
10.
11. <%
12. /////////////////////////////////////////////////////////
13. // Create dynamic subcategory navbar
14.
15. sql = "SELECT distinct data_subcategory FROM data
    where data_category = " + current_category + " order
    by data_subcategory";
16. rs = Server.CreateObject("ADODB.RecordSet");
17. rs.Open (sql, Conn, 2,3);
18.     if (rs.EOF){        // check to see if rs is empty
19.             out += "no subcategories in this
                category.";
```

```
20.      }
21.      else{                          // rs not empty
22.              Response.Write("<center>");
23.              while (! (rs.EOF)){
24. %>
25.                      <a href="#<% =
                        String(rs.fields.item
                        ("data_subcategory"))%>"><% =
                        String(rs.fields.item
                        ("data_subcategory"))%></a>
26.                            
27. <%
28.                      rs.move(1);
29.                      } // end while recordset
30.      } // end else (rs not empty)
31.
32. rs.Close ();
33.
34. %>
35. <form action="<% = edit_subcategories_form_script
    %>">
36. <input type="submit" name="toss" value="Edit
    Subcategories">
37. </form>
38. </center>
39. <%
40. /////////////////////////////////////////////////////
41. // Create list of records:
42.
43. sql = "SELECT * FROM data where data_category = " +
    current_category + " order by data_subcategory,
    data_name";
44.
45. // events should be ordered by date:
46. if (current_category == 2){
47.     sql = "SELECT * FROM data where data_category =
        " + current_category + " order by
        data_subcategory,data_main_date, data_name";
48. }
49.
50. rs = Server.CreateObject("ADODB.RecordSet");
51. rs.Open (sql, Conn, 2,3);
52. if (rs.EOF){             // check to see if rs is empty
53. %>
54. <p>There are no records in this category
55. <%
56. }
57. else{                          // rs not empty
58.
59.     temp_subcat= "";  //this string used to group
        records by subcategory
```

```
60.    fields = new Object(); // this object used to
       store fields in records
61.
62. while (! (rs.EOF)){
63.
64.    // clean up data and put it into the fields
       object:
65.    for ( field_number = 0; field_number <
       rs.fields.count ; field_number++ ){
66.
67.       temp_field =
          String(rs.fields(field_number).Name);
68.       temp_content =
          String(rs.fields.item(temp_field));
69.       temp_content =
          temp_content.replace(/&#039;/g,"'");
70.       if (temp_field.search(/date/) > 0 )
          //check for date fields
71.             {temp_content =
                slash_date(temp_content);}
72.       else if (temp_content == "null")
          {temp_content = ""; }
73.       fields[temp_field] = temp_content
74.    } // end looping through fields in current
       record
75.
76.       // subcategories: when we get to a new one,
          display it
77.       if (temp_subcat != fields.data_subcategory){
78.             temp_subcat = fields.
                data_subcategory;
79. %>
80.             <div align="center"><b><a name="<% =
                temp_subcat %>"><% = temp_subcat
                %></a></b></div>
81. <%
82.       }
83.
84.       //////////////////////////////////////////
85.       // What happens next is entirely category
          dependent
86.       //////////////////////////////////////////
87.
88.       //////////////////////////////////////////
89.       // PEOPLE (1)
90.       if (current_category == 1){
91. %>
92. <p><b><% = fields.data_name%></b> -  <% =
    fields.data_description %>
```

```
93.    <a href ="<% = edit_record_form_script
     %>?current_category=<% = current_category
     %>&current_record=<% = fields.data_uid %>">Edit</a>
94.  <table width=80%><tr>
95.  <td width=50%>
96.     Company: <% = fields.data_company %>
97.     <br>Address1: <% = fields.data_address1 %>
98.     <br>Address2: <% = fields.data_address2 %>
99.     <br>City: <% = fields.data_city %>
100.    <br>State: <% = fields.data_state %>
101.    <br>Zip: <% = fields.data_zip %>
102.    <br>Country: <% = fields.data_country %>
103. </td><td>
104.    Email: <% = fields.data_email %>
105.    <br>Work Phone: <% = fields.data_phone_work %>
106.    <br>Fax: <% = fields.data_phone_fax %>
107.    <br>Cell Phone: <% = fields.data_phone_cell %>
108.    <br>Home Phone: <% = fields.data_phone_home %>
109. </table>
110. <%
111.        } //end if cat is 1
112.
113.        ///////////////////////////////////////////
114.        // EVENTS (2)
115.        else if (current_category == 2){
116.
117.
118. %>
119. <p><b><% = fields.data_main_date %>: <% =
     fields.data_name%></b>
120.   <a href ="<% = edit_record_form_script
     %>?current_category=<% = current_category
     %>&current_record=<% = fields.data_uid %>">Edit</a>
121. <br>Description: <% = fields.data_description %>
122. <br>Start Date: <% = fields.data_start_date %>, End
     Date: <% = fields.data_end_date %>
123.
124. <%
125.        } // end if category is 2
126.
127.
128.        ///////////////////////////////////////////
129.        // WEB SITES (3)
130.        else if (current_category == 3){
131. %>
132. <p>
133. <a href="<% = fields.data_url %>">
134. <b><% = fields.data_name%></b></a>
135.   <a href="<% = edit_record_form_script
     %>?current_category=<% = current_category
     %>&current_record=<% = fields.data_uid %>">Edit</a>
```

```
136.  <br><% = fields.data_description %>
137.  <%
138.          } //end if cat is 3
139.
140.
141.          ///////////////////////////////////////////
142.          // CATCH-ALL TEMPLATE
143.          else {
144.  %>
145.  <p>
146.  <a href="<% = fields.data_url %>">
147.  <b><% = fields.data_name%></b></a>
148.    <a href="<% = edit_record_form_script
      %>?current_category=<% = current_category
      %>&current_record=<% = fields.data_uid %>">Edit</a>
149.  <br><% = fields.data_description %>
150.  <br>Note: no template has been created for this
      category
151.  <%
152.          }
153.
154.
155.          rs.move(1);
156.      } // end while recordset
157.  } // end else (rs not empty)
158.  rs.Close ();
159.
160.
161.
162.  // Form to set up "Create New Record" button:
163.  %>
164.  <hr><center>
165.  <form action="<% = blank_record_form_script %>">
166.  <input type="hidden" name="current_category"
      value="<% = current_category %>">
167.  <input type="submit" name="toss" value="Create New
      Record">
168.  </form></center>
169.
170.  <%
171.  Conn.Close ();
172.  %>
173.  </body>
174.  </html>
```

HOW THE SCRIPT WORKS

ch4_list_records.asp creates a template-based list of all the records in a single category, creates "Edit" links to let users edit specific records, and displays buttons that let people go to ch4_edit_subcategories.asp (the Edit Subcategories button) and ch4_blank_record_form.asp (the Create New Record button).

Most of the code in this script is identical to ch3_view_records.asp, which was discussed in detail in the previous chapter. This script is different only in that it creates the "Edit" link and buttons mentioned above.

Thus, rather than pursue the grail of redundancy, **the sections of the script that are different from ch3_view_records have been bolded, and only those sections are discussed.**[4]

> **7.** For some reason, few users seem willing to skim through the source code to figure out what a script is supposed to do. Fortunately, a bit of documentation here and there seems to do the trick.

> **35–37.** This button takes users to ch4_edit_subcategories.asp. The use of a button here is an interface decision. A simple link could also have been used:
>
> ```
> <a href="<% = edit_subcategories_form_script
> %>">Edit Subcategories</a>
> ```

---

4. If you're like me, you might be wondering, Why have two practically identical scripts in the book? Isn't this, after all, the beginning of a version control nightmare? Wouldn't it make more sense to have a single script?

The answer is a qualified yes. If you're going to be using the scripts in both Chapter 3 and Chapter 4, you'll probably want to maintain only a single script. It's not all that hard: Just add if statements to execute the bold code when you're editing. Probably the best thing to check for is the session variable used to protect the scripts in Chapter 4. For example:

```
if (Session("edit_db_pass") == "OK")
       {
       // bold code goes here.
       }
```

However, if you're going to use only the scripts in Chapter 3, you may appreciate the fact that it's not unnecessarily complicated by code that is used to edit the database via the Web.

The `edit_subcategories_form_script` variable is set in the include file described earlier in this chapter.

93, 120,
135, 148. The code on each of these lines is the same, repeated because each category has its own template (see discussion of `ch3_view_records.asp` if you're not clear on why there are templates). In each case, the code creates an "Edit" link to the `edit_record_form_script` (`ch4_edit_record_form.asp`). The link includes the form variable `current_record`, which contains the uid of the record to be edited.

162–168. The form on these lines generates a Create New Record button that will take the user to `ch4_blank_record_form.asp`. The `current_category` variable is passed to the blank record form script so that it will be able to set the category scroll box to the appropriate value.

Script 4-10
ch4_edit_record_form.asp

```
1.  <%@ Language=JavaScript %>
2.  <!-- #include file="ch4_include.js" -->
3.
4.  <html><head><title>Edit Record
    Form</title></head><body>
5.
6.  <% = nav_header %>
7.
8.  <%
9.  // grab information about record we want to edit:
10. sql = "SELECT * FROM data where data_uid = " +
    current_record ;
11. rs = Server.CreateObject("ADODB.RecordSet");
12. rs.Open (sql, Conn, 2,3);
13. if (rs.EOF){        // check to see if rs is empty
14.     out += "no records found. This shouldn't
        happen unless multiple people are using the
        database simultaneously";
15. }
16. else{                    // rs not empty
17. %>
18. <!-- Table: Delete and save buttons -->
19. <table border=0>
20. <tr><td valign=top>
```

```
21.    <!-- Delete button sends user to the delete
       script -->
22.    <form action="<% = delete_record_script%>">
23.    <input type="hidden" name ="current_category"
       value="<% = current_category %>">
24.    <input type="hidden" name ="current_record"
       value="<% = current_record %>">
25.    <input type="submit" name ="toss"
       value="Delete This Record">
26.    </form>
27. </td><td valign=top>
28.    <!-- Save button sends user to the update
       script -->
29.    <!-- Note that this form spans most of this
       script -->
30.    <form action="<% = update_record_script%>">
31.    <input type="submit" name ="toss" value="Save
       Changes">
32. </td></tr></table>
33.
34. <!-- Table: holds all of the fields that get
    displayed -->
35. <table>
36. <%
37. for ( field_number = 0; field_number <
    rs.fields.count ; field_number++ ){
38.
39.    temp_field =
       String(rs.fields(field_number).Name);
40.    temp_content =
       String(rs.fields.item(temp_field));
41.
42.    //data cleanup: nulls, dates, field names
43.    if (temp_content == "null") {temp_content =
       ""; }
44.    else if (temp_field.search(/date/) >= 0 )
       // check for date fields
45.                {temp_content =
                    slash_date(temp_content);}
46.    // we can get rid of "data_" on labels, but
       not in the form fields
47.    temp_field_label =
       temp_field.replace(/data_/,"");
48.
49.    // uid field should not be editable:
50.    if (temp_field.search(/uid/) >= 0){
51.            out += '\n\n<tr><td>' +
               temp_field_label + ': </td><td>' +
               temp_content + '</td></tr>';
52.    }
53.
```

```
54.    // category needs a scroll box:
55.    else if (temp_field.search(/data_category/)
       >= 0){
56.          out +=
             '\n\n<tr><td>'+temp_field_label+'
             </td><td>';
57.          out += '\n<select name="' + temp_field
             + '">';
58.          for (i=0; i < cat_object.qty ; i++){
59.                out += '\n<option
                   name="data_category" value="' +
                   cat_object[i].uid + '"';
60.                if (current_category ==
                   cat_object[i].uid)
                   out += ' selected ' ;
61.                out += '>' +  cat_object[i].name;
62.          }
63.          out += '\n</select></td></tr>\n\n';
64.    }
65.
66.    // subcategory also needs a scroll box:
67.    else if (temp_field.search(/data_subcategory/) >=
       0){
68.          sql = "SELECT * FROM subcategories where
             category = " + current_category;
69.          rs2 =
             Server.CreateObject("ADODB.RecordSet");
70.          rs2.Open (sql, Conn, 2,3);
71.          if (rs2.EOF){  // check to see if rs is
             empty
72.                out += "<tr><td>error: no
                   subcategories exist for this
                   category!</td><td></td></tr>";
73.          }
74.          else{                    // rs not empty
75.                out +=
                   '\n\n<tr><td>'
                   +temp_field_label+'</td><td>';
76.                out += '\n<select name="' +
                   temp_field + '">';
77.                while (! (rs2.EOF)){
78.                      out += '\n<option name="'+
                         temp_field +'" value="' +
                         String(rs2.fields.item
                         ("subcategory")) +  '" ';
79.                      if (temp_content ==
                         String(rs2.fields.item
                         ("subcategory")))
80.                            {out += ' selected '
                             ;}
```

```
81.                              out += '>' +
                                 String(rs2.fields.item
                                 ("subcategory"));
82.                              rs2.move(1);
83.                      } // end while recordset
84.                              out +=
                                 '\n</select></td></tr>\n\n';
85.              } // end else (rs not empty)
86.              rs2.Close ();
87.      } // end subcategory scrollbox
88.
89.      // <textarea> for description field
90.      else if (temp_field.search(/description/) >= 0){
91.              out += '\n\n<tr><td>' + temp_field_label +
                 ': </td><td><textarea name="' + temp_field
                 + '" cols=50 rows=3> ' + temp_content +
                 '</textarea></td></tr>';
92.      }// end description field
93.
94.      // standard text box
95.      else {
96.              out += '\n\n<tr><td>' + temp_field_label +
                 ': </td><td><input type=text name="' +
                 temp_field + '" value="' + temp_content +
                 '" size=60></td></tr>';
97.      }
98.
99. }// end of looping through incoming form fields
100.
101. } // end else (rs not empty)
102.
103. rs.Close ();
104. %>
105. <% = out %>
106. </table>
107.
108. <!-- Table: Delete and save buttons -->
109. <p><table border=0>
110. <tr><td>
111.    <!-- Save button sends user to the update
         script -->
112.    <!-- also, close form that spans most of this
         script-->
113.    <input type="hidden" name ="current_record"
         value="<% = current_record %>">
114.    <input type="hidden" name ="current_category"
         value="<% = current_category %>">
115.    <input type="submit" name ="toss" value="Save
         Changes">
116.    </form>
117. </td><td>
```

```
118.    <!-- Delete button sends user to the delete
        script -->
119.    <form action="<% = delete_record_script%>">
120.    <input type="hidden" name ="current_category"
        value="<% = current_category %>">
121.    <input type="hidden" name ="current_record"
        value="<% = current_record %>">
122.    <input type="submit" name ="toss" value="Delete
        This Record">
123.    </form>
124. </td></tr></table>
125.
126. <%
127. Conn.Close ();
128. %>
129. </body></html>
```

HOW THE SCRIPT WORKS

When a user clicks on the "Edit" link next to a record on the page generated by `ch4_list_records.asp`, this invokes `ch4_edit_record_form.asp` and passes it the uid of the record that the user wants to edit. This generates a form that a user can use to edit the information for that record or to delete the record.

`ch4_edit_record_form.asp` does pretty much the same thing as `ch4_edit_category_form.asp`, discussed earlier in this chapter: it generates a form dynamically, based on the information that is retrieved from the database. The script is more complex, however, because where the category form involved only string data that could be edited using a text box, this script deals with a more complicated set of data involving strings, dates, and multiple-choice fields that require not only simple text boxes but also select boxes and a `<textarea>` field. If reading JavaScript ASP code is not yet second nature to you, you'll probably want to make sure that you completely get the code to edit category scripts before you move on to the code to edit record scripts.[5]

---

5. On this note, it might be worth noting that probably the single most important thing to learn in order to be able to code effectively is the ability to discern between things you understand well and things that don't completely make sense to you.

Over and over, I notice an easily preventable bad habit that cripples people's ability to work effectively: using code without really understanding it and not being aware of the fact.

We all have to do deal with things that we don't fully understand—that's part of life. Whether it's nested tables, objects, HTTP headers, the

You'll notice going through this script that all of the output is collected into a string variable called `out`. Because of the ratio of JavaScript code to HTML, this seems like a fine way to go. The alternative would be to be constantly opening and closing the ASP tags (`<%...%>`), which would probably make the script a little harder to read than it is this way.

Which is, of course, what makes this stuff fun. Here goes:

1,2. Set language and grab include file.

6. Insert `nav_header` variable (set in include file).

10. Create SQL statement that will grab the record we want from the database: all the fields for any record where the `data_uid` field is equal to the value of `current_record` (`current_record` is a form variable that the include file grabs and uses to create the JavaScript variable of the same name).

11,12. Create a Recordset object called `rs`.

13–15. In the unlikely event that nothing is found, generate an error message. Given that the record has to exist to create the "Edit" link that got the user to this form, it seems unlikely that it will very often get deleted between when the "Edit" link is created and when a user clicks on it.

16. If the script has a record, lines 17–102 get executed.

18–32. The first thing that happens is that two buttons are created at the top of the page: a Delete button and a Save button.

22–26. The Delete this Record button that gets created here requires three pieces of information to work: the name of the script that will do the actual deleting (`delete_record_script`,

---

relational algebra underlying SQL, or how TCP/IP really works, we can probably all think of things that we used to have trouble conceptualizing or still have trouble conceptualizing that we are, nevertheless, able to use. The individual who is conscious of this weakness will be able to work more effectively than the individual who doesn't take the time to understand the limits of his or her knowledge.

So if you don't completely "get" the scripts in this chapter, by all means, go ahead and use them. But just because you're able to get them to work, don't pretend to yourself that you really understand them until your grasp of HTML, ASP, JavaScript, SQL, ODBC, and how Web browsers and servers work is, in fact, refined to the point that you ontologically know what they are. In the meantime, feel free to let others think what they will. But don't fool yourself.

which resolves to `ch4_delete_record.asp`), the uid of the current record (`current_record`, so that the delete script knows what to delete), and the uid of the current category (`current_category`, so that after deleting the record, the delete script can forward the user to the appropriate list of records).

30. The form that gets created on this line spans most of the page, including all of the form fields that let the user edit the contents of the current record.

37. The `for()` loop on this line is used to iterate through every field in the recordset `rs` in turn. `rs.fields.count` tells the `for()` loop how many fields there are and is used to determine the upper limit of the variable `field_number`, which is used to store the index value of each field in turn.

There are 22 fields, so `field_number` will increment from 0 to 21. On each iteration of the loop, the code on lines 38–100 is executed, and on each occasion, another row is added to the table that starts on line 35.

39. `field_number` is used to set `temp_field` to the name of a field using the `rs.fields` object.

40. `temp_field` is used to set a value for `temp_content`.

42–45. After getting the field name and its contents from the `rs.fields object`, the first task is to clean up the data. First, any null fields are converted to empty strings (""), which is more user-friendly. Next, in 44–45, the `slash_date()` function is applied to any non-null date fields to convert the date to a friendlier format. (Without it, a date like `"1/6/2000"` would come out as `"Thu Jan 6 00:00:00 PST 2000"`).

47. Again, in the interest of being user-friendly, a regular expression is used to yank the prefix `/data_/` from the field name and create a new variable `temp_field_label`.

49–97. Next, a series of `if(){...}else if(){...}else if(){...}else{}` blocks are used to execute different blocks of code, depending on the field.

In each case, the decision is made by applying a regular expression to the `temp_field` string. If a match is found, the corresponding block of code is executed. For example, to find the `data_uid` field, the regular expression search-es for the `/uid/` pattern.

49–52. `data_uid` field: This is the simplest case. Because the `data_uid` is set by the database, it should not be editable by the user. Displaying the field is a matter of creating a table row with two cells in it, and putting `temp_field_label` in the first field and `temp_content` in the second.

Alternatively, you might decide that there's no point in displaying this information at all, in which case, you might want to do something like:

```
if (temp_field.search(/uid/) >= 0){
        // do nothing
}
```

43–64. `data_category` field (scroll box): The category scroll box is a little tricky. Because the categories are fixed, users need to be constrained to choosing from a list. This can be done either with a scroll box or radio buttons. For this kind of thing, I think scroll boxes are more conventional.

Getting the categories is fairly easy, because category information is put into `cat_object` in the include file. In line 57, the `<select>` form field is started, with the name set to `temp_field`.

In lines 58–62, the script iterates through `cat_object` once for each category, using `cat_obect[i].uid` to set a value (an integer) for each option that will appear in the select box and `cat_object[i].name` to create a human-readable label (the category name) for each option. The `for()` loop used here is complicated by the fact that, on each iteration, the script checks to see whether the cate-gory being put into the `<select>` box matches the cur-rent category (stored in the `current_category` object). If a match is found (line 60), the `selected` option is set for the `<option>` tag being assembled, so that the correct category will be displayed by the select box.

66–87. `data_subcategory` field (scroll box): The subcategory scroll box needs to be populated with valid subcategories for the current category. The process is similar to how a scroll box was set up for the category field above, except that because this information has not yet been collected (there is no `cat_object` to turn to), a list of valid subcategories must be collected by querying the database.

In lines 68–70, a new recordset, `rs2`, is created that contains all of the subcategories that exist for the current category. Subcategories are stored in the `subcategories` table. Lines 71–73 generate an error message if no subcategories are found. If you find that you don't necessarily want to use subcategories, you might want to change the message in line 72.

77–83. Loop through `rs2` and populate the `<select>` box that is opened on line 76 and closed on line 84. Again, there is a check on each iteration to make sure that the appropriate subcategory is selected.

89–92. `data_description` field (`<textarea>`): The description field is the last field that gets special treatment. Because it may contain more than one line of information, it is set up as a `<textarea>` form field. This is quick work, a matter of dropping the variables `temp_field_label`, `temp_field`, and `temp_content` into the appropriate HTML.

94–97. All the other fields: The remaining 18 fields can all be handled the same way—a text box (an `<input>` tag with the `type` attribute set to `text`) is generated with the same three variables dropped in the appropriate place: `temp_field_label`, the human-readable field label, `temp_field`, which is the full name of the field, and `temp_content`, the contents of the field that were retrieved from the database.

Note that neither this script nor any of the other scripts in this chapter make any effort to perform error checking. If you're going to be setting novice users loose on this, it's probably something that you'll want to add, using either client-side or server-side code.[6]

99, 101. These lines close blocks of code that were started toward the beginning of the script.

103. Closes the `rs` object that will not be used again.

---

6. For information on client-side error checking with JavaScript, see *JavaScript for Web Professionals*, also in this series.

105. The out string, which is by now quite large, is sent to the browser at this point.

106. The table that contains the editable fields is closed.

Finally, another set of Save and Delete buttons is placed at the bottom of the page.

113–116. The Save button has to go first, because it is part of the form that has been running since line 30. Both current_record and current_category are set as hidden form variables. current_category is necessary because it contains the primary key of the current record, which the update script will need in order to save edits to the database. current_category is used so that the user can be returned to the list of records for the current category (otherwise, the user would have to be returned to the list of categories, which would be disorienting).

127. The Conn object that is opened in the include file is closed.

When a user has completed her edits, she clicks on the Save Changes button, which submits the form to ch4_update_record.asp, which is next.

Script 4-11
ch4_update_record.asp

```
1.  <%@ Language=JavaScript %>
2.  <!-- #include file="ch4_include.js" -->
3.
4.  <%
5.  temp_update = "";
6.
7.  for ( field_number = 1; field_number <=
    Request.QueryString.count ; field_number++ ){
8.
9.      temp_field =
        String(Request.QueryString.Key(field_number));
10.     temp_content =
        String(Request.QueryString.item(temp_field))
11.
12.     // make sure field is one we want to use
13.     if (temp_field.search
        (/current_record|current_category|toss/) < 0 ){
14.
15.         // nulls
16.         if (temp_content == "null" || temp_content
            == ""){
17.
```

```
18.                      temp_update += " "+ temp_field + "
                         = null,";
19.            }
20.
21.            //int fields
22.            else if (temp_field.search
               (/data_category/) >= 0)
23.                     {temp_update += " "+ temp_field +
                        " = " + temp_content +",";}
24.
25.            //this works for non-null char fields
26.            else {
27.
28.                     temp_content =
                        temp_content.replace
                        (/'/g,"&#039;");
29.                     temp_update += " "+ temp_field + "
                        = '" + temp_content +"',";
30.            }
31.
32.      } // end if we want to use field
33. } // end for loop
34.
35. // remove last character, which is a trailing comma
    that we don't want
36. temp_update =
    temp_update.substring(0,temp_update.length-1);
37.
38. update_sql = "update data set " + temp_update + "
    where data_uid = " + current_record;
39.
40. Conn.Execute(update_sql);
41.
42. Conn.Close ();
43.
44. Response.Redirect(list_records_script +
    "?current_category=" + current_category)
45.
46. //Response.Write("<hr>\n\n\n" + update_sql +
    "\n\n\n<hr>");
47. //Response.Write(list_records_script +
    "?current_category=" + current_category)
48. %>
```

HOW THE SCRIPT WORKS

This script works pretty much the same as `ch4_update_catego-ry.asp` (discussed earlier in this chapter). I wrote an overview of how that one worked before diving into the code. Here, I'll just dive into the code:

1,2. Tell Bill to use open protocols, grab bag of tricks.

5. Declare variable `temp_update` that will be used to store key/value pairs for the SQL `update` statement that is created by this script.

7. Rather than explicitly call out form variables, the script uses the `for()` loop that starts on this line to iterate through the `Request.QueryString` object and grab all the incoming form information. The block of code in the loop (lines 8–33) then looks at each incoming variable in turn and decides whether and how to put the incoming form information into the update statement used to update the database.

Note that `field_number`, the counter that is used to iterate through the `Request.QueryString` object, starts at one, rather then zero. I think I've already complained to you about that one. The `count` property of `Request.QueryString` is used to set the upper limit of `field_number`.

9,10. `temp_field` and `temp_content` are used to store, in turn, the values of each form variable and its contents as they are retrieved from `Request.QueryString`.

13. A regular expression is used to eliminate variables that we're not interested in. Any field that matches the regular expression (`/current_record|current_category|toss/`) will cause the `search()` method to return a value of 0 or higher, so that the `if()` statement resolves to false. Any field that fails to match is presumed to be a database field, and lines 14–32 are executed.

14–37. The `if(){…} else if(){…} else{}` statement that runs from line 14 to line 32 ensures that, depending on the field in question, the field name and its contents are added to the `temp_update` string.

16–19. The first thing the script checks for is null values in `temp_content`, looking for the keyword `null` or an empty string ("”). If this is the case, that field is set to `null`.

22–24. The next step checks for integer fields, which, unlike string fields, should not have single quotes around them. Because some of the string fields might contain integers, checking the contents is not an option. And because I didn't set up a naming convention to deal with integer fields, there is no generic way to identify integer fields. As a result, they need to be explicitly identified in the regular expression used on line 22, which checks for /data_category/. This works because data_category is the only nonstring field in the data table.

26–30. Fields that do not contain nulls or integer values can all be treated the same: It is simply a matter of first replacing any single quotes within the field with their HTML equivalent (line 28, with a regular expression), then of encapsulating the contents of the field with single quotes (line 29).

32. Close the if() started on line 13.

33. Closes the for() loop.

36. Because the script deals with an indeterminate number of fields, each time a field is added to temp_update, a trailing comma is added in anticipation of the next. The last comma is superfluous and is removed here, using the substring() method that can be applied to any JavaScript string.

38. Here, the SQL statement that lies at the core of this script is finally put together. The temp_update string at this point consists of a series of comma-separated key/value pairs:

```
field_1 = 'field_1', field_2 = field_2, … field_n =
'field_n'
```

Meanwhile, current_record contains the uid of the record that is to updated, so that for a record whose id is "i", update_sql will be:

```
update data set field_1 = 'field_1', field_2 =
field_2, … field_n = 'field_n' where data_uid = i
```

The fields, of course, will be actual field names with actual values or the SQL special value null.

40. Finally, the SQL `update` statement is executed through the `Conn` object (created in the include file).

42. The `Conn` object is closed.

44. `Response.Redirect` is used to redirect the browser to `ch4_list_records.asp`.

46–47. I left these lines here in case you ever need to debug this script. To debug, comment out lines 40 and 44, and comment in lines 46 and 47. This will let you take a look at the SQL code being generated and the URL that the browser is being redirected to.

Script 4-12
ch4_delete_record.asp

```
 1. <%@ Language=JavaScript %>
 2. <!-- #include file="ch4_include.js" -->
 3.
 4. <%
 5. delete_sql = "delete from data where data_uid = " +
    current_record;
 6.
 7. Conn.Execute(delete_sql);
 8.
 9. Conn.Close ();
10.
11. Response.Redirect(list_records_script +
    "?current_category=" + current_category)
12.
13. //Response.Write("<hr>\n\n\n" + delete_sql +
    "\n\n\n<hr>");
14. //Response.Write(list_records_script +
    "?current_category=" + current_category)
15. %>
```

HOW THE SCRIPT WORKS

Give this script the primary key of a record in the `data` table, and it will delete a record for you.

5,7. The work is performed on lines 5 and 7. Using the form value `current_record`, line 5 creates an SQL statement that will delete any record whose `data_uid` field is set to that value. The SQL `delete` statement is then executed on line 7.

9,11. Line 9 closes the `Conn` object, and line 11 redirects users to `ch4_list_records.asp`.

13,14. Lines 13 and 14 are there in case you get creative and need to do some debugging. Note that, as long as you give this script a valid value for `current_record`, the `delete` statement should work, and as long as you give it a valid value for `current_category`, the `redirect` statement should do fine as well.

Script 4-13
ch4_blank_record_form.asp

```
1. <%@ Language=JavaScript %>
2. <!-- #include file="ch4_include.js" -->
3.
4. <html><head><title>Blank Record
   Form</title></head><body>
5.
6. <% = nav_header %>
7. <%
8. sql = "SELECT * FROM data where data_uid=0" ;
9. rs = Server.CreateObject("ADODB.RecordSet");
10. rs.Open (sql, Conn, 2,3);
11.
12. out += '<form action="' + insert_record_script +
    '">';
13. out += '<input type="submit" name="toss"
    value="Create New Record">';
14. out += '<table>';
15.
16. // loop through form fields and create a form based
    on fields we found
17. // in recordset.
18. for ( field_number = 0; field_number <
    rs.fields.count ; field_number++ ){
19.
20.     temp_field =
        String(rs.fields(field_number).Name);
21.
22.     // we can get rid of "data_" on labels, but not
        in the form fields
23.     temp_field_label =
        temp_field.replace(/data_/,"");
24.
25.     // uid field should not be editable:
26.     if (temp_field.search(/uid/) > 0){
27.         // do nothing!
28.     }
```

```
29.
30.     // category needs a scroll box:
31.     else if (temp_field.search(/data_category/) >=
        0){
32.            out += '\n\n<tr><td>'+temp_field_label+
               '</td><td>';
33.            out += '\n<select name="' + temp_field +
               '">';
34.            for (i=0; i < cat_object.qty ; i++){
35.                   out += '\n<option value="' +
                      cat_object[i].uid +  '"';
36.                   if (current_category ==
                      cat_object[i].uid) {out += '
                      selected ' };
37.                   out += '>' +  cat_object[i].name;
38.            }
39.            out += '\n</select><br></td></tr>\n\n';
40. }
41.
42.     // subcategory also needs a scroll box:
43.     else if (temp_field.search(/data_subcategory/) >=
        0){
44.            sql = "SELECT * FROM subcategories where
               category = " + current_category;
45.            rs2 =
               Server.CreateObject("ADODB.RecordSet");
46.            rs2.Open (sql, Conn, 2,3);
47.
48.            if (rs2.EOF){  out += "<tr><td>error:
               no subcategories exist for this
               category!</td><td></td></tr>"; }
49.            else{                    // we have
               subcategories
50.                   out +=
                      '\n\n<tr><td>'+temp_field_label
                      +'</td><td>';
51.                   out += '\n<select name="' +
                      temp_field+ '">';
52.                   while (! (rs2.EOF)){
53.                          out += '\n<option value="' +
                             String(rs2.fields.item
                             ("subcategory")) +  '">' +
                             String(rs2.fields.item
                             ("subcategory"));
54.                          rs2.move(1);
55.                   } // end while rs2
56.                   out += '\n</select></td></tr>\n\n';
57.            } // end else (rs2 not empty)
58.            rs2.Close ();
59.     }// end subcategory scroll box
60.
```

```
61.    // <textarea> for description field
62.    else if (temp_field.search(/description/) >= 0){
63.        out += '\n\n<tr><td>' + temp_field_label +
           ': </td><td><textarea name="' + temp_field
           + '" cols=50 rows=3>
           </textarea></td></tr>';
64.    }// end description field
65.
66.    // standard text box
67.    else {
68.        out += '\n\n<tr><td>' + temp_field_label +
           ': </td><td><input type=text name="' +
           temp_field + '" value=""
           size=60></td></tr>';
69.    }
70.
71. }// end of looping through incoming form fields
72. rs.Close ();
73.
74. out += '</table>';
75. out += '<input type="hidden" name="current_category"
    value="'+ current_category +'">';
76. out += '<input type="submit" name="toss"
    value="Create New Record">';
77. out += '</form>';
78.
79. %>
80.
81. <% = out %>
82.
83. <%
84. Conn.Close ();
85. %>
86. </body>
87. </html>
```

HOW THE SCRIPT WORKS

If you compare this script to ch4_edit_record_form.asp, you'll see that it's almost the same, except that, because it creates a blank form, it doesn't put any values into any of the fields. Because ch4_edit_record_form.asp was discussed at length just a few pages ago I'll make this discussion very brief, and focus primarily on what's different about this script.

The basic idea of the script is simple: create a recordset that includes all the fields from the data table and build a form based on those fields so that a user can type in information that will then be stored in that table. By generating the form dynamically from the table, it makes it fairly easy to insert the information dynamically into the table (in SQL, records are created using `insert` statements).

1–7. Unless you've just opened the book to this page, you're probably familiar with this stuff.[7]

8. The SQL statement created on this line is interesting, in that it is guaranteed to create an empty recordset. We can be sure of this because the `data_uid` field is provisioned by MS Access, which will use integers starting with the number 1. Getting an empty recordset is fine, as far as this script goes, because all we care about is the name of all the fields in the `data` table, which we can obtain even if the recordset is empty. Although performance is not likely to be a big issue with this database, which is organized only to deal with relatively small numbers of records, it's nevertheless nice to keep the script's overhead down, and one would hope that an empty recordset would incur less overhead than a bigger recordset (you never really know without testing, and I haven't).

9,10. Create recordset `rs`.

12–14. Start form, Create New Record button, and start table.

18. Beginning of `for` loop that loops through fields in the recordset, accessed through the `rs.fields` object.

20. Create `temp_field` variable that contains the name of a different field each time the script iterates through the `for()` loop.

23. Create human-readable label `temp_field_label`.

26–28. Script won't create form field for `data_uid` field, which is set by database.

31–40. These lines build a scroll box that contains a list of categories pulled out of `cat_object`.

43–59. These lines build a subcategory scroll box, using a second recordset, `rs2`.

62–64. The `data_description` field gets a `<textarea>` tag.

---

7. If you did just open the book, take a look at similar scripts in Chapter 3.

67–69. All the other fields get standard text boxes (<input type=text ...> tags).

74–77. Close table, pass the current_category variable to the next script, build a Create New Record button, and close the <form> tag.

81. Send the out string to the browser.

83–87. Wrap things up.

Script 4-14
ch4_insert_record.asp

```
1.  <%@ Language=JavaScript %>
2.  <!-- #include file="ch4_include.js" -->
3.
4.  <%
5.  fields = "";
6.  values = "";
7.
8.  // loop through incoming form fields to build sql
    statements
9.  for ( field_number = 1; field_number <=
    Request.QueryString.count ; field_number++ )
10.     {
11.         temp_field =
            String(Request.QueryString.Key(field_number));
12.         temp_content =
            String(Request.QueryString.item(temp_field))
13.
14.         if (temp_field.search(/toss|current_category/) <
            0 ){
15.
16.             fields += ' ' + temp_field + ',';
17.
18.             // check for null values
19.             if (temp_content == "null" || temp_content
                == "")
20.                 {
21.                 values += " null,";
22.                 }
23.
24.             // check for int fields
25.             else if (temp_field.search
                (/data_category/) >= 0)
26.                 {values += " " + temp_content
                    +",";
27.                 current_category = temp_content;
28.                 }
```

```
29.
30.              // this works for non-null char fields
31.              else {
32.
33.                      temp_content =
                          temp_content.replace
                          (/'/g,"&#039;");
34.                      values += " '" + temp_content
                          +"',";
35.              }
36.
37.      } // end if
38. } // end looping through incoming form fields
39.
40. // remove last character, which is a trailing comma
    that we don't want
41. values = values.substring(0,values.length-1);
42. fields = fields.substring(0,fields.length-1);
43.
44. insert_sql = "insert into data (" + fields + ")
    values (" + values + ")";
45.
46. Conn.Execute(insert_sql);
47.
48. Conn.Close ();
49.
50. Response.Redirect(list_records_script +
    "?current_category=" + current_category)
51.
52. //Response.Write(list_records_script +
    "?current_category=" + current_category)
53. //Response.Write(list_records_script +
    "?current_category=" + current_category)
54. %>
```

HOW THE SCRIPT WORKS

Once again, a script whose inner workings are eerily reminiscent of earlier scripts. This script is closest to its baby brother, ch4_insert_category.asp, described earlier in the chapter, but also a lot like the update scripts, also discussed earlier.

Briefly, the script collects incoming form information, grabs the fields that should go in the database, creates an SQL insert statement, executes the statement, then forwards the user back to ch4_list_records.asp. Less briefly:

1,2. Declare language and grab include file discussed earlier in this chapter.

5,6. Create two variables, `fields` and `values`, that will be used to generate an SQL statement that contains the information typed in by the user in `ch4_blank_record_form.asp`.

9. Start looping through incoming fields in `Request.QueryString`.

11,12. Populate the temporary variables `temp_field` and `temp_content`.

14. Use a regular expression to eliminate fields that we're not interested in.

16. Add `temp_field` to the `fields` string.

19–22. In the case of `null` fields and empty strings, the `null` value is appended to `values`.

25–28. For `data_category`, which is an `int` field, single quotes are not necessary when adding `temp_content` to `values`.

31–35. Any other fields will be noted, primarily for their need for single quotes on the outside and no single quotes on the inside. Thus, line 33 gets rid of any of the undesirable kind, and line 34 puts a single quote on either side of `temp_content`, and a comma on the end, and concatenates the whole thing into `values`.

37,38. Close a couple of blocks of code.

41,42. Get rid of extra commas that are hanging onto the end of `values` and `fields`.

44. At last, `insert_sql`, the point of the entire exercise, with `fields` and `values` in their proper place, so that the resulting SQL statement will be in the form:

```
insert into data field_1, field_2 values value_1,
value_2
```

46. The SQL statement is delivered to the database.

48. The database connection is closed.

50. The user is redirected to `ch4_list_records.asp` or whatever URL is assigned to `list_records_script` in the include file.

52,53. A couple of lines that may come in handy if you ever need to debug this script.

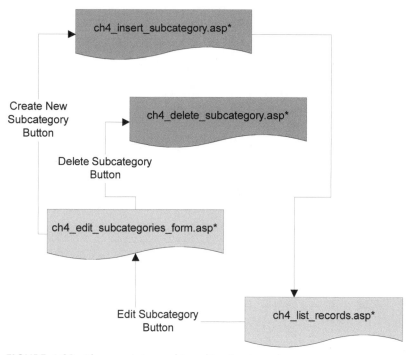

FIGURE 4-10: Three scripts used to edit subcategories

CODE TO EDIT SUBCATEGORIES

As Figure 4-10 implies, when a user clicks on the Edit Subcategory button on ch4_list_records.asp, they are taken to ch4_edit_subcategories_form.asp, where they can create new subcategories (ch4_insert_subcategory.asp does the work) or delete existing ones (ch4_delete_subcategory.asp). There is no mechanism to edit existing subcategories, short of deleting an existing subcategory and creating a new one. If you've read this far, perhaps you'll be tempted to figure out how to do it yourself. :)

Script 4-15
ch4_edit_subcategory_form.asp

```
1.  <%@ Language=JavaScript %>
2.  <!-- #include file="ch4_include.js" -->
3.
4.  <html><head><title>Edit
    Subcategories</title></head><body>
5.
6.  <% = nav_header %>
```

```
7.  <center><font size="+2"> Edit Subcategories
    </font><br></center><hr>
8.  You can use this form to delete existing
    subcategories or to create new ones.
9.
10. <%
11. sql = "SELECT categories.category_uid,
    categories.category_name, subcategories.subcategory
    FROM categories INNER JOIN subcategories ON
    categories.category_uid = subcategories.category
    ORDER BY categories.category_name"
12. rs = Server.CreateObject("ADODB.RecordSet");
13. rs.Open (sql, Conn);
14. if (rs.EOF){   // check to see if rs is empty
15.     out += "no subcategories found. ";
16. }
17.
18. else{                    // rs not empty
19.     category_header = ""
20.     while (! rs.EOF){
21.             temp_category =
                String(rs.fields.item("category_uid"))
22.             temp_category_name =
                String(rs.fields.item("category_name"))
23.             temp_subcategory =
                String(rs.fields.item("subcategory"))
24.
25.                     // categories: when we get to a
                        new one, display it
26.                     if (category_header !=
                        temp_category_name){
27.                             category_header =
                                temp_category_name;
28. %>
29.                             <div align="center"><b><% =
                                category_header %></b></div>
30. <%
31.                     }
32. %>
33. <br><b><% = temp_subcategory %></b>   
34. <a href="<% = delete_subcategory_script
    %>?current_category=<% = temp_category
    %>&current_subcategory=<% = temp_subcategory %>">
35. <font size="-1"
    face="arial,helvetica">Delete</font></a>
36. <%
37.             rs.move(1);
38.     } // end while
39. } // end else
40. %>
41.
```

```
42.  <hr>
43.  To create a new subcategory, select a category and
     type in the name of the subcategory you want to
     create:
44.  <form action="<% = insert_subcategory_script %>">
45.  <select name="current_category">
46.  <%   for   (i=0; i < cat_object.qty ; i++){ %>
47.             <option value="<% = cat_object[i].uid
                %>"><% = cat_object[i].name %>
48.  <%       } %>
49.  </select></td></tr>
50.  Subcategory<input type=text name=current_subcategory
     value="">
51.  <input type=submit name=toss value="Create New
     Subcategory">
52.  </form>
53.
54.  <%
55.  Conn.Close ();
56.  %>
57.  </body></html>
```

HOW THE SCRIPT WORKS

This script creates a Web page (Figure 4-11) that lists all of the subcategories for all of the categories and makes it easy to delete subcategories or to create new ones.

Note that there is no way to edit subcategories. Subcategories are stored in each record as strings, rather than using an id, so editing a subcategory would mean not only changing the value of a subcategory name in the subcategories table but also changing the name of that subcategory every time it occurs in a record in the data table. This is perfectly doable, but it's not what this script does, because doing it this way is simpler, albeit less powerful.

The first half of the script lists all of the subcategories that already exist in the database and creates links that can be used to delete subcategories that are no longer useful.

The second half of the script creates a form that can be used to create new subcategories.

1. Set language to JavaScript.

2. Grab the include file described earlier in this chapter.

6. Drop navigation header created in the include file at the top of the page.

8. You might want to add more documentation here if you find that people are not figuring out how to use this page.

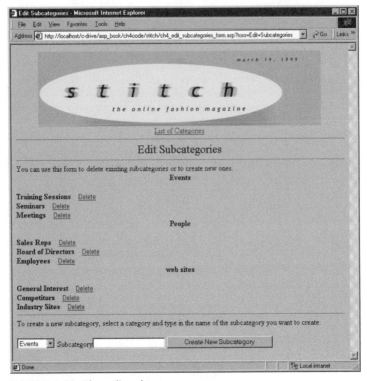

FIGURE 4-11 The edit subcategory page

11. This SQL statement is a bit of a mouthful, but it makes sense once you look at it: To organize subcategories by category, the script needs to know which category a subcategory is in. Because category names are stored in the categories table (only category uids are stored in the subcategories table), it's necessary to do an inner join on the two tables to create a recordset that will look like this (only the first few records are shown):

Category_uid	category_name	subcategory
1	People	Employees
1	People	Board of Directors
1	People	Sales Reps
2	Events	Rock
2	Events	Easy listening
3	Web sites	Industry Sites
3	Web sites	Competitors

Kind of neat how everything in SQL looks like a table, isn't it?

12,13. Create a recordset called `rs`, based on the above SQL statement.

14–16. If the recordset is empty, in which case `rs.EOF` will be true, generate a graceful error message. Otherwise, execute lines 18–39.

19. Create an empty string called `category_header`. This will be used to see whether any given record is in the same category as the previous record. If not, the script will decide that we're dealing with a new category and will display the name of the category.

20–38. This `while()` loop goes through the recordset one line at a time. Each record will be added to the HMTL output by the script. If appropriate, a new category heading will be created, as well.

21–23. Three variables are created to collect the three fields in the recordset shown in the table above.

26–31. These lines deal with deciding whether to create a category heading (see table above to see how subcategories are grouped by category).

26. Checks to see whether the `category_header` variable created in line 19 is **not** equal to `temp_category_name`, which contains the category associated with the current subcategory record. If they are the same, nothing happens. If they are different (which will be the case for the first record and any time the category changes—remember that the subcategories in the recordset are ordered by category), lines 27–30 are executed.

27. This line resets `category_header` to a new value—the value of the current category (`temp_category_name`).

28–30. These lines close the ASP tags and create the HTML for the category heading, which is simply the name of the new category, centered on the page. Once again, evidence that I am not a designer.

33–36. Regardless of whether a heading is created above, every subcategory in the recordset gets added to the page being created. This is where it happens. Once again, the ASP tags are closed, because there's a fair amount of HTML involved.

The only tricky part here is the "Delete" link that is created on lines 34 and 35. This includes a link to the `delete_subcategory_script` that includes the form variables `current_category` and `current_subcategory`. The latter will be used to figure out which subcategory to delete by the script, which is described later in this chapter.

37. Important line: Never forget to go to the next record when using a `while()` loop to iterate through a recordset. Otherwise, it takes a very long time.

Then there's some HTML...

44. This is the first line of the form that collects the information required to create a new subcategory record. As the `action` attribute suggests, the new subcategory will be created by the `insert_subcategory_script`, described next.

45–49. These lines create a select box by looping through the `cat_object` object created in the include file that knows all there is to know about categories. Note that the value of each item in the select list is set to the uid of a category while the human-readable name is displayed for public consumption.

50. Every subcategory must have a name, and a name every subcategory shall have. This is where it all starts.

51. Yet another Submit button called `toss`, so that it can easily be edited without affecting the functionality of anything. Customers are always weirdly picky about what buttons say. Maybe because it gives them the illusion of control. `<Existential Moment>`

55. Good practice to close the recordset, even if IIS will do it for us.

Script 4-16
ch4_insert_subcategory.asp

```
1. <%@ Language=JavaScript %>
2. <!-- #include file="ch4_include.js" -->
3.
4. <%
```

```
 5. insert_sql = "insert into subcategories
    (category,subcategory) values (" + current_category +
    ", '" + current_subcategory + "')";
 6.
 7. Conn.Execute(insert_sql);
 8.
 9. Conn.Close ();
10.
11. Response.Redirect(edit_subcategories_form_script)
12. //Response.Write("<hr>\n\n\n" + insert_sql +
    "\n\n\n<hr>")
13. //Response.Write("redirect: "+
    edit_subcategories_form_script)
14.%>
```

HOW THE SCRIPT WORKS

Aren't short yet useful scripts the best? As the title indicates, this one creates a new subcategory, based on information collected in `ch4_edit_subcategories_form.asp`, discussed above.

1. Language set to JavaScript.

2. Grab the include file, which creates the database connection `Conn` as well as a couple of variables that we'll use.

5. This is the SQL statement that will create a new subcategory record by adding two fields, `category` and `subcategory`, to the `subcategories` database. Both fields are passed to the script as form variables and set as the local variables `current_category` and `current_subcategory` by the include file.

7. Execute the SQL statement created in line 5.

8. Close the database connection that was created in the include file.

11. That's it. This script produces no output. Instead, it redirects users to the `edit_subcategories_form_script`. On good days, the subcategory that they just tried to create is there, waiting to be used.

Script 4-17
ch4_delete_subcategory.asp

```
 1. <%@ Language=JavaScript %>
 2. <!-- #include file="ch4_include.js" -->
 3.
```

```
 4. <%
 5. delete_sql = "delete from subcategories where
    category = " + current_category + " and subcategory
    = '" + current_subcategory+  "'";
 6.
 7. Conn.Execute(delete_sql);
 8.
 9. Conn.Close ();
10.
11. Response.Redirect(edit_subcategories_form_script)
12.
13. //Response.Write("<hr>\n\n\n" + delete_sql +
    "\n\n\n<hr>")
14. //Response.Write("redirect: "+
    edit_subcategories_form_script)
15. %>
```

HOW THE SCRIPT WORKS

A mildly destructive script designed to delete a single record from the `subcategories` table when someone clicks on a delete link in `ch4_edit_subcategories_form.asp`.

1. Set JavaScript as the scripting language.

2. Grab the include file, which creates the database connection `Conn` and the variables `current_category` and `current_subcategory`.

5. This line creates the SQL statement that is designed to delete a single record from the `subcategories` table. Note that the `where` clause of the statement specifies a value for both the `category` field and the `subcategory` field. Because subcategories are category-specific, this is required to prevent deleting more than one subcategory if the same subcategory name is assigned to more than one category.

7. This is where the `delete` statement actually gets executed.

9. This is where the database connection is closed.

10. This is where the user gets redirected to `ch4_edit_sub-categories_form.asp`.

RECAP

This chapter demonstrates fairly conclusively that creating an HTML front end to let a lot of users edit a database is often more trouble than it's worth. Used correctly, however, it can save you a lot of tedious work. This script, at the very least, can make the task of maintaining and publishing a simple database like a phone list a lot less boring than it used to be. In a company of any size, having a phone list that's reasonably up to date will probably save the company a surprising amount of money.

Oh yeah. Technology:

- Some neat tricks to collect data submitted by a form, even if you don't know what the data is.
- Storing that data in a database.
- Create template-driven interfaces.
- Using a password to limit who can use a script.
- Organize a set of scripts to work together relatively efficiently.

IDEAS FOR HACKING THIS SCRIPT

The main challenge with a script like this is to figure out how to use it in a way that's actually useful. Ideally, take a look at processes within an organization that require collecting information from a number of people and storing it in a single place. If this is information that then needs to be published to a lot of people, so much the better. If it's information that's constantly changing and causing people endless headaches, you may have yourself a useful application.

The interfaces on the scripts in this chapter are probably too rough for most applications. Take some time to customize them. If you can, get a good graphic designer to help you. Listen to the people who use this stuff. If you pay attention, you may be able to figure out ways to make simple changes that will make a big difference. I'm always surprised by how nontechnical users are constantly assuming that what they need can't be done. So they don't ask for the easy stuff that can be tweaked in a few minutes, although that seems to be changing as people spend more time with computers and start to expect more.

I made a note to myself a while back that it'd be nice to modify the delete script so that it won't delete a category if there are any records in that category. You could create a recordset that contains all of the records in that category and delete the category only if the recordset is empty. I'm sure you can think of a thousand other tweaks.

5 Shopping Cart

IN THIS CHAPTER

- A complete shopping cart system
- A text-file database
- Storing information in the ASP Session object
- A simple keyword search engine

As I write this, e-commerce dot-coms are going out of business with the same manic intensity as they burst on the scene last year or the year before. So long as your customers are other businesses, it's probably safe to admit to being in the Internet business—at least for the moment.

The case for doing business online, of course, continues to be more and more compelling, and, although large sites will need industrial-strength systems, the shopping cart system in this chapter will easily handle a few sales—or even a few hundred sales per day.

Two of the critical ingredients of business success are cost control and execution. With this chapter, you can have a shopping cart up and running in the time it takes you to put the files on your server, for the cost of a paperback computer book. Give yourself a couple of days to customize the look and feel to meet your needs and set up a database of items you want to sell, and you're in business.[1]

---

1. Don't forget to budget time and, perhaps, money for marketing. Time is the critical ingredient. Get your site registered with search engines and participate in online communities that your customers are active in.

◆ Project: Building a Shopping Cart

Just as the last two chapters presented groups of scripts that worked together toward a common goal, the scripts in this chapter work together to allow a user to browse the contents of a catalog of goods for sale, select some of those items, and purchase them.

With a little bit of design work, these scripts offer a quick and functional solution. Because any of the scripts can be easily edited, customizing the shopping cart is often simple. Except, as ever, when it isn't. :)

Security

This chapter does not deal with security issues, which are beyond the scope of this book. However, security is a very real issue, so here's a quick list of things to think about:

- Communication between a browser and a server can be encrypted using SSL. Without SSL, any information (for example, credit card information) that is being passed to a Web server can be intercepted. SSL is not only safer than unencrypted communication, it makes people more comfortable giving you credit card information. Comfort is good.
- This script stores payment information (credit cards, prepaid Internet cards, etc. ...) unencrypted on the server. This is a security issue. You have a couple of solutions here. The best would be to encrypt the information. This can be done by the operating system, I think (I've never done it). I've also seen a JavaScript MD5 library that you could use. If you do store unencrypted information on your server, make sure that the server is as secure as you can make it and that you take the information off the server quickly. It's equally important to protect names and addresses of your customers, who generally expect the information they give you to be protected.
- If a merchant ships products to someone using stolen credit cards, the merchant is liable for the product. So make sure that your credit card validation process includes antifraud measures. Talk to your bank for more information on this subject.
- A lot of people argue (and I'm one of them) that you should be more worried about people you know than unknown bad guys on the Internet. Password-protect computers that store important information and don't share the passwords. Keep computers in locked rooms.

Exercise common sense! You probably wouldn't leave a pile of credit cards or information about your customers unattended in a public place. Digital valuables also need to be protected.

That said, security is an engineering problem. There are good solutions to security problems that make it possible for you to protect yourself to whatever level you think is appropriate. Take the time to educate yourself on the issue so that you are competent to create a working environment that is secure enough to meet your needs. And because security involves cool software and hardware, you can usually have a lot of fun with it. ;)

A Quick Tour

The cart in Figure 5-1 lets buyers browse items for sale by category or via keyword search. Each item supports an unlimited number of

FIGURE 5-1 View items available for sale; search by category or keyword

different options, any of which can be selected by clicking on a "Buy" link (which you can rename or replace with an image).

The cart is pretty much what you'd expect it to be. Item quantities can be edited using a text box and Submit button while "Delete This Item" links make it easy to remove unwanted items. A link lets shoppers check out when they're ready (See Figure 5-2).

FIGURE 5-2 View contents of cart, change quantities, remove items

There is a two-step purchase process. The first step requires that the buyer submit shipping information—how the item will be shipped and where it will be sent (Figure 5-3).

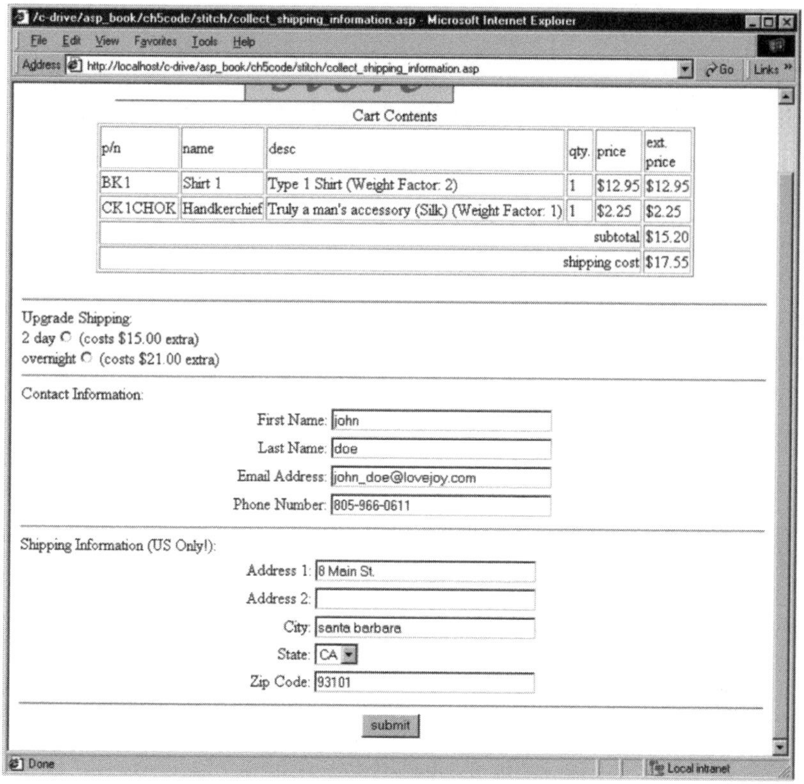

FIGURE 5-3 First, shipping information is collected ...

Next, the customer types in payment information (tax is automatically applied to in-state orders). Because only the front end of the cart is automated, it is possible to accept international orders, although you'll probably want to tweak the interface a little bit to do that (see Figure 5-4).

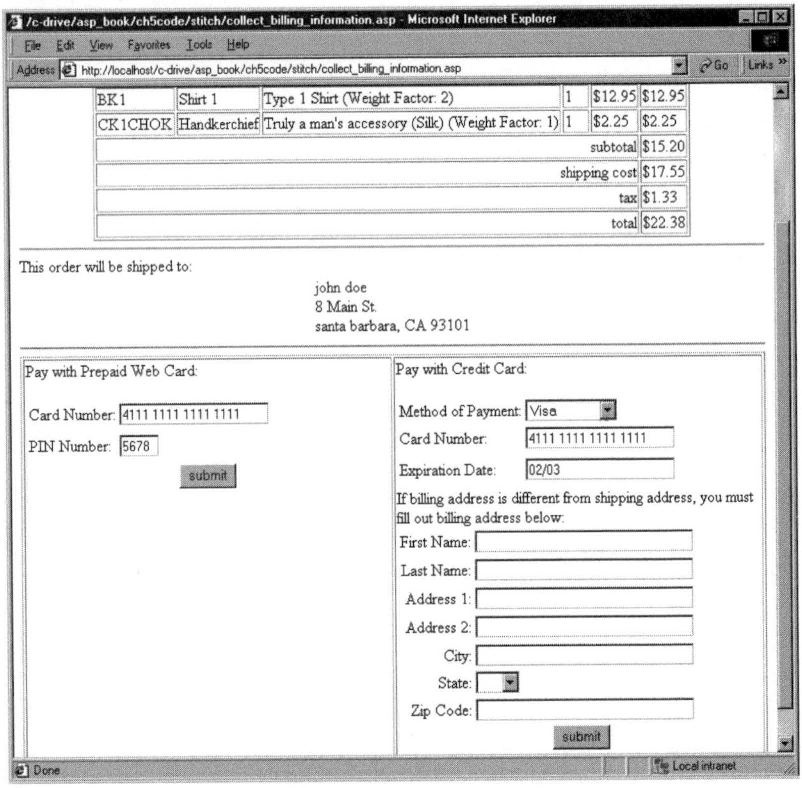

FIGURE 5-4 ... then billing information

At this point, the order is complete.

The cart generates an "Order Complete" page that summarizes the order information and gives the customer a unique order number (see Figure 5-5).

FIGURE 5-5 Order acknowledgment screen

At the same time, orders are written to a folder on the hard drive of your Web server, where they can easily be collected (see Chapter 6 for information on how to have orders emailed to you). See Figure 5-6.

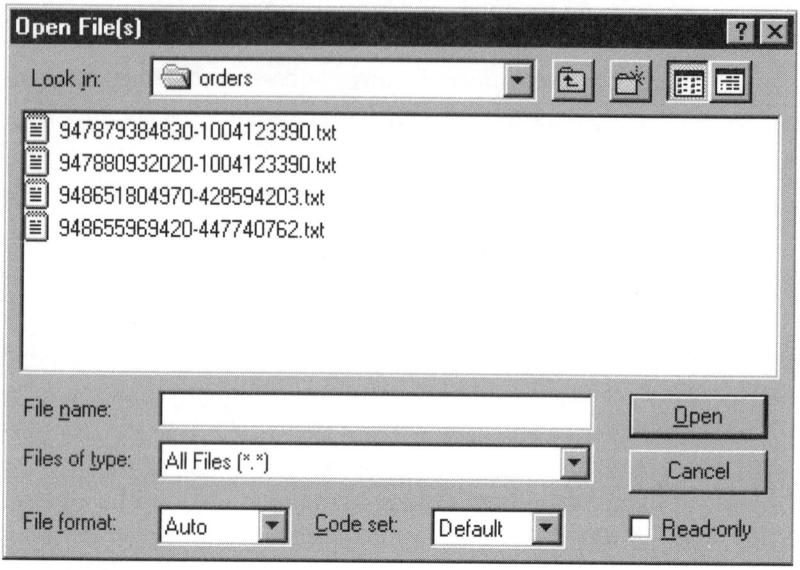

FIGURE 5-6 Orders in the orders folder

Each order file looks like this:

```
Order Number:960800441188-623866419

Order Summary:
1: BK2PB (The dilemma of 2 (paperback))
Ship Method: basic
Grand Total: $11.68

Contact Information:
john doe
john_doe@lovejoy.com
805-966-0611

Shipping To:
john doe
8 Main St.
santa barbara, CA 93101

Billing Information:

Visa
4111 1111 1111 1111
02/03
```

NEW FEATURES

Storing Information in the Session Object

No sooner was HTML successful than it became necessary to figure out how to get around the fact that HTML is a stateless protocol. As originally conceived, Web servers were supposed to forget about who they were dealing with as soon as they were done sending a user a Web page.

This creates a real problem for a number of Web applications, including shopping carts. The whole point of a shopping cart is that it lets you browse a Web site, looking for stuff that you want to buy, picking stuff out to add to your "cart," then buying it all when you're ready. Not what HTML was designed for.

Early innovators figured out a way to get around this by passing form information on every single link on their sites, so that, for example, a link to a Web page would include an id of some kind:

```
http://www.lovejoy.com/cgi-
bin/store/page2.cgi?user=123451234512345
```

This is pretty cumbersome. Some sites still do this, because to let people who don't have cookies shop on your site, you pretty much need to do something along these lines. Just make sure that you pass that id field on every single link, because otherwise the contents of a person's shopping cart are gone. Another irate customer.

The cookie was the next step in the evolution of things. With cookies, you could store a limited amount of information on the user's browser, which would be accessible to only you because the browser would share cookie information for a given domain only with a Web server for that domain.

Cookies are actually a very cool thing, even if they are kind of creepy ("You mean a Web site can put something on my computer?!?! Outrage!") and horribly unsafe (there have been too many security holes that have allowed unauthorized users to get hold of cookies).

Although cookies are poorly suited for storing credit card numbers and phone numbers, they are well suited to storing meaningless information, which means that it's possible to use cookies to assign unique ids to everyone who visits your site—then to store information that one would not want to share (credit card info, etc. ...) in a safe place and reference the private information with the unique id stored in the cookie.

Which is what the ASP Session object does.

This means that one of the great challenges of building a shopping cart—keeping track of unique visitors to a site—is already taken care of with ASP. Any user-specific information that you want to keep track of can be stored in the ASP Session object. It's very sweet.

The scripts in this chapter take full advantage of this to store two sets of information in the Session object: things that users put into their carts and information that they give us about themselves. Only when all the information necessary for an order has been collected is an order file created and saved on the hard drive.

CART_ITEMS

cart_items is an object that is used to store items that a user has placed in his or her cart. In the interest of simplicity, all the information that the scripts will need about items that a user wants to purchase is stored here: item part numbers, quantities, names, descriptions, prices, etc.

ORDER_INFO

The order_info object is used to store all the other information that is collected about a user, which is basically shipping and billing information (you can always get additional information by modifying the scripts).

Creating Templates

Creating an effective Web site is wonderfully complicated. One of the more interesting challenges is that Web sites are increasingly built by teams. Although in the first half of the 1990s, I used to kid myself that I could design an effective site, for the last few years I've left navigation and interface design to graphic designers and information architects.

In some cases where I've done all of the maintenance on a site, design and navigation elements have been freely mixed in with the code, so that only someone who was very comfortable with my scripts could actually edit a page.

Increasingly, however, I've lost interest in the day-to-day maintenance of Web pages, and this has meant structuring the programmatic elements of a Web application in such a way that people unfamiliar with the function of the application could work on that application's interface. This has meant using templates that contained as little code as possible, so that people who were familiar with HTML would be able to more or less easily modify the front end of a script.

In this chapter, the interface has been to a large extent separated from the functional elements of the script, so that the interface consists of templates that are relatively easy for people who don't understand the underlying ASP to edit. There's still some code but, fortunately, most people who are familiar with HTML are hard to intimidate, and I've had good luck letting designers put the front end on these scripts without having to go through the files with me line by line to figure out what's going on.

Storing Related Data in Two Text Files

To make it as easy as possible to set up the shopping cart, information about items that are for sale is stored in two text files: `catalog_file.txt` and `option_file.txt`.

Each item that is for sale is listed in `catalog_file.txt`. Every item in this file must have at least one option, which is, in turn, stored in `option_file.txt`. Thus, if you're selling a T-shirt that is available in three sizes, you would create one record in `catalog_file.txt` and three records in `option_file.txt`. A record is a line of information about an item. For example, a simplified illustration of how the data is organized can be depicted in a table:

`catalog_file.txt`		`option_file.txt`			
Part Number	**Description**	**Part Number**	**Extension**	**Option Desc.**	**Price**
b_shrt	A nice blue shirt	b_shrt	-Sm	Small	$12.00
		b_shrt	-Md	Medium	$15.00
		b_shrt	-Lg	Large	$17.00
w_shrt	A good white shirt	w_shrt		One size fits all	$16.00

The table above illustrates two cases: A blue shirt, which is available in three sizes, and a white shirt, which is available in only one size. Both shirts have a single line of information in `catalog_file.txt`. In `option_file.txt`, however, it's a different story: Here, there are three lines for the blue shirt, which has three options, and one line for the white shirt, which has one option.

Note that the part number field appears in both files, which makes it possible to map records in the catalog file to records in the option file. The full part number of an item consists of a concatenation of the part number and the extension fields (extensions can be blank if an item has only one option). Thus, w_shrt and b_shrt-sm are valid part numbers, whereas b_shirt is not a valid part number, because it does not include an extension, and there is more than one option for the blue shirt.

The actual text files used by the shopping cart are only slightly more complicated than the table above. catalog_file.txt has five fields:

- id: Same as Part Number, above.
- category: A field that can be used to organize items for sale into categories.
- name: The name of an item that is for sale.
- description: A description of an item.
- image: Usually an HTML image tag, but any legal HTML is fine.

For example (wraps indented for clarity):

```
//id|category|name|description|image
bk1|Books|Book 1|The story of the number 1|<img
  src="images/logo.gif">
bk2|Books|Book 2|The dilemma of 2|<img
  src="images/logo.gif">
ck1|Pastries|Croissant|Snooty French pastry|<img
  src="images/logo.gif">
ck2|Pastries|Bagel|Bread disguised as a donut|<img
  src="images/logo.gif">
```

option_file.txt also has five fields:

- id: Same as part number, above
- ext: An extension to the id used to identify an option uniquely. This field can be blank if an item has only one option.
- price: The price of an option.
- weight: The weight factor of an option. This is used to calculate shipping and can be an actual weight or an arbitrary value used to calculate how much shipping to charge for a given item.

- description: A description of an option. Note that this should be used only to describe the option, not the item itself, which should be described in the description field in catalog_file.txt.

For example:

```
//id|ext|price|weight|description
bk1||12.95|2|
bk2|pb|8.95|1|paperback
bk2|hb|23.22|2|cloth cover
ck1|chok|2.25|1|Chocolate Croissant
ck1|plain|2.15|1|Plain Croissant
ck2|on|4.25|3|Onion (dozen)
ck2|pl|4.25|3|Plain (dozen)
ck2|po|4.25|3|Poppy Seed (dozen)
```

THE ASP SHOPPING CART CODE

Many of the scripts in this chapter make use of the cart.js file, which is discussed last. So if you run into an undefined variable or function that you're curious about, you can always jump back there and see how it works.

HOW THE PIECES FIT TOGETHER

Figure 5-7 shows the files for the ASP shopping cart scripts and gives you a preview of how they all fit together.

BROWSING THE CATALOG AND FILLING THE SHOPPING CART WITH GOODIES

The scripts in this section let users browse items that are for sale, add them to their carts, and later remove them if they are so inclined.

Script 5-1
cart_list_items_for_sale.asp

```
1.  <%@ Language=JavaScript %>
2.  <!-- #include file="cart.js" -->
3.
4.
5.  <%
6.  cart_header();
7.  items = create_items_object ();
8.  %>
9.
10. <!---------------start item display template-------->
```

FIGURE 5-7 How the scripts in this chapter fit together

```
11.  <%
12.  for (key in items){
13.  %>
14.  <!--------- start header ------------->
15.  <table border=1 width=80% align=center>
16.  <!--------- end header ------------->
17.  <!--------- start item ------------->
18.    <tr><td colspan=2>
19.    <% = items[key].name %>
20.    </td></tr>
21.    <tr><td>
22.    <% = items[key].image %>
23.    </td><td valign=top>
24.    <% = items[key].description %><p>
25.      <!------ start item option information --------->
26.      <% for (key2 in items[key].options){
27.      if (String(items[key].options[key2].
         description) != "none"){
28.        %>
29.        <div align=right><% =
           items[key].options[key2].description %>: $<% =
           items[key].options[key2].price %> (<% = key
           %><% = items[key].options[key2].ext %>) <% =
           items[key].options[key2].buy_link %></div>
30.      <% }
31.      else {
32.        %>
33.        <div align=right>$<% =
           items[key].options[key2].price %>(<% = key %><%
           = items[key].options[key2].ext %>)  <% =
           items[key].options[key2].buy_link %></div>
34.      <% }
35.      }// end for key2 loop %>
36.      <!------- end item option information ---------->
37.  </td></tr>
38.  <!--------- end item ------------->
39.  <!--------- start footer ------------->
40.  </table>
41.  <!--------- end footer ------------->
42.  <%
43.  } //end looping through items
44.  %>
45.  <!--------------end item display template---------->
46.  </BODY></HTML>
```

HOW THE SCRIPT WORKS

Most of the functionality used in this script is actually stored in the include file `cart.js` to make this as much as possible a "template" that can be edited by any designer who is comfortable with HTML.

Before diving into the details, it's worth remembering that this script essentially does only two things: First, it creates the HTML for a header that lets visitors navigate the cart; second, it displays information about one or more products or services that are for sale, using an object called `items`.

As always, the devil is in the details:

1. Set JavaScript as the scripting language.

2. Include `cart.js`, the file that contains many of the functions that are used throughout the shopping cart.

6. The `cart_header()` function (from the `cart.js` include file) generates the HTML for a header that lets users browse cart products by category, perform a keyword search, or view the contents of their carts (See Figure 5-8).

FIGURE 5-8 `cart_header( )` creates a header used throughout the shopping cart

7. This line creates an object called `items`, using the function `create_items_object()`. `create_items_object()`, which is in the `cart.js` include file, performs most of the work required to display a list of products and/or services that are for sale through the shopping cart.

Depending on whether parameters are passed to the current script, `create_items_object()` will contain either all of the items that are available for sale, only those items that are in a specific category, or those items that match a keyword search.

To display the products or services stored in the `items` object, all that's required is to loop through the `items` object and put the information stored within it into an HTML page--which is, curiously enough, exactly what the rest of this script does.

8–46. While there is a lot of ASP code in these lines, it's mostly little bits and pieces embedded in an HTML page. The purpose here is to abstract the look of the page (HTML) from the functionality of the page (ASP) as much as possible. Thus, even someone who'se entirely unfamiliar with ASP can edit the HTML portion of this page, so long as he or she is reasonably careful not to break any of the ASP pieces.

12–43. Line 12 is the beginning of a `for()` loop that loops through the `items` object, displaying the information about each product or service stored in `items`.

One of the great things about objects and arrays is that it's possible to loop through them without having to know exactly what's inside of them. `items` is actually an object that consists of zero or more things that we want to sell (also objects, which are nested inside of `items`). In this case, the `for` loop works by creating the string `key`. By using each value of key in turn, it is then easy to access all of the good stuff stored inside of `items`.

For example, if all you wanted to do was get a list of the stuff inside of `items`, you could do that as follows:

```
for (key in items){
Response.Write("\n<br> " + items[key].name );
}
```

The `name` property of any given object inside of the `items` object is what you would expect—the name of a product as it was typed in one of the data files used by the cart scripts. If, for example, `items` contains information about three items called `item1`, `item2`, and `item3`, the output generated would be:

```
<br> item1
<br> item2
<br> item3
```

Of course, it's always possible that, for any given product or service, there are several versions of any particular product: books may be available in both hard cover and soft cover. Other items may be available in several different colors. This is addressed by yet another nested object, called `options`, which is created for each cart item stored in the `items` object.

Each product or service in the cart, by definition (see description of data files earlier in this chapter), has at least one option. Thus, to get not only the names of the various items for sale, but also the part numbers and the prices of the items, we need to loop not just through the `items` object, but also through the `options` object within each item. Simply done, this would look like this:

```
1.for (key in items){
2.  Response.Write("\n<br> " + items[key].name );
3.  for (key2 in items[key].options){
4.    Response.Write("\n<br>---" + key +
      items[key].options[key2].ext)
5.    Response.Write(": "
      +items[key].options[key2].price)
6.  } // end looping through options
7.} // end looping through items
```

Assuming that we're working with the same three items posited above and that each is available in two colors, we might get something like this:

```
<br> item1
<br> ---item1-yellow: $1.00
<br> ---item1-purple: $2.00
<br> item2
<br> ---item2-yellow: $5.00
<br> ---item2-purple: $6.00
<br> item3
<br> ---item2-yellow: $10.00
<br> ---item2-purple: $9.00
```

In fact, this is pretty much what happens in this script: Lines 12–43 loop through the `items` object, while lines 26–35 loop through the `options` object that is created for each item. During the loop through, various properties are dropped into the page. These are, including the properties we've described so far:

Table 5-1 The properties of the `items` object

items[key].name	the name of the item
items[key].image	the filename of the image associated with the image.
items[key].description	text description of the item
items[key].options [key2].description	description of a specific option
key	the unique id of the item
items[key].options[key2].ext	the unique id of the item's extension
items[key].options[key2].buy_link	a link that lets a visitor add the item to the cart
items[key].options[key2].price	the price for a specific item/option pair (only options have prices)

There is only one other piece of code in the script:

27. Here, the script checks to see whether `items[key].options[key2].price` is set to `none`, so that the information displayed will be different, depending on whether a description exists for an option.

If no option exists, the HTML generated on lines 28–30 is displayed. Otherwise, we get lines 31–34.

Warning

To keep the cart as simple as possible to use and to hack, the cart relies on pricing information stored in `items[key].options[key2].buy_link` (described above). This means that a malicious shopper could attempt to defraud you by creating a fraudulent `buy_link`. All orders should be reviewed to make sure that the total amount is correct.

Script 5-2
cart_set_session.asp

```
1. <%@ Language=JavaScript %>
2. <!-- #include file="cart.js" --><%
3. //Session.Timeout=1
4. var add = String(Request("add"));
5.
6. add_array = add.split("---")
7.
```

```
 8. if (Session(add_array[2]+".qty") > 0){
 9. Session(add_array[2]+".qty")++
10. }
11.
12. else{
13.    Session(add_array[2]) = new Object()
14.    Session(add_array[2] + ".qty")= 1
15.    Session(add_array[2] + ".name")= add_array[0]
16.    Session(add_array[2] + ".desc")= add_array[1]
17.    Session(add_array[2] + ".price")= add_array[3]
18.    Session(add_array[2] + ".weight")= add_array[4]
19. }
20.
21.
22. Response.Redirect(cart_view_contents_script)
23. %>
```

HOW THE SCRIPT WORKS

cart_set_session.asp is a relatively simple script that is used to add an item to the cart. Once it's done its work, it redirects a shopper to the cart_view_contents_script.

cart_set_session.asp is invoked when a user clicks on a link that was created by the create_items_object (). The format of the link is:

```
<a
href="cart_set_session.asp?add=Book+1%2D%2D%2DThe+story+
of+the+number+1%2D%2D%2Dbk1%2D%2D%2D12%2E95%2D%2D%2D2"
>Buy</a>
```

Information is stored in a multipart form variable called add, which includes the name, description, part number, price, and weight of the item being added to the cart. In the example above, the item being added is called Book 1; the item description is The story of the number 1; the part number of the item is bk1; the price of the item is 12.95 (currency is not specified); and the weight of the item is 2.

So here's how the script works:

1. Set JavaScript as language.

3. This line, which is commented out, is useful if you're tinkering with things and you want to start with a clean slate. Setting Session.Timeout to one means that after one minute, the session object will be dumped.

If you're modifying the cart and want to zap the Session object, all you have to do is comment out the line and add something to the cart, comment the line back in, then wait a minute. If you can't stand the thought of waiting a minute, you should probably set it to five and force yourself to take a break. ;)

4. As discussed above, incoming form information is stored in a variable called add. Here, it gets shoved into a local variable of the same name.

6. Because the add variable is actually a multifield variable, the first thing to do is to use the split() method intrinsic to any JavaScript string to create an array called add_array.

8–19. As discussed in the section on storing information in the Session object earlier in this chapter, order information for the cart is stored using the ASP Session object. What happens next depends on whether the item being added to the cart already exists in the cart. If it does, all that needs to happen is to increment the qty property of that item by executing the code on lines 8–10. If the object does not exist, all of the information that we have about the item needs to be added to the object, which is what happens on lines 12–19.

8–10. If the item already exists in the cart, its quantity will be zero or greater, and all that needs to happen is for the quantity to be incremented using the ++ operator.

12–19. If the item's quantity is not greater than zero, the script assumes that the item does not exist, and the item is added to the Session object.

13. The first step is to create a new object inside of the Session object. The object is named after the third element of add_array (add_array[2]), which is the item's part number (a concatenation of the item number and the option number), which is unique.

14. Next, the qty property of the object is set to one, because this is the first time that we're adding this object to the cart.

15–18. Finally, the name, desc, price, and weight properties of the item are set, using information from the appropriate fields of add_array.

At this point, the item has either been added to the cart, or, if it was already in the cart its quantity has been increased.

22. The last line forwards the shopper to the `cart_view_contents_script`, where the shopper can view all of the items that have been added to the cart so far.

Script 5-3
cart_view_contents.asp

```
1.  <%@ Language=JavaScript %>
2.  <!-- #include file="cart.js" -->
3.
4.      <center><% = cart_header() %></center>
5.
6.      <center>View/Edit Shopping Cart
        Contents</center>
7.
8.  <form action="<%=change_qty_script%>">
9.  <table border=1 align=center>
10. <% = cart_contents_header_row() %>
11. <% = cart_contents_editable_row () %>
12. <% = cart_contents_subtotal_row() %>
13. </table>
14. <div align=center><input type=submit name=toss
    value="Change Qty"></div>
15. </form>
16.
17. <div align=right><a href="<% =
    collect_shipping_information_script %>">Check Out ->
18. <hr width="50%">
19. <a href="<% = cart_remove_all_from_cart_script
    %>">Clear Cart</a>
20. </div>
21. </BODY></HTML>
```

HOW THE SCRIPT WORKS

Like `cart_list_items_for_sale.asp`, `cart_view_contents.asp` displays information to the shopper. Again, to make it as easy as possible to edit the look and feel of the page, most of the code that gets executed on this page actually lives in the `cart.js` include file.

Although the page generated by the script is fairly complex (it can be used to edit the quantity of items being purchased or remove items from the cart, as well as contains links to continue shopping or "check out"), the ASP on this page is not:

1. Set JavaScript as the scripting language.

2. Grab the include file, which contains all of the functions that will be executed on this page.

4. The `cart_header()` function creates the header that lets shoppers navigate around the cart.

8. None of the cart scripts contain links to specific URLs. Instead, URLs are defined in variables set in `cart.js`. The form that starts on line 8 is configured to send shoppers to the `change_qty_script` if they click on the Submit button on line 14, which would be used if they wanted to change the quantity of one or more items in their carts.

10–12. Create the table that displays the contents of the cart.

10. `cart_contents_header_row()` spits out the HTML for the top row of the table.

11. `cart_contents_editable_row()` is a more sophisticated function that creates a row for every item in the ASP Session object that has a quantity of one or more. The row contains information about the item, a text box that can be used to change the quantity of a particular item being purchased, and a "Delete This Item" link that can be used to remove the item from the cart altogether.

12. `cart_contents_subtotal_row()` creates a row that shows the subtotal for the items currently being purchased.

17,19. The link to the checkout scripts is set using a variable defined in `cart.js`, rather than being hard-coded. The same is true of the link to `cart_remove_all_from_cart_script`, which zaps everything from the cart.

Script 5-4
`cart_change_qty.asp`

```
1. <%@ Language=JavaScript %>
2. <!-- #include file="cart.js" -->
3. <%
4. var uid = String(Request("uid"));
5.
6. // delete links use the "uid" variable:
7. if (uid != "undefined"){
```

```
 8. var set_qty = parseInt(Request("set_qty"));
 9. Session(uid+".qty")=set_qty
10. Response.Redirect(cart_view_contents_script)
11. }
12.
13. // change qty button requires resetting qty on all
    items in the basket.
14. else{
15. // change button scrolls through all items:
16. for ( field_number = 1; field_number <=
    Request.QueryString.count ; field_number++ ){
17.
18.   temp_item =
      String(Request.QueryString.Key(field_number));
19.   temp_qty =
      String(Request.QueryString.item(temp_item))
20.
21.   // make sure field is one we want to use
22.   if (temp_item.search(/uid_/) >= 0 ){
23.     temp_uid =
        temp_item.substring(4,temp_item.length)
24.     //Response.Write(temp_uid + "<br>");
25.     Session(temp_uid+".qty")=temp_qty
26.
27.   }// end if
28. }// end for loop through incoming fields
29. Response.Redirect(cart_view_contents_script)
30. } // end else
31. %>
```

HOW THE SCRIPT WORKS

cart_change_qty.asp can be invoked in two ways: when a shopper clicks on a "Delete This Item" link for a specific item or when
someone clicks on the "Change Qty" Submit button, which can be
used to change the quantity of any number of items in the cart.

In both cases, the script makes the desired change, then sends
people back to the cart_view_contents_script.

1. Language is JavaScript.

2. Include cart.js.

4. The "Delete This Item" link sets a form variable called
uid, which is assigned to a local variable of the same
name.

7–11. If the value of uid is set to something (and is, therefore,
not equal to "undefined"), someone clicked on the

"Delete This Item" link, and lines 8–10 get executed. Otherwise, we know that someone clicked on the Change Qty button, and lines 14–30 get executed.

8. The "Delete This Item" link sets a form variable called set_qty, which is used to set the value of a local variable of the same name. Unless you hack it to do something else, set_qty will always be set to zero, because the point of the link is to delete the item.

9. Each item in the cart has a corresponding object within the ASP Session object. This line sets the qty property of the desired item to the value of set_qty (zero). Note that the item is not actually deleted: Rather, its qty property is set to zero.

10. At this point, the script is done, and the shopper is redirected to the URL assigned to the cart_view_contents_script variable.

14. Start of an else block triggered by the logic in line 7.

16. The script that lets people view the contents of their carts contains a relatively simple form that consists of zero or more text fields, where the users can edit the quantity of every item in their carts. There is also a Submit button that is used to submit the form.

Each text box is named uid_part-number, where part-number is the actual unique id of an item in the cart's database (described in the section on storing related data in two text files, earlier in this chapter).

What happens next is that the script loops through the incoming form data, looking for form fields that start with the string uid_. When it finds one, it uses its value to set the quantity for that item to the value assigned to it by the text box. This might be the value it already had or a new value, if it was changed by the shopper.

16–28. The for() loop started on line 16 loops through each form variable in the ASP Request.QueryString object. The for() loop uses a variable called field_number, which is a simple counter and starts at one rather than zero because that seems to be the Microsoft way. Whatever.

18,19. Starting with the value in the field_number counter, two variables are created: temp_item and temp_qty.

temp_item is the the name of a form variable, and temp_qty is its value.

22. If temp_item matches the regular expression /uid_/, the script decides that it has a winner, and lines 23–25 are executed.

23. As discussed a few lines up, the unique part number (or uid) of the item whose quantity is being set is part of the form variable's name--which is now the variable temp_item. This line creates a new variable called temp_uid by extracting a substring from temp_item that runs from its fifth character (the first character after the prefix uid_) all the way to its last character (temp_item.length).

25. Now that the script knows the part number of the item (temp_uid) and the quantity that it needs to be set to (temp_qty), the information stored in the Session object is updated.

29. Finally, its work complete, the script redirects the shopper to the URL assigned to the cart_view_contents_script variable in cart.js.

Script 5-5
cart_remove_all.asp

```
1. <%@ Language=JavaScript %>
2. <%
3. for (i = 1 ; i <= Session.Contents.Count ; i++){
4.   if ((typeof Session.Contents(i) == "object") &&
     (Session(Session.Contents.key(i)+".qty") > 0)){
5.       Session(Session.Contents.key(i)+".qty") = 0
6.   }
7. }
8. Response.Redirect("cart_view_contents.asp")
9. %>
```

HOW THE SCRIPT WORKS

When shoppers are looking at the contents of their carts (cart_view_contents.asp), they can use the "Clear Cart" link to remove the entire contents. This is the script that gets executed when this happens.

Zapping the contents of a user's shopping cart does not actually involve deleting the information that's been stored in the Session object about that user. Instead, the script scans the Session object for shopping cart objects and sets their quantity attribute to zero. Here's how it works.

1. Set language to JavaScript.

3. Start a `for()` loop that will loop through everything that is in the Session object. `Session.Contents.Count` gives us an integer that tells us how many things we have in the Session object (which we'll access via the Session.Contents object).

Using a counter `i` that gets incremented from 1 to `Session.Contents.Count` (another special Microsoft array that starts at one instead of zero), we can access each item in the Session.Contents object by treating it as an array and using the syntax:

```
Session.Contents(i)
```

4. If the thing that we find is an object and it has a `qty` attribute that is greater than zero, line 5 gets executed, which sets the `qty` attribute to zero.

Thus, once the script has looped through everything in the Session.Contents object, every item in the cart will have its `qty` set to zero, and for all practical purposes the cart will be empty.

The `if` block started on line 4 closes on line 6.

7. End of the `for()` loop.

8. Our work done, the bereft shopper is returned to `cart_view_contents.asp`. Note that this link, unlike most in the script, is hard-wired. You might want to fix that sometime.

COLLECTING SHIPPING AND BILLING INFORMATION AND GENERATING AN ORDER

Once a shopper's decided what to buy, the scripts below collect shipping and billing information, and finally create an order file.

Script 5-6
collect_shipping_information.asp

```
1.  <%@ Language=JavaScript %>
2.  <!-- #include file="cart.js" -->
3.
4.       <center>Cart Contents</center>
5.
6.  <table border=1 align=center>
7.  <% = cart_contents_header_row() %>
8.  <% = cart_contents_non_editable_row () %>
9.  <% = cart_contents_subtotal_row() %>
10. <% = cart_contents_shipping_row() %>
11. </table>
12.
13. <form action="<% = set_shipping_info_script %>">
14. <hr>
15. Upgrade Shipping:
16. <br>2 day<input type=radio name=ship_upgrade
    value="2_day"> (costs <% =
    dollarise((order_info.weight*two_day_ship_cost)-
    (order_info.weight*basic_ship_cost)) %> extra)
17. <br>overnight<input type=radio name=ship_upgrade
    value="1_day">  (costs <% =
    dollarise((order_info.weight*one_day_ship_cost)-
    (order_info.weight*basic_ship_cost)) %> extra)
18.
19. <hr>
20. Contact Information:
21. <table align = center>
22. <tr>
23.   <td align=right>First Name: </td>
24.     <td><input type=text name="f_name"
        value="john" size=30></td>
25. </tr>
26. <tr>
27.   <td align=right>Last Name: </td>
28.     <td><input type=text name="l_name"
        value="doe" size=30></td>
29. </tr>
30.     <td align=right>Email Address: </td>
31.       <td><input type=text name="email"
          value="john_doe@lovejoy.com" size=30></td>
32. </tr>
33.     <td align=right>Phone Number: </td>
34.       <td><input type=text name="phone"
          value="805-966-0611" size=30></td>
35. </tr>
36. </table>
37. <hr>
```

```
38. Shipping Information (US Only!):
39. <table align = center>
40. <tr>
41.    <td align=right>Address 1: </td>
42.       <td><input type=text name="address_1"
          value="8 Main St." size=30></td>
43. </tr>
44. <tr>
45.    <td align=right>Address 2: </td>
46.       <td><input type=text name="address_2"
          value="" size=30></td>
47. </tr>
48. <tr>
49.    <td align=right>City: </td>
50.       <td><input type=text name="city" value="santa
          barbara" size=30></td>
51. </tr>
52. <tr>
53.   <td align=right>State: </td>
54.      <td><select name="state" >
55.      <% for (i in array_of_states){ %>
56.        <option value=<% = array_of_states[i]
           %> ><% = array_of_states[i] %>
57.      <% } %>
58.      </select>
59.      </td>
60. </tr>
61. <tr>
62.   <td align=right>Zip Code: </td>
63.      <td><input type=text name="zip" value="93101"
          size=30></td>
64. </tr>
65. </table>
66.
67. <hr>
68.
69. <center> <input type=submit name=toss
    value="submit"></center>
70. </form>
71.
72.
73. </BODY></HTMLx>
```

HOW THE SCRIPT WORKS

This script allows shoppers to:

- Review their orders.
- Select a shipping option.
- Enter contact information.
- Enter the address to which they want their product shipped.

The cart supports simple shipping options based on a "weight factor" that is specified for each item that is for sale. The weight factor is multiplied by one of three values that are defined in the cart.js include file:

```
basic_ship_cost = 1.95
two_day_ship_cost = 6.95
one_day_ship_cost = 8.95
```

Thus, if a visitor purchases a croissant with a ship factor of 1 and two dozen bagels, each dozen of which has a ship factor of 2, the order will have a ship factor of 5, which will be multiplied by either \$1.95, \$6.95, or \$8.95, depending on the shipping option selected (basic_ship_cost is used by default).

Increasingly, sites include shipping costs in an item's price. If this is the case with your business, you can simply set the variables above to zero, and no shipping cost will be added to orders.

Details:

1. Set language to be JavaScript.

2. Include cart.js, which will do a lot of our work for us.

6, 11. These lines open and close a table that will be generated by some functions in the cart.js file.

7–10. The functions cart_contents_header_row(), cart_contents_non_editable_row(), cart_contents_subtotal_row(), and cart_contents_shipping_row() are used to print the contents of the cart to the page. See Figure 5-9 for an example.

The functions are described in detail later in this chapter. Basically, they grab order information that is stored in the Session object and put it into table rows that are easy to stack together in an HTML page.

13. The purpose of this page is to collect shipping information, using a form that will be sent to the set_ship-

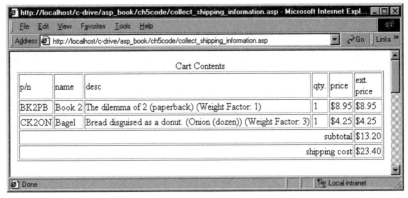

FIGURE 5-9 Lines 7–10 generate cart contents, shipping cost, and subtotal

ping_info_script, a variable set in cart.js that resolves to the string set_shipping_information.asp, which will collect the information entered in the form.

16,17. These lines create two radio buttons that can be used to upgrade from the basic shipping option to the 2_day or 1_day options. Next to each line, the script calculates how much will be added to the cost of the order for that option. This is done by multiplying the weight factor (which is set for each item in option_file.txt) by the rate for 1-day or 2-day shipping. The cost of basic shipping is then subtracted, so that only the difference between the two costs is shown (Figure 5-10).

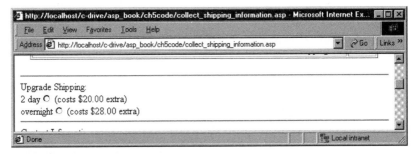

FIGURE 5-10 Shipping radio buttons

The balance of the script, with one exception, is a standard HTML form consisting of a series of text boxes that set the value for a number of variables that store contact and shipping information. Note that the variable names are not arbitrary. If you change their names, you'll probably break a couple of things and need to track down where the variables are used and change the names there, as well.

The one place where there is some ASP code is on lines 55–58, to create the select list that lets shoppers select the state where they live.

The select list is more than just a convenience: To figure out whether or not to charge sales tax, it's necessary to know what state things are being shipped to. By using a select list, it's easy to control how the name of a state is spelled, which makes it easy for the script to determine whether or not to charge sales tax.

Making long select lists is kind of boring, so the task is automated here by using an array that contains the names of all the states. The array is created in `cart.js` (for the sake of simplicity, only three states are included—you can add the rest):

```
array_of_states = new Array("CA","PA","NV")
```

The select list is created as follows:

54. Normal HTML is used to open a `<select>` tag with a name attribute of `"state"`.

55–57. A `for()` loop is used to loop through the array `array_of_states` and create an `<option>` tag for each state in the array.

That's about it. At that point, the script once again lapses into HTML. As done elsewhere in the book, the value of the submit tag is set to `toss` because it is not used except as a means of submitting the form.

One last thing: A lot of the form fields already have their value attributes set. This is for debugging purposes: Getting all the different pieces of the cart to work together often requires going through the shopping process from start to finish a few times. Having the fields filled out makes the first part of debugging a whole lot easier.

Once you're pretty sure that everything works, you can set the `value` attribute of the various form elements to empty string (`" "`)

for a final round of testing, but until then, do the easy thing and leave everything filled in.

Script 5-7
set_shipping_information.asp

```
1.  <%@ Language=JavaScript %>
2.  <!-- #include file="cart.js" -->
3.
4.  <%
5.  //Session.Timeout=1
6.
7.
8.  // set ship type and ship cost info:
9.  if (String(Request("ship_upgrade")) == "2_day"){
10.     order_info.ship_type = "2_day";
11.     order_info.ship_cost =
        order_info.weight*two_day_ship_cost;
12. }
13. else if (String(Request("ship_upgrade")) ==
    "1_day"){
14.     order_info.ship_type = "1_day";
15.     order_info.ship_cost =
        order_info.weight*one_day_ship_cost;
16. }
17. else {
18.     order_info.ship_type = "basic"
19.     order_info.ship_cost =
        order_info.weight*basic_ship_cost;
20. }
21.
22.
23. // loop through other shipping info
24. shipping_info_array = new
    Array("f_name","l_name","email","phone","address_1",
    " address_2","city","state","zip")
25.
26. for (i in shipping_info_array){
27.     if (String(Request(shipping_info_array[i])) != ""
        || shipping_info_array[i] == "address_2"){
28.       order_info[shipping_info_array[i]] =
          String(Request(shipping_info_array[i]))
29.     }
30.     else{ // required fields:
31.       out += "<br> " + shipping_info_array[i];
32.     }
33. }
34.
35. if (String(Request("state")) == "CA"){
36.     order_info.tax = order_info.subtotal * .0875
```

```
37. }
38. else {
39.    order_info.tax = 0;
40. }
41.
42. // concatenate ship address into easy-to-use
    information
43. order_info.ship_address = order_info.f_name + " " +
    order_info.l_name;
44. order_info.ship_address    += "\n" +
    order_info.address_1
45. if (order_info.address_2.length > 0) {
46. order_info.ship_address    += "\n" +
    order_info.address_2 }
47. order_info.ship_address    += "\n" +
    order_info.city + ", " + order_info.state + " " +
    order_info.zip;
48.
49. // create contact info string:
50. order_info.contact_info = order_info.f_name + " " +
    order_info.l_name;
51. order_info.contact_info += "\n" + order_info.email
52. order_info.contact_info += "\n" + order_info.phone
53.
54. // create order summary string:
55. order_info.order_summary = "";
56. for (i in cart_items){
57.    order_info.order_summary += cart_items[i].qty + ":
       " + cart_items[i].uid
58.    order_info.order_summary += " (" +
       cart_items[i].desc + ")" + "\n"
59. }
60. order_info.order_summary += "Ship Method: " +
    order_info.ship_type
61. order_info.order_summary += "\nGrand Total: " +
    dollarise(order_info.subtotal + order_info.ship_cost
    + order_info.tax);
62.
63.
64.
65.
66. // if mandatory field is missing, tell user to fix
    it. otherwise, redirect to billing information page
67.
68. if (out != ""){
69. %>
70. The following field must be filled out:
71. out:    <% = out %>
72. <%
73. }
74.
```

```
75. else {
76.       Session("order_info") = new Object()
77.       for (i in order_info){
78.         Session("order_info." +  i) =
            order_info[i]
79.         }
80.         Response.
            Redirect(collect_billing_info_script)
81. } // end else
82. %>
```

HOW THE SCRIPT WORKS

This script takes the information collected by `collect_bill-ing_information.asp` and stores it in the session variable via an object called `order_info`.

In addition to simply collecting the data and placing it in the Session object, the script checks to make sure that required fields are filled out and begins the process of creating an order by assembling different pieces of information in the correct order.

1. Set Language to JavaScript.

2. Grab `cart.js`.

5. This line is some debug code that I left in there in case you need it later. This line sets the `Timeout` value of the Session object to one second, which is a convenient way to zap the Session object and get a new one (if you don't mind waiting a second. Maybe you should set it to 60 and get up for a minute and stretch. I dunno).

   You could also use the `Timeout` property if you felt that shoppers' sessions were timing out too quickly. For example, if you wanted sessions to last an hour (the default is usually 20–30 minutes, if memory serves), you could set it to 3600 (60 seconds times 60 minutes). Of course, you'd want to do this in one of the scripts that gets used earlier in the process, like `cart_list_items_for_sale.asp`.

8–20. The first thing that the script does is to store information about how the item is being shipped in the `order_info` object, which is an object created in the `cart.js` include file and used to organize information before it is put in the Session object. Note that `order_info` doesn't have any properties: It's essentially an associative array. But it works, and I guess that's really what matters, right?

Anyhow, if you take a look at the form that we're collecting information from (the form generated by the previous script) you'll see that shoppers have three options: They can select the "2 Day" shipping upgrade, which will set a form variable called `ship_upgrade` to a value of 2_day; They can select the "Overnight" shipping upgrade, which sets the same variable to 1_day; or they can do nothing, in which case, we know that they want basic shipping, and `ship_upgrade` will not have a value of 1_day or 2_day.

Thus, the logic of this section is that in line 9 the script checks to see whether `ship_upgrade` is set to 2_day. If it is, `order_info.ship_type` is set to 2_day (in line 10), and `order_info.ship_cost` is set to the product of `order_info.weight` and a variable called `two_day_ship_cost` (in line 11). The values of both `order_info.weight` and `two_day_ship_cost` are set in `cart.js`, which is discussed later in this chapter. `two_day_ship_cost` is an arbitrary string set to whatever the suits decide they want to gouge people for shipping. `order_info.weight` is simply the sum of the weight factors of all the items in the shopper's cart (times the number of each item purchased).

Okay. If you're still reading at this point, you're probably realizing that this isn't exactly how you want cost of shipping to work. I'll cover that in a second.

You'll notice that lines 10, 13, and 17 create an `if` ... `else` `if` ... `else` statement. This means that if `ship_upgrade` isn't set to 2_day, the next thing the script does (line 13) is to check to see if it's set to 1_day. If so, the `ship_type` and `ship_cost` properties of the `order_info` object are set to the appropriate values, this time using the cost stored in the `one_day_ship_cost` variable.

17. `else`, that is, if `ship_upgrade` is not set to either 1_day or 2_day, `order_info.ship_type` is set to basic, and the cost of shipping is calculated using `basic_ship_cost`.

Hacking the ship cost:

You might decide that you want to set a base shipping fee that gets applied to any order, then incremented based on the weight factor (I talk about weight factor rather than weight because, for some items, dimensional weight is more of an issue than physical weight). To do this, you'd want to add a base cost, perhaps using a variable such as `base_ship_cost`. Net result might be:

```
order_info.ship_cost = base_ship_cost +
(order_info.weight*two_day_ship_cost);
```

Don't forget that you'd need to define `base_ship_cost` before you use it.

Another option would be to assign ship costs based on the dollar value of the order. One of the properties of the `order_info` object is `order_info.subtotal`. This value could be multiplied by a fixed amount in order to set the `order_info.ship_cost` property.

That's probably enough about shipping.

26–33. The script makes sure that required fields are filled out and puts them into the `order_info` object. You might want to fancy this up, because all the script does is check for empty strings in required fields.

24. `shipping_info_array` is an array used to list the fields that we want to put into the `order_info` object, so called because that's where this script puts all its order information before storing it in the Session object. Note that fields in this array are not necessarily required fields—the `address_2` field can be left blank. These are simply the fields we care about.

26–33. The next step is to loop through the fields in `shipping_info_array` and do two things.

First, in line 27, we check to make sure that required fields are filled out. This is done by making sure that the fields are not empty (`!=  ""`). The `address_2` field is exempt, because it's an optional field that many shoppers may not use. If a field is empty, that field's name gets concatenated into the `out` string on line 31, which will be used to generate an error message asking the shopper to fill in that field.

Second, assuming the condition set in line 27, in line 28, the information collected by the form is added to the `order_info` variable. Thus, for example, the form variable `f_name` becomes `order_info.f_name`.

The next step is to figure out whether the order is taxable.

35. Using an `if... else` statement, the form variable `state` is checked to see whether its variable is set to the string "CA" (I live in California. You'll need to change this if you're in a different state).

36. If the order is being shipped to California, the `tax` property of `order_info` is set to 8.75% (that's the same thing as .0875) of `order_info.subtotal`.

39. If the order is not being shipped to California, `order_info.tax` is set to zero.

order_info.tax will be used to create a grand total later in this script.

Next, various properties of the `order_info` object are concatenated into three summary strings: `order_info.ship_address`, `order_info.contact_info`, and `order_info.order_summary`.

43–47. These lines create a shipping address by concatenating the shopper's name and address information into a single string. Note that Newline characters "\n" are used to create line breaks in the appropriate places, so that `order_info.ship_address` will end up creating a string that looks something like this:

```
john doe
8 Main St.
santa barbara, CA 93101
```

50–52. The shopper's name, email address, and phone number are put into `order_info.contact_info`, creating a string similar to:

```
john doe
john_doe@lovejoy.com
805-966-0611
```

55–61. The `order_summary` string pulls information both from the `cart_items` object that contains the items that the shopper is purchasing and the `order_info` object.

In lines 56–59, the script iterates through the `cart_items` object. Every item in the shopper's cart is added to the order_summary string.

Once the contents of the order have been collected, the ship method and grand total are added. The grand total is calculated as the sum of `order_info.subtotal`, `order_info.ship_cost`, and `order_info.tax`. The `dollarise()` function is used to make sure that the total is expressed as a figure with two decimal places, the way a dollar figure is expected to look.

For example, the net result might look like this:

```
1: BK2PB (The dilemma of 2 (paperback))
1: CK1CHOK (Snooty French pastry. (Chocolate
Croissant))
Ship Method: basic
Grand Total: $16.08
```

At this point, the script's work is almost finished.

68. The `if()` statement here checks to see whether the `out` variable is empty (it contains a list of mandatory fields that were not filled out, if any).

If `out` is not empty, lines 69–73 are executed, and an error message is displayed, asking the shopper to fill out the missing fields.

If `out` is empty, the `else` statement (lines 75–81) are executed. Two things happen: Order information is passed to the Session object, and the user is redirected to the next script, where billing information will be collected.

Passing information to the Session object is a matter of the following:

76. A new object, called `order_info`, is created inside of the Session object.

77–79. A `for()` loop is used to iterate through the `order_info` object and replicate each of the properties of `order_info` in `Session("order_info")`. It seems like there should be a way just to put the entire object into the Session object, but I couldn't quickly figure out a way to do that, and this works. Good enough.

80. At last, our script's work is done, and the shopper is forwarded to the `collect_billing_info_script`.

Script 5-8
collect_billing_information.asp

```
1.  <%@ Language=JavaScript %>
2.  <!-- #include file="cart.js" -->
3.
4.          <center>Order Summary</center>
5.
6.  <table border=1 align=center>
7.  <% = cart_contents_header_row() %>
8.  <% = cart_contents_non_editable_row () %>
9.  <% = cart_contents_subtotal_row() %>
10. <% = cart_contents_shipping_row() %>
11. <% = cart_contents_tax_row() %>
12. <% = cart_contents_grand_total_row() %>
13. </table>
14.
15.
16. <hr><!-- confirm address -->
17. This order will be shipped to:
18. <table align=center border=0><tr><td>
19. <% = order_info.ship_address.replace(/\n/g,"<br>") %>
20. </td></tr></table>
21. <hr>
22.
23. <table border =1 width="100%">
24. <tr>
25. <td width="50%" valign=top>
26.     Pay With Prepaid Web Card:
27.     <form action="<% =
        set_pwc_billing_information_script %>">
28.       <table>
29.       <tr>
30.         <td>Card Number: </td>
31.             <td><input type=text
                name=card_number value="4111 1111 1111 1111"
                size=20></td>
32.       <tr>
33.       <tr>
34.         <td>Pin Number: </td>
35.             <td><input type=text
                name=pin_number value="5678" size=4></td>
36.       <tr>
37.       </table>
38.       <center><input type=submit name=toss
          value="submit"></center>
39.     </form>
40. </td>
41.
42. <td width="50%">
```

```
43.    Pay with Credit Card:
44.    <form action="<% =
       set_cc_billing_information_script %>">
45.      <table>
46.      <tr>
47.        <td align=right>Method of Payment: </td>
48.          <td>
49.          <select name="payment_method">
50.          <option name="visa">Visa
51.          <option name="mastercard">Mastercard
52.          </select>
53.          </td>
54.      </tr>
55.      <tr>
56.        <td>Card Number: </td>
57.          <td><input type=text
             name=card_number value="4111 1111 1111
             1111"></td>
58.      <tr>
59.      <tr>
60.        <td>Expiration Date: </td>
61.          <td><input type=text
             name=expiration_date value="02/03"></td>
62.      <tr>
63.      </table>
64.
65.      If billing address is different from shipping
         address, you must fill out billing address
         below:
66.
67.      <table>
68.      <tr>
69.        <td align=right>First Name: </td>
70.          <td><input type=text
             name="f_name" value="" size=30></td>
71.      </tr>
72.      <tr>
73.        <td align=right>Last Name: </td>
74.          <td><input type=text name="l_name" value=""
             size=30></td>
75.      </tr>
76.      <tr>
77.        <td align=right>Address 1: </td>
78.          <td><input type=text name="address_1"
             value="" size=30></td>
79.      </tr>
80.      <tr>
81.        <td align=right>Address 2: </td>
82.          <td><input type=text name="address_2"
             value="" size=30></td>
83.      </tr>
```

```
84.      <tr>
85.        <td align=right>City: </td>
86.          <td><input type=text name="city" value=""
             size=30></td>
87.      </tr>
88.      <tr>
89.        <td align=right>State: </td>
90.          <td><select name="state" value="" >
91.          <option value="">
92.          <% for (i in array_of_states){ %>
93.            <option value=<% = array_of_states[i] %>
               ><% = array_of_states[i] %>
94.          <% } %>
95.          </select>
96.          </td>
97.      </tr>
98.      <tr>
99.        <td align=right>Zip Code: </td>
100.         <td><input type=text name="zip" value=""
             size=30></td>
101.     </tr>
102.     </table>
103.     <center><input type=submit name=toss
             value="submit"></center>
104.   </form>
105.
106. </td>
107. </tr>
108. </table>
109. </BODY></HTML>
```

HOW THE SCRIPT WORKS

Briefly, this script:

- Presents the shopper with all the details of the order, including the cost of shipping and tax.
- Displays the shipping address collected by the previous script to prevent stupid mistakes.
- Collects the information required to bill the shopper for the purchase being made.

If you've looked at the script source code or the HTML page that it generates, you've probably noticed a curious thing—a payment option called "Prepaid Web Card." Increasingly, Web sites are accepting non-credit-card payment options, including prepaid Web cards. The prepaid Web card option illustrates how even a simple shopping cart can be set up to accept multiple payment options.

1. Set language to JavaScript.

2. Include the `cart.js` include file.

6–13. Table tags here enclose a series of functions, each of which create one or more rows of a table that displays the contents of the shopper's cart and the grand total of the purchase, including shipping and, if applicable, tax. These functions, which are described in detail in `cart.js`, were also used in `cart_view_contents.asp` and `collect_billing_information.asp`.

19. This line displays the shipping information, which was concatenated into `order_info.ship_address` (full name and address). Note how the `replace()` method, which is intrinsic to any string, including the property of an object, is used to replace Newlines with HTML break tags.

The balance of the script is straightforward HTML. Note that there are two forms on this page. The first collects payment information for shoppers using prepaid Web cards, which is processed by the `set_pwc_billing_information_script`. The second form collects payment information for shoppers using credit cards and is processed by `set_cc_billing_information_script`.

There's another snippet of ASP code on lines 91–93, used to generate a select list of the states contained in the `array_of_states` variable created in `cart.js`.

Script 5-9
set_cc_billing_information.asp

```
1. <%@ Language=JavaScript %>
2. <!-- #include file="cart.js" -->
3.
4. <%
5. // loop through billing info. check for required
   fields & put data into order_info
6. billing_info_array = new
   Array("payment_method","card_number",
   "expiration_date","f_name","l_name",
   "address_1","address_2","city","state","zip")
7.
8. var optional_fields_regex =
   /f_name|l_name|address_1|address_2|city|state|zip/
9.
10. for (i in billing_info_array){
11.   if (String(Request(billing_info_array[i])) != "" ||
   billing_info_array[i].search
   (optional_fields_regex)>=0){
```

```
12.      order_info["billing_" +
         billing_info_array[i]] =
         String(Request(billing_info_array[i]))
13.    }
14.    else{
15.      out += "<br> " + billing_info_array[i];
16.    }
17. }
18.
19. // create a uid:
20.    temp_date = new Date()
21.    order_info.uid = temp_date.getTime() + "-" +
       Session.SessionID
22.
23.
24. // summary of billing info:
25.
26. order_info.billing_info = order_info.billing_f_name +
    " " + order_info.billing_l_name;
27. order_info.billing_info      += "\n" +
    order_info.billing_payment_method
28. order_info.billing_info      += "\n" +
    order_info.billing_card_number
29. order_info.billing_info      += "\n" +
    order_info.billing_expiration_date
30. order_info.billing_info      += "\n" +
    order_info.billing_address_1
31. if (order_info.billing_address_2.length > 0) {
32.    order_info.billing_info      += "\n" +
       order_info.billing_address_2 }
33. if (order_info.billing_city.length > 0) {
34.    order_info.billing_info      += "\n" +
       order_info.billing_city + ", " +
       order_info.billing_state + " " +
       order_info.billing_zip;
35. }
36.
37.
38. // if mandatory field is missing, tell user to fix
    it. otherwise, redirect to billing information page
39.
40. if (out != ""){
41. %>
42. The following field must be filled out:
43.    <% = out %>
44. <%
45. }
46.
47. else {
48.
```

```
49.   // 1st put the information into the session
      variable
50.   Session("order_info") = new Object()
51.   for (i in order_info){
52.     Session("order_info." +  i) = order_info[i]
53.   } // end for
54.
55.   // 2nd, put it into an order file:
56.
57.   // get rid of script name in absolute path
58.   // and replace with name of file we want to open
59.   var abs_path =
      String(Request.ServerVariables("PATH_TRANSLATED"));
60.   var file_to_create =
      abs_path.replace(/\\\w*\.asp/,"\\orders\\") +
      order_info.uid + ".txt";
61.
62.   var fso = new
      ActiveXObject("Scripting.FileSystemObject");
63.   var temp_file = fso.CreateTextFile(file_to_create,
      true);
64.   temp_file.Write("Order Number:" + order_info.uid);
65.   temp_file.Write("\n\nOrder Summary:\n" +
      order_info.order_summary);
66.   temp_file.Write("\n\nContact Information:\n" +
      order_info.contact_info);
67.   temp_file.Write("\n\nShipping To:\n" +
      order_info.ship_address);
68.   temp_file.Write("\n\nBilling Information:\n" +
      order_info.billing_info);
69.   temp_file.Close();
70.
71.   Response.Redirect(order_complete_script)
72. }
73. %>
```

HOW THE SCRIPT WORKS

This script performs the following tasks:

- It makes sure that required billing information is collected.
- It creates a string that summarizes billing information.
- It creates an order file that stores all of the information collected by the various scripts to date as a text (.txt) file.
- It redirects shoppers to the final script in the cart: order_complete.asp.

1. Tell IIS we're using JavaScript.

2. Include cart.js.

6. Create `billing_info_array`, an array that contains all of the incoming form fields that we want to pass to the `order_info` object.

8. Create `optional_fields_regex`, a regular expression that will match the names of fields that are optional. We'll use this in line 11.

10–17. These lines iterate through the form elements in `billing_info_array` using a `for()` loop, making sure that required fields are filled out and stuffing the information collected into the `order_info` object.

11. The first thing that happens in the loop is to verify that either a form field has something in it (so that `String(Request(billing_info_array[i])) != ""` will be true) or that the field name matches one of optional fields in the `optional_fields_regex` regular expression (so that `billing_info_array[i].search(optional_fields_regex)>=0` will be true).

12. If either condition is true, the field is stored in the `order_info` object.

Note that the prefix `billing_` is added to every field to differentiate between the first name of the contact person for the order (`order_info.f_name`) and the first name of the credit card holder (`order_info.billing_f_name`).

15. If one of the required fields is missing, the `if()` statement in line 11 will be false, and the missing field will be added to the `out` variable, which will be used to ask the shopper to fill in the required field later in this script.

20,21. Each order generated by the script gets a unique order number, which can be used to track orders, manage post-order customer questions, etc. ... IIS generates a unique `SessionID` for every visitor, which is guaranteed to be unique unless the server is rebooted. Because servers get rebooted, the script generates order numbers that are a concatenation of the time that the order is created (a rather large number of milliseconds, for example, 958951109525) and the IIS `SessionID` (also a rather large number, for example, 52468604). Net result:

```
958951109525-52468604
```

To generate the time that the order is created, based on when this script is executed, first a new `Date()` object has to be created. This is `temp_date`, in line 20. Next, the `getTime()` method has to be applied to the object, which returns, in this case, something on the order of 959 billion milliseconds.

Getting the `SessionID` is considerably easier, because it is a property of the ASP Session object.

26–34. These lines create a property of `order_info` called `billing_info`, which summarizes the billing information for the order: name, credit card number, etc. ... lines 32 and 34 only add stuff only if there's something to add, which prevents a mysterious comma from appearing in the order when the billing address is the same as the shipping address. The net result is something like this:

```
john doe
Visa
4111 1111 1111 1111
02/03
po box 72
santa barbara, CA 93103
```

40. If `out` is not empty, a required field is missing, and lines 41–45 get executed, printing an error message that asks the shopper to fill out the missing information.

Otherwise, the order is complete and lines 49–72 are executed.

50–53. These lines create a new `Session` object called `order_info` and populate it with the information in the `order_info` object used by the script, overwriting the `order_info` object that already exists in the `Session` object.

59–69. These are the lines that create the order file that stores completed orders as separate files. These files can then be processed automatically or by hand, as you wish.

59,60. The first step is to figure out what the file name of the order file is going to be. The file itself will be named after the order number, so that it'll end up being something like `958951109525-52468604.txt`, which is easy enough. However, to create a file, we need to give the operating system the full path to the file. Rather than hard-coding this information, the script figures out where it is in line 59 by using the Request object (`Request.ServerVariables("PATH_TRANSLATED")`) to create a variable called abs_path.

60. Next, the `replace` method intrinsic to all strings is applied to `abs_path` to substitute the name of the current script for the order file we want to create. Here's how it works:

The regular expression `/\\\w*\.asp/` will match a single backslash (`"\\"`), followed by zero or more word characters (`"\w*"`), followed by a period (`"\."`) and, finally, the string asp (`"asp"`). For example, if the current script is:

```
C:\cart\set_cc_billing_information.asp
```

the regular expression will match the last backslash and the name of the script (in bold):

```
C:\cart\set_cc_billing_information.asp
```

This will be replaced with the string `"\\orders\\"` (backslashes need to be escaped):

```
C:\cart\orders\
```

to which we concatenate `order_info.uid` and the string `".txt"`, for example:

```
C:\cart\orders\958951109525-52468604.txt
```

all of which is tucked away inside of `file_to_create`.

62. Next, we create a FileSystemObject called `fso` that will handle all the file system magic for us.

63. This creates a file object called `temp_file`, using the file name we just created (`file_to_create`).

Note

If you get this error at this point, it means you have to create an `orders` directory inside the directory where this script is running:

```
Microsoft JScript runtime error '800a004c'
Path not found
/c-drive/asp_book/ch5code/set_cc_billing_
information.asp, line 64
```

Just make a folder called `orders` and the error message will go away.

64–68. These lines use the `Write` method of the `temp_file` object to take a bunch of order information out of the `order_info` object: the order number, the order summary, and the contact, shipping, and billing information.

69. At this point, the order information safely stored on the file system, the script closes the file.

71. Finally, the script forwards the shopper to the last script in the cart, the `order_complete_script` (a variable assigned to a real file's name in `cart.js`).

Script 5-10
set_pwc_billing_information.asp

If the shopper uses a prepaid Web card instead of credit card, this script is invoked.

```
1. <%@ Language=JavaScript %>
2. <!-- #include file="cart.js" -->
3.
4. <%
5. // loop through other shipping info
6. billing_info_array = new
   Array("card_number","pin_number")
7. for (i in billing_info_array){
8.    if (String(Request(billing_info_array[i])) != ""
      ){
9.       order_info["billing_" + billing_info_array[i]] =
         String(Request(billing_info_array[i]))
10.   }
11.   else{ // required fields:
12.      out += "<br> " + billing_info_array[i];
```

```
13.    }
14. }
15.
16. // create a uid:
17.    temp_date = new Date()
18.    order_info.uid = temp_date.getTime() + "-" +
       Session.SessionID
19.
20.
21. // summary of billing info:
22.
23. order_info.billing_info = "Prepaid Web Card";
24. order_info.billing_info      += "\nCard Number:" +
    order_info.billing_card_number
25. order_info.billing_info      += "\nPin Number:" +
    order_info.billing_pin_number
26.
27.
28. // if mandatory field is missing, tell user to fix
    it. otherwise, redirect to billing information page
29.
30. if (out != ""){
31. %>
32. The following field must be filled out:
33. out:    <% = out %>
34. <%
35. }
36.
37. else {
38.
39.    // 1st put the information into the session
       variable
40.    for (i in order_info){
41.      //Response.Write(i + ": " + order_info[i] +
         "<br>")
42.      Session("order_info") = new Object()
43.      Session("order_info." +  i) = order_info[i]
44.    } // end for
45.
46.    // 2nd, put it into an order file:
47.
48.    // get rid of script name in absolute path
49.    // and replace with name of file we want to open
50.    var abs_path =
       String(Request.ServerVariables("PATH_TRANSLATED"));
51.    var file_to_create =
       abs_path.replace(/\\\w*\.asp/,"\\orders\\") +
       order_info.uid + ".txt";
52.
53.    var fso = new
       ActiveXObject("Scripting.FileSystemObject");
```

```
54.
55.   var temp_file = fso.CreateTextFile(file_to_create,
      true);
56.   temp_file.Write("Order Number: " + order_info.uid
      );
57.   temp_file.Write("\n\nOrder Completed: " +
      Date());
58.   temp_file.Write("\n\nOrder Summary:\n" +
      order_info.order_summary);
59.   temp_file.Write("\n\nContact Information:\n" +
      order_info.contact_info);
60.   temp_file.Write("\n\nShipping To:\n" +
      order_info.ship_address);
61.   temp_file.Write("\n\nBilling Information:\n" +
      order_info.billing_info);
62.   temp_file.Close();
63.
64.
65.   Response.Redirect(order_complete_script)
66. } // end else
67.
68. %>
```

HOW THE SCRIPT WORKS

This script is almost identical to the previous script, set_cc_bill-ing_information.asp, so I'm going to run through it a bit more quickly. At a high level, this script does exactly the same thing: It collects the payment information (card number and PIN), creates an order number, stores the information it collected in the Session object, and creates an order file.

Why a separate script then? At some point, you may want to automate the order process further and perform payment authorization at the time of the sale, rather than doing it by hand later. Frequently, this will require that credit card transactions be handled by one process and that prepaid Web card payments are handled by a second, separate process. By handling different kinds of payment separately, the cart gives you the flexibility to accept as many different kinds of payment as you want and leaves room to automate it all later.

So let's look at how this script differs from credit card Script 5-9.

6–14. Collecting incoming form information is a little simpler here, because only two fields are collected, and both are required fields. As a result, both fields must have something in them (line 8, where we make sure that they're !=""). Form information is put into the order_info object, and if any fields are empty, the field names are placed in the out variable so that we can generate an error message later in the script.

17–18. The order number (uid) is generated here in the same way as the previous script.

23–25. A summary of the billing information collected (the card number and the PIN) is placed into order_info.billing_info.

30. To make sure that sufficient information to go ahead was collected, the script makes sure that out is empty. If it is not, in lines 31–35, an error message is created. Otherwise, lines 37–66 are executed.

40–44. Information stored in order_info is passed to the Session object.

50–62. An order file is created, and all the information we have about the order is written to the file.

65. Shoppers are redirected to the order_complete_script.

Script 5-11
order_complete.asp

```
1.  <%@ Language=JavaScript %>
2.  <!-- #include file="cart.js" -->
3.  <HTML><HEAD><TITLE>Order Complete</TITLE></HEAD><BODY
    BGCOLOR="#FFFFFF" >
4.
5.  <center>Order Complete</center>
6.  <p><b>Order Number:</b><br>
7.  <% = order_info.uid %>
8.
9.  p><b>Order Summary:</b><br>
10. <% = order_info.order_summary.replace(/\n/g,"<br>")
    %>
11.
12. <p><b>Contact Information:</b><br>
13. <% = order_info.contact_info.replace(/\n/g,"<br>") %>
14.
15. <p><b>Shipping to:</b><br>
16. <% = order_info.ship_address.replace(/\n/g,"<br>") %>
17.
18. <p><b>Billing info</b>:<br>
19. <% = order_info.billing_info.replace(/\n/g,"<br>") %>
20.
21. <p>
22. <p>
```

```
23. <center>
24. Questions? We've hidden contact information somewhere
    on this site. Try and find it!
25. </center>
26. </BODY></HTML>
```

HOW THE SCRIPT WORKS

The script above presents one way of wrapping things up: It gives shoppers a brief message, "Order Complete," then presents them with their order number, what they ordered, who we think they are, where we're sending it, and how they're paying for it.

Note that this script doesn't affect the function of the cart in any way. The cart would work just as well if the code were this:

```
1. <HTML><HEAD><TITLE>Order Complete</TITLE></HEAD><BODY
   BGCOLOR="#FFFFFF" >
2. <CENTER>Thanks for your order</CENTER>
3. </BODY></HTML>
```

So feel free to hack this up in any way you want. For what it's worth, giving shoppers their order numbers and a way to contact you if they have any questions is probably a good idea.

The code:

1. Scripting language is JavaScript.

2. Include `cart.js`, because the script uses the `order_info` object created there.

7. Print out the order number.

10. Print out a summary of the products ordered. Note that the `replace()` method of the String object is applied to substitute break tags for the line breaks.

13. Print out the contact information we collected about the shopper.

16. Print out where we plan to ship the order.

17. Print out how we're billing the shopper for the order. This means displaying the shopper's credit card or prepaid Web card information on the screen, which is obviously less secure than not displaying it.

Order complete. Next, `cart.js`, that does so much of the work for this script.

Script 5-12
cart.js

```
1. <%
2.
3. ////////////////////////////////////////////////////
4. //   misc. strings:
5. ////////////////////////////////////////////////////
6.
7. var current_script=
   String(Request.ServerVariables("SCRIPT_NAME"));
8.
9. out = "";
10.
11. basic_ship_cost = 1.95;
12. two_day_ship_cost = 6.95;
13. one_day_ship_cost = 8.95;
14.
15.
16. array_of_states = new Array("CA","PA","NV");
17.
18. ////////////////////////////////////////////////////
19. //    script mapping
20. ////////////////////////////////////////////////////
21.
22. display_records_script =
    "cart_list_items_for_sale.asp";
23.
24. cart_set_session_script = "cart_set_session.asp";
25. cart_view_contents_script = "cart_view_contents.asp";
26.
27. change_qty_script = "cart_change_qty.asp";
28. cart_remove_all_from_cart_script =
    "cart_remove_all.asp";
29. //clear_session_script = "cart_clear_session.asp";
30.
31. collect_shipping_information_script =
    "collect_shipping_information.asp";
32. set_shipping_info_script =
    "set_shipping_information.asp";
33. collect_billing_info_script =
    "collect_billing_information.asp";
34. set_cc_billing_information_script =
    "set_cc_billing_information.asp";
35. set_pwc_billing_information_script =
    "set_pwc_billing_information.asp";
36.
37. order_complete_script = "order_complete.asp";
38.
```

```
39. view_session_info_script =
    "view_session_contents.asp";
40.
41.
42. ///////////////////////////////////////////////////
43. //    Stuff relating to displaying items for sale
44. ///////////////////////////////////////////////////
45.
46. var catalog_file = "catalog_file.txt";
47. var option_file = "option_file.txt";
48.
49. var category = String(Request("category"));
50. var keyword = String(Request("keyword"));
51.
52. if (category != "undefined"){
53.    var search_term = category
54.    var search_type = "category"
55. }
56.
57. else if (keyword != "undefined"){
58.    var search_term = keyword
59.    var search_type = "keyword"
60. }
61.
62. else {
63.    var search_type = "all"
64. }
65.
66. //// create_items_object () returns an object that
    contains zero or more items that
67. //// are for sale
68.
69. function create_items_object (){
70. var items = new Object();
71.
72. // get rid of script name in absolute path
73. // and replace with name of file we want to open
74. var abs_path =
    String(Request.ServerVariables("PATH_TRANSLATED"));
75. var file_to_open =
    abs_path.replace(/\\\w*\.asp/,"\\") + catalog_file;
76.
77. fso = new
    ActiveXObject("Scripting.FileSystemObject");
78.
79. if (!fso.FileExists(file_to_open)){
80.    Response.Write("can't open " + file_to_open)
81. }
82. else {
83.    fs_stream = fso.OpenTextFile(file_to_open);
84.
```

```
85.    var temp_regex = new RegExp(search_term,"i")
86.    while (! fs_stream.AtEndOfStream){
87.
88.      temp = fs_stream.ReadLine() ;
89.      temp_array = temp.split(/\|/);
90.
91.      if ((search_type=="category" &&
         temp_array[1].search(temp_regex)>=0) ||
         (search_type=="keyword" &&
         (temp_array[1].search(temp_regex)>=0 ||
         temp_array[2].search(temp_regex)>=0 ||
         temp_array[3].search(temp_regex)>=0)) ||
         (search_type =="all" && temp_array[0] != "//id"))
         {
92.        items[temp_array[0]] = new Object();
93.        items[temp_array[0]].category =
           temp_array[1];
94.        items[temp_array[0]].name =
           temp_array[2];
95.        items[temp_array[0]].description =
           temp_array[3];
96.        items[temp_array[0]].image =
           temp_array[4];
97.        items[temp_array[0]].options = new
           Object();
98.        items[temp_array[0]].options_qty = 0;
99.      }
100.
101.   } // end while
102.
103.
104. fs_stream.close();
105. } // end if file opens
106.
107. // open option file and grab option information
108.
109. file_to_open = abs_path.replace(/\\\w*\.asp/,"\\") +
     option_file;
110.
111. if (!fso.FileExists(file_to_open)){
112. Response.Write("can't open " + file_to_open)
113. }
114. else {
115.   fs_stream = fso.OpenTextFile(file_to_open);
116.
117.   while (! fs_stream.AtEndOfStream){
118.     temp = fs_stream.ReadLine() ;
119.     // if there are two pipes next to each
            other, add a space.
120.     temp = temp.replace(/\|\|/g,"| |");
121.     temp_array = temp.split(/\|/);
```

```
122.
123.    if (temp_array[0] != "//id" &&
        String(items[temp_array[0]]) != "undefined"){
124.
125.      temp_qty = items[temp_array[0]].options_qty
126.      items[temp_array[0]].options[temp_qty]
         = new Object
127.      if (temp_array[1] == " "){ temp_array[1] = ""
         }
128.      items[temp_array[0]].options[temp_qty].ext =
         temp_array[1]
129.      items[temp_array[0]].options[temp_qty].price =
         temp_array[2]
130.      items[temp_array[0]].options[temp_qty].weight =
         temp_array[3]
131.
132.      if (String(temp_array[4]) == "undefined"){
133.        items[temp_array[0]].options
           [temp_qty].description = "none"
134.      }
135.      else{
136.        items[temp_array[0]].options
           [temp_qty].description = temp_array[4]
137.      }
138.      temp_buy_link = '<a href="' +
         cart_set_session_script + '?add='
139.      temp_buy_link2 = items[temp_array[0]].name +
         "---" + items[temp_array[0]].description
140.      if (items[temp_array[0]].options
         [temp_qty].description != "none"){
141.        temp_buy_link2 += " ("+
           items[temp_array[0]].options
           [temp_qty].description +")"}
142.      temp_buy_link2 += "---" + temp_array[0] +
         temp_array[1] + "---" + temp_array[2] + "---"
         + temp_array[3]
143.      temp_buy_link +=
         Server.URLEncode(temp_buy_link2) + '">Buy</a>';
144.
145.      items[temp_array[0]].options[temp_qty].buy_link
         = temp_buy_link
146.
147.      items[temp_array[0]].options_qty++
148.      //Response.Write(temp_array+ "<br>")
149.    }
150.  } // end while
151. } // end else
152. return items
153. } // end defining function create_items_object ()
154.
155. ///////////////////////////////////////////////////
```

```
156. //   Create the cart_items and order_info object
157. ///////////////////////////////////////////////////
158.
159. // first create both objects
160.
161. cart_items = new Object();
162. order_info = new Object();
163. order_info.subtotal = 0;
164. order_info.weight = 0;
165.
166. // loop through the Session object and provision
     cart_items:
167.
168. for (i = 1 ; i <= Session.Contents.Count ; i++){
169.   if ((typeof Session.Contents(i) == "object") &&
       (Session(Session.Contents.key(i)+".qty") > 0)){
170.     cart_items[i-1] = new Object;
171.     temp_uid = Session.Contents.key(i)
172.     cart_items[i-1].uid = temp_uid
173.     cart_items[i-1].qty =
         parseInt(Session(temp_uid+".qty"))
174.     cart_items[i-1].name = Session(temp_uid+".name")
175.     cart_items[i-1].desc = Session(temp_uid+".desc")
176.     cart_items[i-1].price =
         parseFloat(Session(temp_uid+".price"))
177.     cart_items[i-1].weight =
         parseFloat(Session(temp_uid+".weight"))
178.     order_info.subtotal +=
         cart_items[i-1].price*cart_items[i-1].qty
179.     order_info.weight +=
         cart_items[i-1].weight*cart_items[i-1].qty
180.   }// end if
181.
182. }// end for
183.
184.
185. // set order_info stuff
186.
187. order_info.uid = Session("order_info.uid")
188.
189. order_info.ship_type =
     Session("order_info.ship_type")
190. order_info.ship_cost =
     Session("order_info.ship_cost")
191.
192. order_info.tax =
     parseFloat(Session("order_info.tax"))
193.
194. order_info.f_name = Session("order_info.f_name")
195. order_info.l_name = Session("order_info.l_name")
196. order_info.email = Session("order_info.email")
```

```
197. order_info.phone = Session("order_info.phone")
198.
199. order_info.address_1 =
     Session("order_info.address_1")
200. order_info.address_2 =
     Session("order_info.address_2")
201. order_info.city = Session("order_info.city")
202. order_info.state = Session("order_info.state")
203. order_info.zip = Session("order_info.zip")
204.
205. // summary fields:
206. order_info.ship_address =
     Session("order_info.ship_address")
207. order_info.contact_info =
     Session("order_info.contact_info")
208. order_info.order_summary =
     Session("order_info.order_summary")
209. order_info.billing_info =
     Session("order_info.billing_info")
210.
211.
212. /////////////////////////////////////////////////////
213. // functions that build rows in the tables used to
     display the
214. // contents of the shopping cart:
215. /////////////////////////////////////////////////////
216.
217.
218. //// zero or more rows that include a text box to
     change the qty of an item
219. //// and a delete link that lets shopper remove an
     item from cart.
220.
221. function cart_contents_editable_row (){
222. if (order_info.subtotal == 0){
223.    %><tr><td colspan=6 align=center>No Items in
        cart</td></tr><%    }
224. else{
225. // loop throught the cart_items object and add the
     contents of the cart to the table
226. for (i in cart_items){
227.    %>
228.    <tr>
229.       <td><% =   cart_items[i].uid %></td>
230.       <td><% = cart_items[i].name%></td>
231.       <td><% = cart_items[i].desc%>   (Weight Factor:
          <%= cart_items[i].weight %>)</td>
232.       <td>
233.          <input type=text
             name="uid_<%=cart_items[i].uid%>" value="<% =
             cart_items[i].qty %>" size=2>
```

```
234.      </td>
235.      <td><% = dollarise(cart_items[i].price)%></td>
236.      <td><% = dollarise(cart_items[i].price *
          cart_items[i].qty)%></td>
237.      <td></td>
238.      <td>
239.        <a href="<%=change_qty_script%>?set_qty=
          0&uid=<%=cart_items[i].uid%>"><font color=red
          size=1>Delete This Item</font></a>
240.      </td>
241.    </tr>
242.  <%
243. } // end looping through cart_items
244. }//end else
245. } // end cart_contents_editable_row ()
246.
247.
248. //// a row of headers
249.
250. function cart_contents_header_row(){ %>
251. <tr><td>p/n</td><td>name</td><td>desc</
     td><td>qty.</td><td>price</td><td>ext.<br>price</
     td></tr>   <%
252. } // end cart_contents_start_table()
253.
254.
255. //// a subtotal row
256.
257. function cart_contents_subtotal_row(){ %>
258. <tr><td colspan=5 align=right>subtotal</td><td><% =
     dollarise(order_info.subtotal) %></td></tr>   <%
259. } // end cart_contents_subtotal_row()
260.
261.
262. //// zero or more rows that display contents of
     cart. not editable
263.
264. function cart_contents_non_editable_row (){
265. if (order_info.subtotal == 0){
266.    %>
267.    <tr><td> </td><td> </td><td>No Items in
       cart</td><td> </td><td> </td><td> 
       </td><td></td><td></td></tr>
268. <%}
269.
270. else {
271.    // loop throught the cart_items object and add the
       contents of the cart to the table
272.    for (i in cart_items){
273.      %>
274.      <tr>
```

```
275.        <td><% = cart_items[i].uid %></td>
276.        <td><% = cart_items[i].name%></td>
277.        <td><% = cart_items[i].desc%> (Weight Factor:
            <%= cart_items[i].weight %>)</td>
278.        <td><% = cart_items[i].qty %></td>
279.        <td><% = dollarise(cart_items[i].price)%></td>
280.        <td><% = dollarise(cart_items[i].price *
            cart_items[i].qty)%></td>
281.      </tr>
282.    <%   } // end looping through cart_items object
283. } // end else
284. } // end function cart_contents_non_editable_row ()
285.
286.
287.
288.
289. //// row with shipping cost
290.
291. function cart_contents_shipping_row() {
292. // if ship_type is null, set it to basic:
293. if (order_info.ship_type == null){
294.   order_info.ship_type = "basic"
295.   order_info.ship_cost =
       order_info.weight*basic_ship_cost
296. }
297. %>
298. <tr><td colspan=5 align=right>shipping
     cost</td><td><% =
     dollarise(order_info.weight*order_info.ship_cost)
     %></td></tr>
299. <%
300. } // end cart_contents_shipping_row()
301.
302.
303. //// row with amount of tax, if any
304.
305. function cart_contents_tax_row() {
306.   %>
307. <tr><td colspan=5 align=right>tax</td><td><% =
     dollarise(order_info.tax) %></td></tr>
308.   <%
309. }
310.
311. //// row with grand total
312.
313. function cart_contents_grand_total_row() {
314.   %>
315.   <tr><td colspan=5 align=right>total</td><td><% =
       dollarise(order_info.subtotal + order_info.tax +
       order_info.ship_cost) %></td></tr>
316.   <%
```

```
317. }
318.
319.
320. ///////////////////////////////////////////////
321. // Misc. Functions
322. ///////////////////////////////////////////////
323.
324. function dollarise(temp_amount){
325. // interesting bug: this returns: 894.9999999999999
326. //temp_amount2 = String(8.95 * 100)
327. if (temp_amount > 0){
328.    temp_amount2 = String(Math.round(temp_amount *
       100))
329.    temp_length = parseInt(temp_amount2.length)
330.    temp_price_1 = temp_amount2.substring(0,
       (temp_length-2))
331.    temp_price_2 = temp_amount2.substring
       ((temp_length-2),temp_length)
332.    return("$"+ temp_price_1 + "." + temp_price_2)
333. }
334. else
335.    return("$0.00")
336. } // end dollarise
337.
338.
339.
340. //// creates a header used by some of the scripts.
     header includes links to a couple
341. //// of categories, a keyword search box, and a link
     to the cart page
342.
343. function cart_header(){
344. %>
345. <HTML><HEAD><TITLE><% = current_script
     %></TITLE></HEAD><BODY BGCOLOR="#FFFFFF" >
346. <table border=1 width=90% align=center>
347.    <tr>
348.      <td colspan=2 align=center>View by Category</td>
349.      <td align=center>Keyword Search</td>
350.      <td align=center>View Contents of</td>
351.    <tr><td align=center>
352.      <a href="<% = display_records_script
         %>?category=books">books</a>
353.    </td><td align=center>
354.      <a href="<% = display_records_script
         %>?category=pastries">pastries</a>
355.    </td><td align=center>
356.      <form action="<% = display_records_script %>">
357.      Search For: <input type=text name=keyword
         value="">
```

```
358.    <input type=submit name=toss
        value="Go->"></form>
359.  </td><td align=center>
360.    <a href="<% =cart_view_contents_script
        %>">Cart</a>
361.
362.    </td></tr>
363.
364. </table>
365. <hr>
366. <%
367. } // end cart_header
368.
369.
370. //// session_contents() creates a snapshot of the
     contents of the session object
371. //// which is useful for debugging.
372.
373. function session_contents(){
374.
375. for (i = 1 ; i <= Session.Contents.Count ; i++){
376.   if (typeof(Session.Contents(i)) == "object") {
377. //   cart_items[i-1] = new Object;
378. %>
379.     <% = i + ". " + Session.Contents.key(i) %> (<% =
        typeof(Session.Contents(i)) %>):
380.     <% //= Session(Session.Contents.key(i))%>
381. <blockquote><table border=1>
382.
383. <%   // loop through and find "properties" of object:
384.     var temp_regex = new
        RegExp(Session.Contents.key(i))
385.     for (ii = 1 ; ii <= Session.Contents.Count ;
        ii++){
386.       if (Session.Contents.key(ii).search
          (temp_regex) >= 0 &&
          typeof(Session.Contents(ii)) != "object"){
387.       %>
388.       <tr><td>
389.       <% = Session.Contents.key(ii) %> (<% =
          typeof(Session.Contents(ii)) %>)
390.       </td>
391.       <td align=left>
392.       <pre><% =
          Session(Session.Contents.key(ii))
          %></pre>
393.       </td></tr>
394.       <%
395.       } // end if search good
396.     } //end inside for
397. %>
```

```
398. </table></blockquote>
399. <%
400.
401.   } // end if
402. } // end outside for
403.
404. } // end function session_contents
405.
406. %>
```

HOW THE SCRIPT WORKS

Something of a catch-all script, `cart.js` performs a number of different functions:

- Does most of the work of creating lists of items that are for sale by reading the configuration files (`catalog_file.txt` and `option_file.txt`), implementing category and keyword searches, and creating an object that can easily be used to display one or more items that are for sale.
- Helps manage two objects that are fundamental to how the cart works: `cart_items`, which stores the contents of a shopper's cart, and `order_info`, which stores shipping, contact, and billing information about an order.
- Defines some variables and functions that are used by the different scripts discussed in this chapter.
- Helps minimize the amount of code that goes into scripts that are visible to users in order to make it as easy as possible to edit the look and feel of those pages.

Let's dive in.

1. Notice that we don't need to tell IIS that we're using JavaScript. This is an include file, and setting the language is done in the script that is using the include file.

7. `current_script` contains the URL of the current script, something that often comes in handy.

8. The `out` variable is used in a number of different places in the cart as a place to store output. In some cases, code may assume that `out` already exists, which is why it's worth defining `out` as an empty string (otherwise, an error message would be generated).

11–13. Variables that are used to calculate cost of shipping an order. See the section on `set_shipping_information.asp`, earlier in this chapter, for how these are used.

16. The `array_of_states` array is used to generate select boxes when collecting shipping and billing information. You may want to add more states.

22–39. Script mapping: For some reason, files always seem to move and get new names over time. This leads to broken links that are sometimes difficult to find. Mapping script names to variables helps solve this problem by creating a single variable to update if a file name is changed.

The last script, `view_session_info_script`, is a debugging script that is discussed later in this chapter.

46–159. These lines do most of the work involved in taking zero or more records from the text configuration files and putting information about them into an object that is used in `cart_list_items_for_sale.asp` to display items that are for sale.

There are three ways to define the scope that determines how many items are displayed. This is done by passing or not passing form variables to the display script:

- If a variable called `category` is passed, all the items in that category are displayed. For example, the sample configuration file includes two categories, `books` and `pastries`.
- If a variable called `keyword` is passed, the script searches for an exact match of the keyword or keywords entered in information stored in `catalog_file.txt`. Note that keyword searches will not match information in `option_file.txt`.
- If neither a `category` nor a `keyword` variable are passed, all the items for sale are displayed.

46,47. The names of the catalog file and the option file are stored in variables here to make it easy to move or rename the files.

49,50. The form variables `category` and `keyword` are collected and assigned to local variables of the same name.

52–64. Using an `if/else if/ if` statement, the variables `search_type` and `search_term` are defined. `search_type` is used to determine how the `create_items_object` will parse `catalog_file.txt` (whether it will grab records in a category, records that match a keyword search, or grab everything). `search_term` contains the category or keyword used by the category and keyword searches, respectively.

69–158. The `create_items_object()` function: This function creates and returns an object that contains zero or more items that are for sale. It is used in `cart_list_items_for_sale.asp` to create an object called `items`:

```
items = create_items_object ();
```

Once the function has been used to create an object, in this case an object called `items`, it is easy to iterate through the items object to display them using a `for()` loop:

```
for(key in items) {…}
```

70. The first thing that the function does is create an object called `items` that will be used to store the records that are collected by the function. Note that, because `items` is defined within the function, its scope will be limited to within the function. Using the name `items` twice—once inside, and once outside the function—is not particularly clever on my part, because it's an easy way to get confused. That said, the code works, and if it ain't broke…

74,75. Using a regular expression described in detail in the discussion of the previous script, the variable `catalog_file`, assumed to be the name of a file that is in the same directory as the current script, is used to create a variable called `file_to_open,` which contains the full path to the file.

77. A new FileSystemObject called `fso` is created. (See Chapter 2 for an introduction to working with the file system if this stuff is new to you.)

79–81. Rather than assuming that `file_to_open` exists, the script uses the `fso.FileExists()` method to make sure that the file is there before trying to open it. This makes it possible to generate a custom error message (line 80), rather than to have a user confronted with a cryptic Microsoftian error. So maybe you should edit the message in line 80 to make it less cryptic. Whatever.

If the file exists, which it usually does, once we're done debugging (although you're more or less guaranteed that it'll eventually get moved, renamed, or deleted if you let a novice edit it...), lines 82–110 get executed.

82–110. These lines will open the file, find records that match the criteria defined by the `search_type` and `search_term` variables, store them in the `items` object, then close the file.

83. Using the `fso.OpenTextFile()` method, a Textstream object called `fs_stream` is created.

85. The variable `search_term` may contain the name of a category or a string typed into the keyword search box. Here, it is turned into a regular expression using the JavaScript `RegExp()` function. The parameter `"i"` is used to make the search case-insensitive, so that the users trying to use the keyword search feature don't have to worry about what case they're using.

86. This line creates a `while()` loop that will repeat itself until the script gets to the end of the file, at which point, the `fs_stream.AtEndOfStream` condition will be true. This works well in conjunction with the next line...

88. This line creates a variable called `temp`, which contains one line of the file `fs_stream`. The `ReadLine()` method does two things: It returns one line from the file and it moves to the next line, so that the next time the `ReadLine()` method is invoked, the next line will be returned.

The `temp` variable now contains one line from the file `catalog_file.txt`, for example:

```
bk1|Books|Book 1|The story of the number 1|<img
src="images/logo.gif">
```

89. The record above consists of a number of fields, specifically (in order): `id`, `category`, `title`, `description`, and `image`. The fields are separated using pipes ("|"), which makes it easy to turn the record into an array, using the `split()` method. Note that the pipe needs to be escaped in the regular expression because pipes are normally used to delimit patterns.

91. This rather unreadable line performs the task of deciding whether or not to add the record currently being evaluated to the `items` object that is being created. Although the line is a bit long-winded, the logic is straightforward.

There are three separate sets of conditions, separated by logical ORs ("||"). If any one of them is true, lines 92–98 get executed. First condition:

```
(search_type=="category" &&
temp_array[1].search(temp_regex)>=0)
```

This will resolve to true if search_type is set to category and search_term (which is inside of temp_regex) matches the second field in the record, which is the category field. Thus, if search_type is set to category and the category being searched for is books, a record of category books will be put into the items object (in lines 92–98), while a record of category pastries will be ignored.

Second condition:

```
(search_type=="keyword" &&
(temp_array[1].search(temp_regex)>=0 ||
temp_array[2].search(temp_regex)>=0 ||
temp_array[3].search(temp_regex)>=0))
```

This will be true if search_type is set to keyword and search_term can be found in the category, name, or description fields. You can muck with this if you want to change how the keyword search behaves. For example, if you want people to be able to look up items using an id, you could modify the script so that it also looked for a match in the first field of the array:

```
temp_array[0].search(temp_regex)>=0
```

And the third condition:

```
(search_type =="all" && temp_array[0] != "//id")
```

This will be true if search_type is set to all and the first element of the array isn't "//id", which is the first element of the comment row at the top of the file. So every item in the file gets put into items, which is then used to create a page listing items for sale.

For sites with a large amount of items for sale, the all search_type may not be particularly useful.

92–98. Having determined that the information stored in a line of `catalog_file.txt` should be put into `items` so that it can be displayed, these lines do the work of adding records to items.

Before we look at what happens here, it's worth understanding how `items` works. To do this, the first step is to understand how our data is structured: The shopping cart is designed to support any reasonably small number of items for sale, each of which must have one or more options.

Thus, if we have a book that is available in both paperback and hardcover, that book would have one record in `catalog_file.txt` and two records in the option file (one record for each option).

Another book, which was available only in hardcover, would have a single record in each file. At a minimum, an item that is for sale must have a record in each file.

This means that this cart is quite adequate for selling items that have a reasonably small number of options associated with them and less well suited to selling something like an automobile, where the large number of different option combinations might require hundreds of lines in the option file.

Finally, it is important to understand how the part numbering system works: Each item that is for sale must have a unique part number (sometimes referred to as an `id`). Each option for that item must have a unique identifier as well, which is an extension to the basic part number. The part number and unique option identifier can thus be concatenated, and this concatenated identifier can also be thought of as a part number.

`items` is designed to store information about one or more objects that are for sale efficiently, as follows:

- For each item stored in the `items` object, there is an object whose name is the unique part number stored in `catalog_file.txt`. Thus, if `items` contains two books that are for sale, `items` might consist of two objects:

```
items.bk1       // an object that stores information
                // about the first book.
items.bk2       // an object that stores information
                // about the second book.\
```

Note that these objects are nested inside of `items`, which is also an object.

- Each object inside of `items` has properties that store information taken from `catalog_file.txt`. Thus, if the information about `bk1` in `catalog_file.txt` is:

```
bk1|Books|Book 1|The story of the number 1|<img
src="images/logo.gif">
```

then `items.bk1` will have the following properties:

```
items.bk1.category    // which will be set to "Books"
items.bk1.name        // "Book 1"
items.bk1.description // "The story of the number 1"
items.bk1.image       // "<img src="images/logo.gif">"
```

- Furthermore, an object is created for every option that an item has, inside of yet another object, called `options`.

  For example, `bk1` is available only in paperback, so it has only one option, which will be called `option[0]`:

```
items.bk1.option[0]
```

This `option` object then has properties like `price` and `description`:

```
items.bk1.option[0].price    // an amount, like 12.95
items.bk1.option[0].description // an optional string
```

Some items, of course, have more than one option. `bk2`, for example, has two:

```
items.bk2.option[0]
items.bk2.option[1]
```

which makes for a lot of objects. In the case of `bk2`, we have: the `items` object, which stores all of the items that are going to be displayed; the `bk2` object, which stores information about `bk2`; the `option` object, which stores information about bk2's options, the 0 object, that stores information about one of bk2's options; and the 1 object, which stores information about bk2's second option.

Although this is a bit complicated, the structure makes it very easy to loop through items and retrieve any number of objects, each of which can have any number of options.

So that's how items works. Let's go back to lines 92–98:

92. This line creates a new object using the part number stored in the first item of temp_array. Thus, if the part number is bk1, this is the line where items.bk1 is created.

93–96. Pulling more information from temp_array, the category , name , description , and image properties of the object created in line 92 are assigned string values.

97. This line creates the options object that will be used to store information about options.

98. The options_qty property of the item being created is set to zero. It will be incremented later when the script parses option_file.txt.

104. After going through every line in catalog_file.txt, the script closes the fs_stream object used to read the contents of the file.

On to the option file!

109. Using the same trick used to get the fully qualified path of catalog_file.txt, file_to_open is now set to the full path to option_file.txt.

111–114. Once again, an if/else statement is used to make sure that the file exists before proceeding to execute lines 115–150.

114. A TextSream is created to look at the options file.

117. A while() loop is used to go through the file one line at a time.

118. On each iteration through the while() loop, a line is stuffed into the temp variable.

120. This line looks for empty fields (two pipes with nothing in between them) and inserts a single space between them. This fixes something that wasn't working correctly, though I can't recall what at the moment.

121. Again, the `temp` variable is split into an array of fields called `temp_array`.

123. The `if` statement on this line determines whether the current record we're looking at is used to add information to the `items` object.

The first thing we check for is simple enough: If the first element in `temp_array` is `"//id"`, we know that we're looking at the first row of the file, which is a comment, and we want to ignore it.

The second thing that the `if` statement does is to make sure that `String(items[temp_array[0]])` is not equal to the special JavaScript value `"undefined"`. This is a way of checking to make sure that the only options that are added to the `items` object are those that match items that are currently stored in the `items` object. Recall that, in most cases, `items` is storing a subset of the items that are for sale—items that are in a particular category or match a particular keyword.

The first field in `temp_array` is the `id` field, which gives us the part number of the item to which the current option record applies. For example, if a record in the option file looks like this:

```
bk1||12.95|2|
```

we know that this is an option for part number `bk1`.

So if this record is the current record in the loop, the `if()` statement will check to see whether `String(items[bk1])` is not equal to `"undefined"`. If it is, we know that the `items` object does not include an object called `bk1`, and the `if()` statement will resolve to false. On the other hand, if the `items.bk1` exists (this is the same thing as `items[bk1]`), then `String(items[temp__array[0]])` will not be equal to `"undefined"`, the `if()` statement will be true, and lines 125–148 will be executed.

Although this is a kind of a tricky way to go about it (which makes it hard to remember how it works), it has the advantage that, for the `create_items_object()` function to execute, the two configuration files have to be parsed only once each. So, overall, it seems like a fairly efficient way to go.

125–148. These lines take information from the current record and store it in the `items` object.

125. The first step is to set `temp_qty`, which is obtained from the value of the `options_qty` property of the current item. If this is the first option we've discovered, this will be zero. If it's the second, it will be one, and so on.

126. This line creates a new options object. Options are named using the value retrieved from the current `item`'s `options_qty` field. Thus, the first option will be `options[0]`, the next `options[1]`, and so forth.

127. Because the option extension field is optional for items that have only one option, in some cases, `temp_array[1]` will consist of a single space (created by the regular expression on line 120). Should this be the case, this line substitutes the single space for an empty string, which avoids ending up with a part number that ends in a space, something that can cause havoc.

128–130. These lines take the option extension, price, and weight information taken from the text file and assign them to the appropriate property of the option object created in line 126.

132–137. In the display script `cart_list_items_for_sale.asp`, option information is displayed differently, depending on whether a particular option has a description. This is handled by checking to see whether an option's description is set to `"none"`. These lines check to see whether the last field in the option record is undefined. If it is, the `description` property of the option object is set to `"none"`. Otherwise, the description is assigned to the property as expected.

138–145. The last property of the option object that needs to be set is `buy_link`. This is the link that a shopper can click on to purchase an item. It consists of a link to the `cart_set_session_script`, a form variable called add, and the word Buy, a clever subliminal message designed to prey on the subconscious consumer impulse. If you take a look at all the variables that get stuffed into the add form variable (everything that goes into `temp_buy_link2`), you'll notice that basically every bit of information that we have about the current part number/option combination goes into it: the name of the item,

its part number and extension, description, price, etc. ...
When a shopper clicks on the "Buy" link, the information
is stored in the Session object, and from there is used by
most of the scripts in the cart.

Note that, in line 143, `Server.URLEncode()` is used to
make sure that all the information that gets stuffed into
`temp_buy_link2` is URL-friendly.

147. Having finished setting up the current option object, the
current item's `options_qty` property is incremented by
one.

152. Once the script has iterated through the entire options file
and stored the information collected into the `items`
object, the `items` object is returned before the function
ends on line 153.

155–211. As shoppers add items to their carts and enter their shipping and payment information during checkout, information about a shopper's order is managed in two objects
that are stored in the ASP Session object: `cart_items`
stores the list of items that have been placed in the shopper's cart, and `order_info` stores summary information
about the order, as well as the shipping and payment
information that is submitted by the shopper.

Not only do these objects store information in the Session
object, making it possible to maintain state as the shopper moves from page to page, but many of the scripts in
the cart make changes to the information that is stored in
these objects. To make it easier to work with the two
objects, `cart.js` pulls all the information stored in these
Session objects and stores it in to local JavaScript objects
of the same name. Then, if a script makes any changes to
either object, the changes are often made first to the local
object, then transferred to the Session object at the end of
the script. Because the variables have the same name, it
may be kind of confusing. The key thing is to remember
that there are two sets of objects:

```
Session("order_info") // an object that is inside of
                      // Session

order_info  // a local object that contains the same
            // information as Session("order_info")

// body of script
```

```
// makes changes to order_info

order_info // order_info no longer contains the same
           // information as Session("order_info")

Session("order_info") = new Object() // overwrite
                            // the old Session object.
for (i in order_info){     // Take information
   Session("order_info." +  i) = order_info[i]
}                          // from order_info
                           // and store it in
                           // new Session("order_info")
```

The example above illustrates the relationship between Session("order_info") and the local variable order_info. A similar relationship exists between Session("cart_items") and cart_items.

Note that order_info and cart_items are not necessary: Everywhere that these variables are used, it would be probably be perfectly possible to use their two Session counterparts (which do not behave the same way, so it's not an easy switch). However, working with order_info and cart_items is more convenient (or it seemed like it until I had to sit down and write about it <grin>), if only because it means not having to type Session() all the time (and have it clutter up the code).

At any rate, that's the story, and lines 155–211 do the work of creating the variables cart_items and order_info, based on the information stored in the Session objects of the same name.

161–162. The two objects are created.

163–164. Two properties of order_info, subtotal and weight are declared and set to zero. Because the value of these variables depends on which items are in the cart, their value is dynamically set while the script iterates through Session("cart_items"), below.

168. This is the start of a loop that runs until line 182 that loops through every element in an object called Session.Contents using a property Session.Contents.Count, which tells us how many goodies we have inside of Contents.

169. What the script looks for inside of the Session object is objects, because the only objects that are stored inside of the Session object are items that have been added by the cart. This line uses an `if()` statement to test whether the current item in the `Session.Contents` object (`Session.Contents(i)`) is an object by using the JavaScript `typeof` function. Furthermore, because it's possible for an item to have a quantity of zero (if the item was selected then removed from a shopper's cart), the script makes sure that there is one or more of any object it finds by checking the `qty` property of that object.

When an object that matches these criteria is found, the script decides that it has found one of the items in the shopper's cart, and lines 170–79 are executed.

170. This line creates a new object inside of the `cart_items` object. The use of `[i-1]` to identify the object is interesting because it is so specific and so useless: My recollection is that the original idea was that, when the first object was added to `cart_items`, `[i-1]` would resolve to `[0]`, the next to `[1]`, and so forth, which would be nice and tidy, just like an array.

Of course, I miscalculated. Because the objects that the script looks for here are interspersed throughout `Session.Contents`, `[i-1]` is much more likely to end up being first `[0]`, then `[6]`, and so on. In the end, it ends up being completely irrelevant what `[i-1]` is, because it is never used. Ah, well. It was a nice idea.

171. Using the method `Session.Contents.key(i)`, it's possible to transform an index value (that's basically what i is) into a key. The key is the `id` of an object in the cart that was used to create a Session object in the first place in the `cart_set_session.asp` script, discussed earlier in this chapter. This key is stored in a variable called `temp_uid`. (Which would have made a much better choice than `[i-1]`, don't you think?)

172–177. Once the key is known, it's a relatively simple matter to use `temp_uid` to collect the quantity, name, description, price, and weight of the current item and to set the `uid`, `qty`, `name`, `desc`, `price`, and `weight` properties of the object that was created on line 170. Note the use of `parseInt()` on line 173 and of `parseFloat()` on lines 176 and 177. Because JavaScript is loosely typed, you never really know what you're getting when you grab a variable. `parseInt()` and `parseFloat()` force numbers to be integers and floating points, respectively, which makes life easier in very much the same way that the `String()` function makes life easier with strings.

178,179. These two lines update the value of `order_info.subtotal` and `order_info.weight` based on the price, weight factor, and quantity of the item currently being added to `cart_items`.

187–209. These lines are fairly straightforward: Properties of the `Session("order_info")` object are assigned to the same properties of the local `order_info` object. Note that I'm not entirely sure that `Session("order_info.zip")` is a property of `Session("order_info")` in the same way that `order_info.zip` is a property of the JavaScript object `order_info`. If you play around with the Session object a little, you'll see what I mean.

217–312. The functions that are defined in these lines create the tables that are used by the three scripts that display the contents of the shopping cart: `cart_view_contents.asp`, `collect_shipping_information.asp`, and `collect_billing_information.asp`.

221. This line begins the work of defining the function `cart_contents_editable_row()`. Depending on how many items are currently in the shopper's cart (stored in the `cart_items` object, describe above), this function generates one or more rows that make up the body of the table that is displayed on `cart_view_contents.asp`. The word `editable` is included in the function name because these row(s) created by the function allow the shopper to edit the number of items being purchased or to remove the item from the cart.

222,223. The first thing that the function does is to check to see whether the subtotal of the order is zero, which would mean that there are not any items in the cart. If this is the case, line 223 creates a row that contains the message that there are "No Items in cart."

224. If the subtotal is not equal to zero, there is presumably something in the cart, and lines 225–243 are executed.

226. This line begins a `for()` loop that runs from line 227 to line 243. This loops through the contents of the `cart_items` object. Because `cart_items` contains objects that store information about items the shopper has selected, this is an easy way to loop through each item in turn.

227–242. These lines create a row of an HTML table for each item that is found inside of `cart_items`.

229. The first cell gets the item's part number.

230. The next, its name.

231. The third displays the description of the item and its weight factor.

Tip

Although you may not want to display the weight factor in the finished cart, it's useful to have when you're getting it set up, because it helps you to make sure that the shipping amount is correct.

232–234. The number of items being purchased (default is one, editable by user) is displayed in the next cell inside of a text box that the user can then edit. The name of the text box is a concatenation of the string `"uid_"` and the part number of the item. The name of this field is important, because it determines how the field is used by the script that updates item quantities when the user edits this field.

235. Displays the price of the item, using the `dollarise()` function, defined later in this file, to express the price as a dollar amount.

236. Displays the product of the price times the quantity.

237. An empty cell. I'm not sure why it's there.

238–240. This cell creates a link that can be used to remove an item from the cart. This works by sending the user to the `change_qty_script` and passing two form variables: `set_qty`, which is set to zero (same effect as deleting the item), and `uid`, which is the part number of the item being removed from the cart.

250–252. The next function is `cart_contents_header_row()`, which returns the HTML code for the first row. There is no code within the function, which is a function, rather than a variable, for the sake of consistency.

257–259. `cart_contents_subtotal_row()` generates a subtotal row with the subtotal `order_info.subtotal`, which was calculated earlier in `cart.js` (line 178). Once again, the `dollarise()` function is used to make sure that the subtotal has the right number of decimal places.

264–284. The `cart_contents_non_editable_row()` function is simply a pared-down version of its cousin, `cart_contents_editable_row()`, described above. The text box and delete button, the editable aspects of the row, have been removed.

291–300. The `cart_contents_shipping_row()` function generates a single piece of information: the amount that the shopper will be billed for shipping, generated by multiplying the total weight factor of the order by the `order_info.ship_cost`.

Because the first time this function is invoked, `order_info.ship_cost` will not yet have been set, the function checks whether `ship_type` is null. If it is, the `ship_type` and `ship_cost` properties are set.

305–309. `cart_contents_tax_row()` generates a row that adds the tax to the order, if any. This is already calculated and stored in `order_info.tax`.

313–317. The last row function is `cart_contents_grand_total_row()`, which calculates the grand total for the order. This is calculated by adding the subtotal, tax, and shipping cost that are stored in the `order_info` object.

Script 5-13
view_session_contents.asp

```
1. <%@ Language=JavaScript %>
2. <!-- #include file="cart.js" -->
3.
4. <%
5. session_contents()
6. %>
```

HOW THE SCRIPT WORKS

DEBUGGING THE CART

Because so much is going on in the ASP Session object, sometimes it's hard to figure out what the script is doing.

view_session_contents.asp helps to deal with this: It invokes the session_contents() function defined in cart.js to display all the information that is stored in the Session object.

I'm often surprised by how the code I write is doing something that is not quite what I thought it was doing. Scripts like this one help me to figure out how to whip my code into line.

RECAP

The scripts in this chapter create a fairly useful and simple shopping cart by putting the ASP Session object to work.

The flat-file database used to store information about items for sale is also worth taking a look at.

IDEAS FOR HACKING THIS SCRIPT

This is a fairly simple, fairly standard shopping cart. These days, you can't go three clicks on the Web without landing on a commerce site that's got some kind of slick features. With a little thought, many of the things you see out there could be grafted to these scripts. Some good places to start might include:

- Limiting how many records are displayed on one page. If you get to the point where you have a large number of items for sale, you may want to let people look at only 10 or 15 items at a time.
- You can connect the shopping cart to a card authentication system. There is a number of companies out there that will make sure that payment information is valid and then transfer funds to a merchant account.
- Make an additional lookup against the database before collecting payment information to make sure that the prices stored in the session object are valid. The way the cart currently works, it is possible for a malicious shopper to edit price information and try to purchase an item for less than the price listed.

6 Email

IN THIS CHAPTER

- Sending email with CDONTS
- Putting the output of a form into an email
- How email works

The head of sales is looking at you with doe eyes. One of his customers wants to be able to send him email directly from the corporate Web site. Given that he hasn't had a laptop that works for three out of the last five years, his skepticism is understandable. When you call him an hour later to tell him that the form is live on the Web site, there's a stunned silence on the line.

Sure, you get a fat head, start treating interns rudely, and take to wearing stained T-shirts to work—because you can. But what can you say, you're a miracle worker.

Maybe the tricks in this chapter won't turn you into a sartorial criminal and a raving egomaniac. Even so, you may get a small kick over how easy it is to incorporate email into your Web site with ASP.

◆ Project: Simple Email Script

This script implements one of the most common Web site applications out there—it redirects the output of a form to an email.

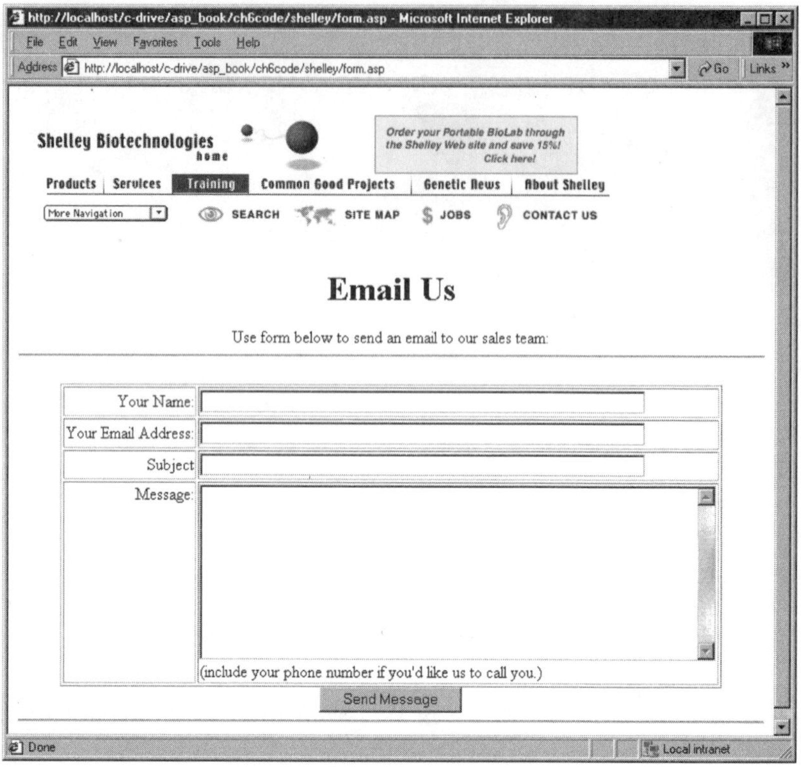

FIGURE 6-1 This form is used to create an email

The form is fairly standard, as in Figure 6-1.

The form's output is then put into an email. In this case, the information is sent to the email address `form-recipient@love-joy.com` (see Figure 6-2).

That's about all there is to it: whatever gets typed into the form ends up in an email sent to the address of your choice. What's more, the code for it isn't much more complicated than the idea.

NEW FEATURES

SMTP, POP, IMAP, Etc.... An Introduction to How Email Works

Like most computer technologies, somewhere along the way, the folks who've made email possible forgot to make email easy enough that people could understand how it works. Probably two-thirds of the questions I field from relatives, friends, and co-workers have to do with email. If I have time, I often try to explain how the pieces fit together, in the hope I

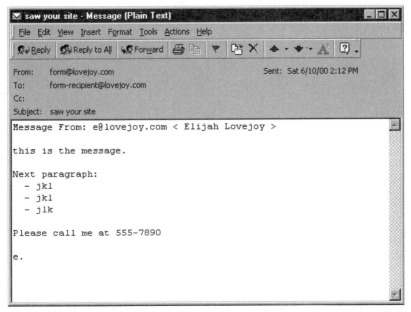

FIGURE 6-2 Information submitted with the form ends up in an email

won't have to answer their questions all over again in six months. Because they usually end up coming back with the same set of questions, I've concluded that email is too complicated to explain to mere users—it couldn't have anything to do with my ability to explain the basic concepts. My hubris wouldn't allow for that.

Why so complicated? Because there are too many pieces to the puzzle:

- **Email addresses** come in the form something@gooblety-gook.com. For example, my email address is Elijah@Lovejoy.com. At this point, it's worth noting that email addresses consist of two critical pieces of information:

  1. The part of the email address that comes after the "@" is an Internet domain name (it could just as well be a more complicated domain, like mail.click.lovejoy.com).[1] This tells mail servers (the applications

---

1. Since Internet domain names are what URLs are built with, I'm not going to go into how domains work. Grab just about any HTML book for an explanation.

that make sure that email gets to where it needs to go) that any email addressed to `Elijah@Lovejoy.com` should be sent to the mail server that is responsible for the `Lovejoy.com` domain.

2. The part of the email that goes in front of the "@" is a unique name that can be mapped to a mail account that is managed by the mail server that is responsible for the mail server that handles all of the email for the domain. In this case, there's a mail server that keeps track of all of the email accounts in the `Lovejoy.com` domain that knows that anything for `Elijah` should go into my mailbox.

• **Mailboxes:** Mail servers, the programs that manage where email goes, often maintain mailboxes for local users. There are numerous different kinds of mailboxes. These days, POP3 mailboxes are the most common. A fair number of people now have IMAP mailboxes, which are a little fancier.

There are two things that are confusing about email boxes. First, to be able to access their email on most systems, users need to remember a username and a password. Because people's email software tends to remember people's passwords for them, people tend to forget their passwords. I get a lot of calls about this.

Second, mailboxes are almost always stored on servers that have a different domain name than the email address. For example, even though my email address is `Elijah@Lovejoy.com`, my mailbox is on a server called `pop.lovejoy.com`. There are good reasons for this, but I'm not convinced that they're worth all the confusion that results.

• **Mail Servers**: Finally, there are the server applications that are in charge of getting email where it needs to go, called "mail servers" (also sometimes called "message transfer agents"). Sometimes, the mail server that manages a users's mailbox also knows how to deal with outgoing mail. Other times, that's not the case. For example, I have to send my outgoing mail to SMTP server `smtp.lovejoy.com`.

Most mail servers these days support SMTP (Simple Mail Transport Protocol, or something like that), which is the Internet standard for email. But a lot of people still use proprietary systems like AOL or Microsoft Exchange, so that their outgoing emails start their travels using one technology, then get passed to an SMTP network somewhere along the way (another piece of software, called a "gateway" handles this transition between different email networks).

Okay, this is getting out of hand. Let's recap: There's an email address (1), a mailbox server (2) that needs a username (3), and a password (4), and, finally, a mail server (5). Never mind that it's useful to know that email addresses can be split into user names (6) and domain names (7) and what the difference is between technologies like POP (8), IMAP (9), and SMTP (10).

Oh bother. I suppose it's a wonder that anybody ever gets any email at all.

CDONTS: Email and Why Microsoft Should Hire More Poets

As we've seen so far in this book, the ASP environment provides built-in objects that make it easy to get things done. This is true with email, as well: A technology called "CDONTS" does most of the work required to take care of things.

For some reason, the name bothers me. CDONTS. It just doesn't roll off the tongue. It's times like this that I think that software companies should all have a poet-in-residence to name things. `</soapbox>`

CDONTS stands for Collaboration Data Objects for Windows NT Server. It's not always installed as part of IIS, so you might want to make sure that you have a file called `Cdonts.dll` installed on your system if you're having trouble getting the scripts in this chapter to work. You can use CDONTS to create an object called a "NewMail object." And that's where the fun begins. For example:

```
1. mail_ob = Server.CreateObject("CDONTS.NewMail");
2. mail_ob.Send("sender@lovejoy.com","
   recipient@lovejoy.com","subject","body");
```

And that's how you can create an object and use it to send a message in two lines of code. The first line creates a NewMail object called `mail_ob` using the `Server.CreateObject()` function, used a couple of other times in this book to use Microsoft technologies that were not intrinsic to ASP. The next line applies the `Send()` method to the `mail_ob` object and passes it four parameters: a From address, a To address, a subject, and a body.

In fact, the only required argument to the `Send()` method is a From address, which means that it's possible to set the To address, subject, and body of the message using properties of the NewMail object before using the `Send()` method. For example:

```
1. mail_ob = Server.CreateObject("CDONTS.NewMail");
2. mail_ob.Subject = "Tomorrow's Meeting";
3. mail_ob.Body = "Jane, I won't be able to make the
   meeting. Can we reschedule?";
4. mail_ob.To = "Jane@lovejoy.com";
5. mail_ob.Send("Elijah@lovejoy.com");
```

Functionally, there's no difference between the this snippet with five lines of code and the block above with two lines of code. Breaking it up like this makes it easier to read, which is nice, but it's simply a matter of taste.

CODE

Two files are described below:

- `form.asp` is the form that collects information to put into an email message.
- `catch_form.asp` is a script that takes the information collected in `form.asp` and fires it off in an email.

Script 6-1
form.asp

```
1. <HTML><HEAD><TITLE></TITLE></HEAD><BODY>
2.
3. <center><h1>Email Us</h1>
4.
5. <p>Use form below to send an email to our sales
   team:
6. <hr>
7. <form action="catch_form.asp">
8. <table align=center border=1>
9.  <tr>
10.    <td align=right>Your Name:</td>
11.    <td><input type=text name=name value=""
       size=60></td>
12.  </tr>
13.  <tr>
```

```
14.     <td align=right>Your Email Address:</td>
15.     <td><input type=text name=email value=""
        size=60></td>
16.  </tr>
17.  <tr>
18.     <td align=right>Subject</td>
19.     <td><input type=text name=subject value=""
        size=60></td>
20.  </tr>
21.  <tr>
22.     <td align=right valign=top>Message:</td>
23.     <td><textarea name=message cols=60
        rows=10></textarea><br>(include your phone number
        if you'd like us to call you.)</td>
24.  </tr>
25.  </table>
26.  <input type=submit name=toss value="Send Message">
27.  <form>
28.  <hr>
29.  </center>
30.  </BODY></HTML>
```

HOW THE SCRIPT WORKS

As you can see, not much code on this page, because it's all
HTML. Key things to note are that the action attribute of the
form tag is set to the URL of the script below, and that all the field
names on the form match the field names that the script below is
expecting.

Script 6-2
`catch_form.asp`

```
1.  <%@ Language=JavaScript %>
2.  <%
3.  mail_ob = Server.CreateObject("CDONTS.NewMail");
4.
5.  mail_ob.Body = String("Message From: " +
    String(Request("email")) + " < " +
    String(Request("name")) + " >"+ "\n\n" +
    Request("message"));
6.
7.  mail_ob.Subject = String(Request("subject"));
8.
9.  mail_ob.To = "form-recipient@lovejoy.com";
10.
11. mail_ob.Importance = 1; // 0=low; 1=normal; 2=high
12.
```

```
13.  mail_ob.Send("form@lovejoy.com");
14.
15.  %>
16.  <HTML><HEAD><TITLE></TITLE></HEAD><BODY>
17.
18.  <center>Email Sent Successfully!</center>
19.  </BODY></HTML>
```

HOW THE SCRIPT WORKS

As you might expect from the introduction to the NewMail object earlier in this chapter, it doesn't take a lot of code to put it to work. This script simply collects the various form elements that were filled out in the previous script and puts them in an email that goes to `form-recipient@lovejoy.com`.

1. Set language to JavaScript.

3. This line creates a NewMail CDONTS object called `mail_ob`.

5. This line generates the body of the message that will be sent out at the end of the script. The key thing here is that the form elements `email`, `name`, and `message` are being concatenated into one big string.

7. The subject of the message is set using the information collected in the subject field of the previous script.

9. This line tells `mail_ob` to send the email to `form-recipient@lovejoy.com`.

11. I'm not sure that anybody pays attention to the importance flag on emails. If whoever reads these emails pays attention to this sort of thing and the information collected here is considered important, you can set the `Importance` of the message to 2.

13. The last step is to use the `send()` method to have the email go out.

18. Don't forget to give the users some kind of feedback so that they have a sense that the script worked.

RECAP

Sending email is so easy, might as well recap with the code:

```
1. mail_ob = Server.CreateObject("CDONTS.NewMail");
2. mail_ob.Send("sender@lovejoy.com","
   recipient@lovejoy.com","subject","body");
```

That's all there is to it!

IDEAS FOR HACKING THIS SCRIPT

- Modify the script so that it collects fields that are more suited to your needs.
- Use this code to modify the shopping cart stuff in Chapter 6 so that orders get emailed to you, as well as stored on the file system.
- Create a password-protected form that you can use to send quick notes to people when you're on the road. You could use a dropdown list to store the email addresses of people you commonly email.
- Create a script that sends emails to multiple recipients. You can do this by using semicolons to separate addresses:

```
mail_ob.To = "form-recipient1@lovejoy.com;
form-recipient2@lovejoy.com";
```

A JavaScript Cheat Sheet

A very quick cheat sheet of some of the JavaScript features used in this book.

◆ Data Types

JavaScript is loosely typed, which means that, unlike many programming languages, there is a lot of flexibility in terms of how variables are used.

Note that all JavaScript datatypes sometimes act like objects, whether it's a string that can have a method applied to it or a Boolean that can be created using a constructor. That's part of JavaScript's charm.

Strings

Strings are the most generic data type, consisting of zero or more characters that can be concatenated and parsed in a few ways. For example:

```
greeting = "Hello World"
```

creates a variable called greeting with a value of "Hello World."

The first time you use a variable, you can optionally declare it. It's also a good practice to put a semicolon at the end of a line:

```
var greeting = "Hello World";
```

257

Both ways work, so it's your call about how you go about things.[1]

Strings can be concatenated using the "+" operator:

```
greeting = "Hello World" + ", How Goes?";
```

Which means that greetings is now set to "Hello World, How Goes?" Alternatively, the same result can be accomplished as follows:

```
greeting = "Hello World";
greeting += ", How Goes?";
```

Because JavaScript types so loosely, sometimes it's hard to be sure that something is a string. When in doubt, the String() function comes in handy:

```
greeting = String(some_other_variable_or_expression);
```

Note that variable and function names are case-sensitive.

Numbers

Numbers are created in more or less the same way:

```
years = 4;
distance = 3.543;
```

Arithmetic operators work like you'd expect them to:

```
nonsense_value = years + distance; // nonsense_value is
                                   // now 7.543
```

The parseInt() and parseFloat() functions can be used to make sure that what looks like a number really is:

```
parseInt(some_number_thing);
```

---

1. My guess is that browsers may be a little more finicky than ASP on this sort of thing. Certainly IIS is fairly forgiving.

Arrays

Arrays are an ordered set of values. For example, you can create an array of names (note that the new constructor must be used when you create an array):

```
names = new Array("Jane","Michael","Anne");
```

The same result can be achieved:

```
names = new Array();
names[0] = "Jane";
names[1] = "Michael";
names[2] = "Anne";
```

Arrays can be used to store any of the JavaScript data types, including numbers and other arrays:

```
numbers = new Array(1,2,3,4,5);
array_of_arrays = new Array();
array_of_arrays[0] = new Array("Jane","Blue");
array_of_arrays[1] = new Array("Michael","Red");
array_of_arrays[2] = new Array("Anne","Tope");
```

To retrieve a value from an array, you invoke it based on its position:

```
names[1]                 // returns "Michael"
array_of_arrays[1][1]    // returns "Red"
```

Note that arrays start at zero, which can take some getting used to if you're new to this kind of thing.

Objects

JavaScript has pretty decent support for objects, including creating constructors, as well as class and instance methods and properties. I won't go into the details of this, because in this book, objects are used as a way to store related sets of data. I mention this simply to make it clear that the objects are discussed here and in the rest of the book are only the tip of the iceberg in terms of what JavaScript objects can be used for.

Objects are created using the new constructor:

```
sample_ob = new Object()
```

Not much use. Let's put some stuff into it to illustrate how an object can be useful:

```
sample_ob.name = "Jane";          // a string
sample_ob.position = "CEO";       // another string
sample_ob.office = 201;           // an integer
sample_ob.phone_nrs = new Object()// an object
sample_ob.phone_nrs.office = "123.456.7890"
                                  // a string,nested inside of
                                  // of two objects
sample_ob.phone_nrs.cell = "123.456.7891"
                                  // another string…
```

Collections

There are no collections, so far as I know, in JavaScript.

Collections are a data type in VBScript, however (and I've been told in Visual Basic, as well). And although Microsoft has done a great job of making ASP accessible via JavaScript, the fact of the matter is that if you use JavaScript to access certain ASP objects or other Windows Scripting Objects, you're going to be using a collection rather than an object.

Collections are more like recordsets than like objects, although the syntax to use them in JavaScript generally looks like you're working with an object. Or at least, that's how I had it in my pea-sized brain until I figured out that they were really collections masquerading as objects.

End result is that, with ASP, you get an extra JavaScript data type. Sort of. But because this isn't a book that thinks real hard about data types, that's all I'm going to write about this. :)

◆ Statements and Operators

if( )

`if()` statements allow for conditional execution of code. For example, given a variable `cust_number`:

```
if (cust_number == 2){
        Response.Write("Hello Jim")    // prints "Hello
                                       // Jim" in browser
}
```

This would be useful if we knew that Jim was customer number two. We might also want to welcome other customers, which we could do with an `else` clause to handle other values:

```
if (cust_number == 2){
        Response.Write("Hello Jim");
}
else{
        Response.Write("Welcome to our web site");
}
```

Besides the equality operator above (two equal signs, rather than the single equal sign used to assign a value to a variable), JavaScript supports the usual other operators as shown in Table A-1.

Table A-1 More Operators!

Operator	Definition
!=	Not equal
<, <=	Less than, less than or equal to
>, >=	Greater than, greater than or equal to
!	not
||	or
&&	and

The last three operators are useful to modify existing expressions or to make more than one test. To welcome every one except Jim:

```
if (! cust_number == 2){
        Response.Write("Welcome to the site");
}
```

And, using the `else if()` construct, we can get real fancy:

```
if (cust_number == 2){
        Response.Write("Hello Jim");
}
else if(cust_number > 10 && cust_number < 20){
        Response.Write("Welcome Special Guest!");
}
else{
        Response.Write("Welcome to our web site");
}
```

for( )

`for()` loops make it possible to iterate while a condition is true. For example, to count from zero to 9:

```
for (i=0; i>10; i++){
        Response.Write("\n" + i);
}
```

which would return:

```
0
1
2
3
4
5
6
7
8
9
```

Of course, without break tags, this would run together in a browser with everything appearing on a single line.

The `for()` operator can also be used to loop through an object or an array. For example:

```
names = new Array("Bob","Anne","Jane","Wilbur","Don")
for (i in names){
        Response.Write(names[i])
}
```

would print out each name in the array, in order.

while( )

while statements will loop through a block of code so long as a condition is true. For example, while() can be used to generate the same result as the for() loop above:

```
i=0;
while (i >10){
        Response.Write("\n"+i);
        i++;
}
```

while loops are especially useful when iterating through a file or a recordset. See examples in Chapters 2–4 for details.

B Server Configuration

The Microsoft IIS Server works pretty well out of the box, which means that I can get away with not covering a lot of ground here. Given how compli-cated it is (there are numerous books written about IIS), this is nice. However, there are a couple of things that are worth mentioning.

◆ Personal Web Server

Personal Web Server is the version of IIS that is available for the nonserver versions of Windows, such as Windows NT Workstation or even Windows 98. Although a lot of the more sophisticated options are not available, it's basically the same Web server, which means that you can set up just about any recent version of Windows as a development server.

In fact, a lot of the scripts in this book were written on a lap-top running Windows 95. Later, it was easy to move them to com-puters running Windows NT Server and Windows 2000.

◆ Configuring IIS

Like many Windows NT and BackOffice applications, IIS is con-figured using the Microsoft Management Console. For IIS on Windows NT Server version 4.0, the console looks like Figure B-1.

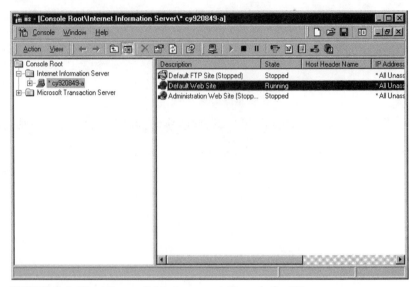

FIGURE B-1 The Microsoft Management Console for IIS

To edit a Web site, the easiest thing to do is to right-click on the site and select Properties, as in Figure B-2.

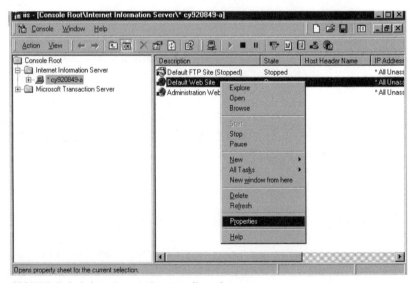

FIGURE B-2 Select Properties to edit a site

By default, IIS is configured to enable ASP. If, for some reason, this is disabled on your server, you can enable this by opening the Properties of the Web site you're working on, going to the Home Directory tab (Figure B-3), and setting the Permissions radio button (in Application Settings) to Script.

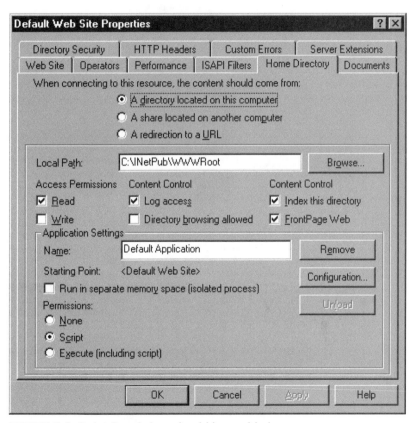

FIGURE B-3 Script Permissions should be enabled

◆ Giving a Script Write Access

The shopping cart script in Chapter 5 stores orders by creating files that are stored on the hard drive. This will usually require modifying the permissions of the Orders folder, where the orders are stored, so that the script is allowed to write to the filesystem.

◆ Creating a DSN to Connect to a Database

A DSN is created by a server administrator, using the ODBC Control Panel. This is covered in detail in Chapter 3.

◆ Getting CDONTS to Work

CDONTS is not always installed with IIS, so the first thing to do is to make sure that you have it on your server. Do a find for Cdonts.dll: if you can't find it, you don't have it. Because it's freely available from the Microsoft Web site, all you have to do is go to the Web site and download it (you'll probably have to register). For example, CDONTS is part of the NT Option Pack 4 (not the service pack).

Index

Symbols
<% ... %>, 2-3
<%Language=JavaScript%>, 3
"=", 2
\n, 29
\t, 29
\', 29
*, 29
\\, 29

A
Active server pages (ASP), xi, xii-xiii
    adding ASP code to an HTML
    page, xiii-xv
    HTML vs., 3
Addresses, email, 249-50
ADODB, xviii
Arrays, 8, 259
ASP, *See* Active server pages (ASP)
ASP objects, xvi-xviii
    Request object, xvi-xvii
    Response object, xvii
    Server object, xvii
    Session object, xvii
ASP Session object, 91-92
ASP tags, 2-3

AutoNumber data type, 53

B
Berners-Lee, Tim, xii

C
cart_change_qty.asp, 189-90
    how it works, 190-92
cart_items, 176
cart.js, 220-30
    how it works, 230-45
cart_list_items_for_sale.asp, 179-81
    how it works, 182-85
cart_remove_all.asp, 192
cart_set_session.asp, 185-86
    how it works, 186-88
cart_view_contents.asp, 188-89
    how it works, 188-89
Case sensitivity, xx
catch_form.asp, 253-54
    how it works, 254
Categories Form, 50-51
CDONTS, xviii, 251-52, 268
CGI, xii
ch3db, 57-58
ch3_include.js, 68-70

how it works, 70-72
ch3_view_categories.asp, 72-73
    how it works, 73-74
ch3_view_records.asp, 74-78
    how it works, 78-82
        creating a header, 78-79
        creating a subcategory
            navigation bar, 79-80
        displaying records, 80-82
        ideas for hacking this script, 82-83
ch4_blank_category_form.asp, 123-24
    how it works, 124-26
ch4_blank_record_form.asp, 150-52
    how it works, 152-54
ch4_delete_category.asp, 121-22
    how it works, 122
ch4_delete_record.asp, 149
    how it works, 147-49
ch4_delete_subcategory.asp, 163-64
    how it works, 164
ch4_edit_category_form.asp, 110-12
    how it works, 112-16
ch4_edit_record_form.asp, 136-40
    how it works, 140-45
ch4_edit_subcategory_form.asp,
    157-59
    how it works, 159-62
ch4_include.js, 100-103
    how it works, 103-7
ch4_insert_category.asp, 127-28
    how it works, 128-29
ch4_insert_record.asp, 154-55
    how it works, 155-57
ch4_insert_subcategory.asp, 162-63
    how it works, 163
ch4_list_categories.asp:
    how it works, 109-10
    to, 108-9
ch4_list_records.asp, 130-34
    how it works, 135-36
ch4_password_form.asp, 98
    how it works, 98-100
ch4_update_category.asp, 116-17
    to how it works, 117-21
ch4_update_record.asp, 145-46

how it works, 149-50
collect_billing_ information.asp,
    206-8
    how it works, 208-9
Collecting information submitted by
    a visitor, 26
Collections, 260
collect_shipping_ information.asp,
    194-95
    how it works, 196-99
Common escape sequences, 29
Concatenation (JavaScript "+"
    operator), 9
Conventions, xix-xx
Cookies, 175
CreateObject() method, Server object,
    58, 61

D

Database, relational, 43
Database Connection object, 57-59
Database-driven pages, 39-84
    categories table, 59
    ch3_include.js, 68-70
        how it works, 70-72
    ch3_view_categories.asp, 72-73
        how it works, 73-74
    ch3_view_records.asp, 74-78
        how it works, 78-82
    Database Connection object, 57-59
    database-driven ASP pages,
        creating, 53
    DSN (data source name), creating,
        53-57
    fields, 43-44
    foreign keys, 45-46
    for () loop, creating, 64-65
    generating Web pages from a
        database, 40-84
    include files, using for shared code,
        64-67, 70
    information:
        stored in different tables,
            relating, 44-46

storing in tables, 43-44
JavaScript function, creating, 65-66
Microsoft Access, 48-53
    AutoNumber data type, 53
    Categories Form, 50-51
    Data Form, 50-51
    downloading a driver for, 55-56
    tables editor, 52
    Tables tab, 52
    primary keys, 45
    records, 43
    recordset, 47
    Recordset object, 59-64
        collecting field names from,
        62-64
    relational databases, 43
    storing information, creating a
    JavaScript object for, 67-68
    structured query language (SQL),
    46-48
        retrieving data from a database
        using, 47-48
        where clause, 47-48
Data Form, 50-51
Data from a text file, adding to Web
page, 14-23
Data types, 257-60
    arrays, 8, 259
    collections, 260
    numbers, 8, 258
    objects, 259-60
    strings, 8, 257-58
date_fancy.asp, 9
    how it works, 10-11
    modification of, 11-12
Date object, xviii
Date () object, 4, 36
Date script:
    powerful, 7-11
        array (JavaScript data type, 8
        concatenation (JavaScript "+"
        operator), 9
        date_fancy.asp, 9
        modification of, 11-12
        how it works, 10-11

new features, 7-9
number (JavaScript data type),
    8
slash// (comment), 7
string (JavaScript data type), 8
simple, 2-6
    <% ... %>, 2-3
    <%Language=JavaScript%>, 3
    ASP tags, 2-3
    Date() object, 4
    date_simple.asp, 5-6
    how it works, 6
    new features, 2-5
    new operator, 4
    powerful, 7-11
    Response.Write (), 4-5
date_simple.asp, 5-6
    how it works, 6
Domain name, 249-50
DSN (data source name):
    creating, 53-57
        to connect to a database, 268

E
ECMA Script, compared to
JavaScript/JScript, xvi
Editing records, 85-166
    ASP Session object, 91-92
    ch4_blank_category_form.asp,
    123-24
        how it works, 124-26
    ch4_blank_record_form.asp,
    150-52
        how it works, 152-54
    ch4_delete_category.asp, 121-22
        how it works, 122
    ch4_delete_record.asp, 149
        how it works, 149-50
    ch4_delete_subcategory.asp,
    163-64
        how it works, 164
    ch4_edit_category_form.asp,
    110-12
        how it works, 112-16

ch4_edit_record_form.asp, 136-40
  how it works, 140-45
ch4_edit_subcategory_form.asp,
  157-59
  how it works, 159-62
  ch4_include.js, 100-103
  how it works, 103-7
ch4_insert_category.asp, 127-28
  how it works, 128-29
ch4_insert_record.asp, 154-55
  how it works, 155-57
ch4_insert_subcategory.asp, 162-63
  how it works, 163
ch4_list_categories.asp:
  how it works, 109-10
  to, 108-9
ch4_list_records.asp, 130-34
  how it works, 135-36
ch4_password_form.asp, 98
  how it works, 98-100
  ch4_update_category.asp,
    116-17
  to how it works, 117-21
ch4_update_record.asp, 145-46
  how it works, 147-49
code to edit categories, 108-29
code to edit database, 98-108
code to edit records, 129-57
code to edit subcategories, 157-64
ideas for hacking, 165-66
includes, 98
passwords, 87, 98
redirecting users with the Response
  object, 90-91
regular expression, using to
  examine the contents of a string,
  96-97
Request.QueryString object, using
  to collect form data, 95-96
Response.Redirect (), 90-91
security, 87, 93-94
Session object:
  collecting a password, 92-93
  password mechanism, 92
Session variable:

checking validity of, 93
  setting, 92-93
  substring () function (JavaScript),
    97
  updating records, using SQL, 94
else if() construct, 262
Email, 247-56
  addresses, 249-50
  catch_form.asp, 253-54
    how it works, 254
  CDONTS, 251-52
  code, 252-53
  form.asp, 252-53
    how it works, 253
  form for creating, 248
  gateways, 251
  how it works, 248-51
  ideas for hacking, 255
  IMAP mailboxes, 250
  Internet domain name, 249-50
  mailboxes, 250
  mail servers, 250-51
  POP3 mailboxes, 250
  simple email script, 247-56
  SMTP, 250-51
Escape sequences, 29
Escaping with **, in JavaScript, 29
Execute () method, Connection object,
  58-59

F

Fields, 43-44
FileExists() method, 35
FileSystem object, xviii
FileSystemObject, using to the data
  from a file, 17-18
Foreign keys, 45-46
for () loop, creating, 64-65
form.asp, 252-53
  how it works, 253
for () operator, 262
fso object, 35
fs_stream, 36

G

Gateways, 251
guest_book.asp, 23-33
  code, 30-33
  collecting information submitted
    by a visitor, 26
  escaping with **, in JavaScript, 29
  FileExists() method, 35
  fso object, 35
  fs_stream, 36
  guest_book_file variable, 34
  guest_book.txt, 33
  how it works, 33-36
  HTML forms, working with, 25-26
  ideas for hacking, 37
  incoming form information, using
    Request object to collect, 27
  information, appending to a file,
    28
  instructions telling a script what to
    do, 26-27
  linebreaks, in JavaScript, 29
  new features, 25-33
  purpose of, 23
  ReadAll() method, 35
  special characters, in JavaScript,
    29
  to_do tag, 34-36
  undefined, 28
  Write() method, TextStream object,
    36

H

HTML:
  ASP vs., 3
  forms, working with, 25-26
  mixing with scripts, xii-xiii

I

if ... else statements (JavaScript), 18
if () statements, 260-62
IMAP mailboxes, 250
Include files, using for shared code,
  64-67, 70

Includes, and editing records, 98
Incoming form information, using
  Request object to collect, 27
Information:
  appending to a file, 28
  stored in different tables, relating,
    44-46
  storing in tables, 43-44
  submitted by a visitor, collecting,
    26
Internet domain name, 249-50

J

JavaScript, xv
  case sensitivity, xx
  cheat sheet, 257-63
  compared to ECMA Script, xvi
  compared to JScript, xvi
  data types, 257-60
    arrays, 259
    collections, 260
    numbers, 258
    objects, 259-60
    strings, 257-58
  Date () object, 36
  else if() construct, 262
  for () loop, creating, 64-65
  for () operator, 262
  if ... else statements, 18
  if () statements, 260-62
  linebreaks in, 29
  Math object, xviii
    generating a random integer
      with, 19
  objects, xviii
  regular expressions, 15-16
  reverse () method, 37
  special characters in, 29
  statements/operators, 260-63
  substring () function, 97
  while () operator, 263
JavaScript function, creating, 65-66

L

Linebreaks, in JavaScript, 29

M

Mailboxes, 250
Mail servers, 250-51
Math object, xviii
   generating random integer with, 19
Microsoft Access, 48-53
   AutoNumber data type, 53
   Categories Form, 50-51
   Data Form, 50-51
   downloading a driver for, 55-56
   tables editor, 52
   Tables tab, 52
Microsoft IIS server, configuring, 265-68
Microsoft Management Console, 265-66
Microsoft scripting objects, xvii-xviii

N

new operator, 4
Numbers, 8, 258

O

Objects, 259-60
OpenTextFile () method, FileSystemObject, 22
Operators, JavaScript, 260-63
option_file.txt, 178-79
order_complete.asp, 218-19
   how it works, 219
order_info object, 176

P

Passwords, and editing records, 87, 98
PerlScript, xv
Personal Web Server, 265
POP3 mailboxes, 250
Powerful date script, 7-11
   array (JavaScript data type, 8

concatenation (JavaScript "+" operator), 9
date_fancy.asp, 9
modification of, 11-12
how it works, 10-11
new features, 7-9
number (JavaScript data type), 8
// (comment), 7
string (JavaScript data type), 8
Primary keys, 45
Purchase process, shopping cart, 171-73

R

Records, 43
   editing, 85-166
   updating, using SQL, 94
Recordset, 47
Recordset object, 59-64
   collecting field names from, 62-64
Regular expressions, 15-16
   using to examine the contents of a string, 96-97
Relational databases, 43
replace() method, 16
Request object, xvi-xvii
   server variables, 15
   using to collect incoming form information, 27
Request.QueryString object, using to collect form data, 95-96
Response object, xvii
Response.Redirect (), 90-91
Response.Write (), 4-5
reverse () method, 37

S

Script, giving write access, 267
Security:
   and editing records, 87, 93-94
   shopping cart, 168-69
Server configuration, 265-68
   Personal Web Server, 265
Server object, xvii

CreateObject() method, 58
Server-side scripting, 3
Session object, xvii
   password mechanism, 92
   storing information in, 175-76
Session variable:
   checking validity of, 93
   setting, 92-93
set_cc_billing_information.asp,
   209-11
   how it works, 211-15
set_pwc_billing_information.asp,
   215-17
   how it works, 217-18
set_shipping_information.asp,
   199-201
   how it works, 201-5
Shopping cart, 167-246
   ASP shopping cart code, 179-246
   browsing items by
      categories/keyword search, 169
   building, 168-246
   cart_change_qty.asp, 189-90
      how it works, 190-92
   cart_items, 176
   cart.js, 220-30
      how it works, 230-45
   cart_list_items_for_sale.asp, 179-81
      how it works, 182-85
   cart_remove_all.asp, 192
      how it works, 192-93
   cart_set_session.asp, 185-86
      how it works, 186-88
   cart_view_contents.asp, 188-89
   how it works, 188-89
   collect_billing_ information.asp,
   206-8
   how it works, 208-9
   collect_shipping_ information.asp,
   194-95
      how it works, 196-99
   debugging, 245-46
   "Delete This Item" links, 170-71
   generating an order, 193-99
   ideas for hacking, 246

   item quantities, 170
   option_file.txt, 178-79
   order acknowledgment screen, 173
   order_complete.asp, 218-19
      how it works, 219
   order file, appearance of, 174
   order_info object, 176
   orders in the orders folder, 174
   purchase process, 171-73
   related data, storing in two text
      files, 177-79
   security, 168-69
   Session object, storing information
      in, 175-76
   set_cc_billing_information.asp,
      209-11
      how it works, 211-15
   set_pwc_billing_information.asp,
      215-17
      how it works, 217-18
   set_shipping_information.asp,
      199-201
      how it works, 201-5
   shipping/billing information,
      collecting, 193-99
   Submit button, 170
   templates, creating, 176-77
   tour, 169-74
   view_session_contents.asp, 245
      how it works, 245-46
Simple date script, 2-6
   <% ... %>, 2-3
   <%Language=JavaScript%>, 3
   ASP tags, 2-3
   Date() object, 4
   date_simple.asp, 5-6
   how it works, 6
   new features, 2-5
   new operator, 4
   Response.Write (), 4-5
// (comment), 7
SMTP, 250-51
Special characters, in JavaScript, 29
SQL, See Structured query language
   (SQL)

Statements, JavaScript, 260-63
Storing information, creating a JavaScript object for, 67-68
String() function, 27
Strings, 8, 257-58
Structured query language (SQL), 46-48
   retrieving data from a database using, 47-48
   updating records using, 94
   where clause, 47-48
substring () function (JavaScript), 97

T

Tables, storing information in, 43-44
Templates, creating, 176-77
Text file, using as a database, 16-17
TextStreamObject, using to read data from a file, 17-18
tip_of_the_day.asp, 15-23
   code for, 19-21
   FileSystemObject, using to read data from a file, 17-18
   how it works, 21-23
   if à else statements (JavaScript), 18
   Math object, generating a said random integer with, 19
   new features, 15-19
   OpenTextFile () method, FileSystemObject, 22
   regular expressions (JavaScript), 15-16
   Request object server variables, 15
   text file, using as a database, 16-17
   TextStreamObject, using to read data from a file, 17-18
   tips.txt, 20
   while() (JavaScript statement), 17
tips.txt, 20

U

undefined, 28
Updating records, using SQL, 94

V

VBScript, xv, 260
view_session_contents.asp, 245
   how it works, 245-46

W

Web interface, using to edit records in a database, 86-166
Web site home page, incorporating a script into, 14-23
where clause, 47-48
while () operator, 17, 263
Write() method, TextStream object, 36